THE SYNTAX OF
MASORETIC ACCENTS IN
THE HEBREW BIBLE

James D. Price

Studies in the Bible and Early Christianity
Volume 27

The Edwin Mellen Press
Lewiston/Queenston/Lampeter

Library of Congress Cataloging-in-Publication Data

This volume has been registered with The Library of Congress.

This is volume 27 in the continuing series
Studies in Bible and Early Christianity
Volume 27 ISBN 0-88946-510-X
SBEC Series ISBN 0-88946-913-X

A CIP catalog record for this book
is available from the British Library.

All rights reserved. For information contact

The Edwin Mellen Press   The Edwin Mellen Press
Box 450   Box 67
Lewiston, New York   Queenston, Ontario
USA 14092   CANADA L0S 1L0

Edwin Mellen Press, Ltd
Lampeter, Dyfed, Wales,
UNITED KINGDOM SA48 7DY

Printed in the United States of America

DEDICATION

This work is dedicated to my friend and colleague, Dr. Hermann J. Austel, Academic Dean and Professor of Old Testament and Biblical Languages at Northwest Baptist Seminary, Tacoma, Washington. He has been a lifelong example of academic and spiritual excellence.

TABLE OF CONTENTS

Table of Contents

Table of Contents

Table of Contents

LIST OF TABLES

PREFACE

What began as a relatively small project developed into a major undertaking. My original intent was to write a brief chapter on Hebrew accents suitable for second-year students of Biblical Hebrew. As I researched the available literature on Hebrew accents and pondered over the classical nineteenth-century work of William Wickes, I became intrigued with the possibility that the Masoretic accents in the Hebrew Bible were governed by a syntax of their own, independent of the syntax of the Hebrew language itself, but obviously related to it.

To test this hypothesis, I developed computer software to isolate and define such a syntax, if it actually exists. To my delight a phrase-structure grammar emerged which defines a hierarchy of simple rules that do indeed govern the placement of the accents in a verse. The more I studied the rules, the simpler they became, and apparent discrepancies acquired independent explanations of their own in harmony with the general tenor of the grammar. As it turned out, two grammars had to be developed, one for the poetic books (Job, Psalms, and Proverbs), and one for the remaining books (which are regarded as prose).

Although at times I found the syntax to disagree with Wickes, in general it confirms and formalizes the observations and laws he set forth. Considerable help was derived from the work of Israel Yeivin who digested and simplified Wickes' complex discussions.

Part One of this present work consists of an exhaustive analysis of the syntax rules governing the accents used in the Pentateuch, although many references are made to passages in the other prose books. In a few instances I was able to exhaustively check certain details in all of the prose books. It is reasonable to assume that the rules that govern the accents in the Pentateuch will also apply to the remaining prose books, with perhaps very minor modifications. Part Two consists of an exhaustive analysis of the syntax rules that govern the accents used in the poetic books. Oh yes, I finally got the small chapter written for my students.

In each part I have attempted to suggest how the accents should be interpreted in the exposition of Hebrew Scripture. They provide the key to determining the ancient rabbinic understanding of the text. Such rabbinic interpretation has its roots in the deep recesses of antiquity, and it should not be ignored by any serious expositor of Scripture. May the Sovereign LORD grant wisdom to those who seek to understand this aspect of His Word.

Chattanooga, TN.
      1990

ACKNOWLEDGMENTS

The author expresses his appreciation to the following publishers who graciously granted permission to reproduce quotations from their copyrighted material:

The WM. B. Eerdmans Publishing Co., Grand Rapids, for permission to reproduce quotations from Ernst Würthwein, *The Text of the Old Testament* (1979).

The Keter Publishing House, Jerusalem, for permission to reproduce quotations from the *Encyclopedia Judaica* (1971).

The KTAV Publishing House, Hoboken, NJ, for permission to reproduce quotations from William Wickes, *Two Treatises on the Accentuation of the Old Testament* (1970).

The *Jewish Quarterly Review* for permission to reproduce quotations from David Weisberg, "The Rare Accents of the Twenty-One Books," *JQR* (1966) 56(4).

Acknowledgments

The *Journal of the Evangelical Theological Society* for permission to reproduce quotations from Bruce K. Waltke, "The New International Version and Its Textual Principles in the Book of Psalms," *JETS* (March 1989) 32(1); and from Duane L. Christensen and M. Naruchi, "The Mosaic Authorship of the Pentateuch," *JETS* (December 1989) 32(4).

The Oxford University Press, London, for permission to reproduce quotations from E. Kautzsch, *Gesenius' Hebrew Grammar* (1910).

The Scholars Press, Atlanta, for permission to reproduce quotations from Israel Yeivin, *Introduction to the Tiberian Masorah*, SBL Masoretic Studies No. 5.

The Sheffield Academic Press, Sheffield, England, for permission to reproduce quotations from W. G. E. Watson, *Classical Hebrew Poetry* (1984); and from E. R. Follis, ed., *Directions In Biblical Hebrew* (1987).

The Zondervan Publishing House, Grand Rapids, for permission to reproduce quotations from John J. Hughes, *Bits, Bytes and Biblical Studies* (1987).

The author also expresses his appreciation to his young colleague, David L. Brooks, who carefully read the manuscript and offered many helpful suggestions.

INTRODUCTION

Hebrew's Non-Vowel Marks

Beside the familiar diacritical marks known as vowel points, the Masoretic text of the Hebrew Old Testament also uses various other marks of significance. They consist of (1) marks denoting possible textual problems, (2) marks referring to marginal notes, (3) marks signifying phonetic union of words, and (4) marks of accentuation.

Textual Problems

The marks that denote possible textual problems are known as (נְקֻדִּים--dots) *niqqudim* or *puncta extraordinaria*. They consist of prominent dots placed above (and sometimes also below) the characters of the word or words in question. No explanation is given in the text as to why the words are so marked. Their significance has been the object of scholarly research.[1] Ernst Würthwein suggested that "these points register textual or doctrinal reservations on the part of scribes (*sopherim*) who dared not alter the text because they held it to be sacrosanct."[2] They

----

[1] Romain Butin, *Ten Neqqudoth of the Torah*, rev. ed., Library of Biblical Studies (New York: KTAV, 1969).

[2] Ernst Würthwein, *The Text of the Old Testament*, trans. by Erroll F. Rhodes (Grand Rapids: William B. Eerdmans, 1979), 17.

occur   ten   times   in the   Pentateuch   and   five   times
elsewhere.[3]

Masoretic Notes

The   printed editions of the Hebrew Old   Testament
commonly   referred   to as BHK and BHS display   a   small
circle   above a word to which a marginal Masoretic note
refers.   Other printed editions use a star or asterisk.
A companion volume to BHS provides a catalog of all the
Masoretic notes.[4]

Phonetic Union

The   Maqqeph (מַקֵּף--hyphen)   is frequently used   to
join   words   that are closely   related   syntactically.[5]
Such word clusters are run together and pronounced as a
single   word having only one primary stress;   they are
called "phonetic units" in this work.   Secondary stress
occurs   in   such word clusters much like a single   long
word with a corresponding number of syllables.   In the
rules of accentuation,   such phonetic units are treated
as though they were one word.

----

[3]Würthwein,   p. 17;   Gen 16:5;   18:9;   19:33;   33:4;   37:12;   Num
3:39;   9:10;   21:30;   29:15;   Deut 29:28;   2 Sam 19:20;   Isa 44:9;   Ezek
41:20;   46:22;   Psa 27:13.

[4]G.   E.   Weil,   ed.   *Massorah Gedolah Iuxta   Codicem
Leningradensem B19a,*   Vol.   I Catalogi (Rome: Pontifical Biblical
Institute,   1971);   Volumes II,   III,   and IV of that publication
offer further details.   See Weil's forward to BHS for a discussion
of the Masoretic notes.

[5]See   Israel Yeiven,   *Introduction to the   Tiberian   Masorah,*
trans.   and ed.   by E. J. Revell,   Society of Biblical Literature
Masoretic Studies,   Number 5 (Missoula, MT: Scholars Press, 1980),
228-36;   he provides a lengthy discussion of *Maqqeph.*

Accent Marks

The remaining non-vowel marks in the Hebrew Bible are marks of accentuation, otherwise referred to as marks of cantillation. The Hebrew Bible uses accent marks to denote secondary stress and primary stress.

Secondary Accents. Some marks of accentuation are not involved with the syntactic and musical aspects of cantillation. They are used to mark a syllable receiving secondary stress in pronunciation. The most common mark for this purpose is the Metheg (מֶתֶג-- bridle). It consists of a small vertical bar placed below the first consonant of the syllable receiving secondary stress and immediately to the left of any vowel there.[6]

Primary stress usually occurs on the last syllable (ultima) of a word or phonetic unit, less frequently on the next-to-last syllable (penultima), but never earlier in the word than that. Secondary stress may occur on words with more than two syllables, and long words or phonetic units may have two or more syllables with secondary stress.[7] On rare occasions a word with

----

[6] In BHK the editors added *Metheg* and *Silluq* which were lacking in MS Leningrad B19a. These added signs were placed to the right of the vowel. This practice was discontinued in BHS, although the signs were placed at the right of the vowel when found so in B19a. See BHS xii. The older name for this mark (*Ga'ya*) is still used in some literature. Yeivin provided a lengthy discussion of secondary accents in *Tiberian Masorah*, 240-64.

[7] A sequence of three *Methegs* occurs in Gen 2:6; and sequences of two occur in Gen 4:19; 9:15; 15:10; 19:13; 21:14, 21; 24:7; 31:43, 52; 32:32; 38:23; Ex 1:21; 2:3; 3:12; 4:13; 12:13; 13:5, 11; 15:26; 20:3; 21:10; 30:10; Lev 1:5; 15:14, 19; 23:31; 25:28; 27:28; Num 5:21; 15:14; 17:21; 26:31; 30:9, 13; Deut 1:29, 33; 2:29; 8:3; 12:20; 22:7; 28:9, 68.

primary stress on the penultima may have secondary stress on the ultima.[8]

In special cases one of the other accent marks usually used to denote primary stress may replace the *Metheg* to mark secondary stress. When used to mark secondary stress, such an accent should be interpreted as a substitute for *Metheg*, with no conjunctive or disjunctive function in cantillation.

Munach frequently serves as a substitute for *Metheg*.[9] *Azla* occasionally does so;[10] and *Tiphcha*,[11] *Mereka*[12] and *Mahpak*[13] do so, but rarely. This phenomenon is discussed more fully in subsequent commentary on the individual accents.

Primary Accents. The primary accents are the subject of the remaining part of this work. They serve three purposes. This work focuses on an understanding of the laws of accentuation and the relationship of the

----

[8] See פֶּצְמָירֵ (Gen 3:18), הָנֵּנִי (22:7), הִסְבַּלְתָּ (31:28). See also Gen 24:9; 28:2, 5, 6, 7; 37:9; 40:15; 43:9; 45:8; 48:19, 22; 50:18; Ex 33:12, 19; Lev 26:21; Num 9:14; 18:8, 19; 22:28; 24:22; 35:16, 17, 18, 21; Deut 4:33; 17:10, 11; 27:9; 28:68; 29:19; 32:13. So BHS, but some are lacking in BHK, and many are lacking in B and MG.

[9] See וּלְמֹועֲדִים (Gen 1:14), and so 364 times in the Pentateuch.

[10] See הַבְּהֵמָה (Gen 7:8), and so 152 times in the Pentateuch.

[11] See לְחֻמָּיו: (Lev 21:4) and לְדֹרֹתֵיכֶם: (Num 15:21); this use of Tiphcha is referred to by the name *Mayela*.

[12] See לֹא־יֹאכַל־בֹּו: (Ex 12:45) and בֶּן־צוּרִי־שַׁדָּי: (Num 2:12).

[13] According to Yeivin (*Tiberian Masorah*, 196), *Mahpak* serves as a substitute for *Metheg* before *Pashta* five times (Song 1:7, 12; 3:4; Eccl 1:7; 7:10).

accents to the interpreting Hebrew Scripture. However,
a discussion of foundational details must precede a
description of the accents themselves.

The Study of the Accents

The study of the Masoretic accents in the Hebrew
Old Testament has been neglected by most Hebrew
grammarians of this century. Most contemporary
grammarians give only a brief description of the
accents with a meager discussion of their function in
the Hebrew Bible. Even *Gesenius' Hebrew Grammar*[14]
devotes only five pages to them. S. R. Driver[15] wrote
a brief chapter on the accents, but it deals mainly
with their value regarding so-called "tense."

Two nineteenth century grammar books[16] have more
extensive discussions of the accents that are helpful,
but they are limited to the needs of students. Max L.
Margolis[17] wrote a detailed article on the accents, but
it is so terse and complex that it is of little value
except to scholars. William Wickes[18] wrote the most

----

[14]E. Kautzsch, ed., *Gesenius' Hebrew Grammar*, 2nd ed.,
revised by A. E. Cowley (London: Oxford University Press, 1910),
pp. 59-63.

[15]S. R. Driver, *A Treatise on the Use of the Tenses in
Hebrew*, 3rd ed. (London: Oxford University Press, 1892), pp. 99-
113.

[16]S. Lee, *A Grammar of the Hebrew Language* (London: Duncan
and Malcolm, 1844); P. H. Mason, and H. H. Bernard, *An Essay,
Practical Hebrew Grammar* (Cambridge: J. Hall and Son, 1853).

[17]Max L. Margolis, "Accents in Hebrew," *The Jewish
Encyclopedia* (1971).

[18]William Wickes, *Two Treatises on the Accentuation of the
Old Testament*, rev. ed. (1881-87; reprint, New York: KTAV, 1970);

comprehensive work on Hebrew accents in 1881-1887.
Aron Dotan, Head of the Department of Hebrew Language,
Tel Aviv University, wrote the prolegomenon to the KTAV
reprint of Wickes' treatises. After giving a thorough
survey of the literature on Hebrew accents, he stated:

> Wickes was and remains unique, head and shoulders
> above everyone else in the study of Biblical accents,
> and to this day his is a basic standard work and an
> excellent textbook for the student as well.[19]

After reviewing more recent works on the accents,
Dotan concluded that

> in the field of instruction, too, as a method for
> learning the accentuation, no less than in the domain
> of research, Wickes' work was, and still remains, the
> basic standard work with no substitute.[20]

Two books on the accents written in this century
are worthy of mention, the work of Mordecai Brewer[21]
and that of Miles B Cohen.[22] In addition, Israel
Yeivin has written a lengthy section on the accents.[23]

----

note that in this reprint, pp. 32, 33 of "Treatise I" belong in
"Treatise II," and pp. 32, 33 of "Treatise II" belong in
"Treatise I."

[19]Wickes, p. xxvi; see his survey for the historic sources.

[20]Wickes, p. xlii.

[21]Mordecai Brewer, *The Biblical Accents as Punctuation*
(Jerusalem: Hamador Hadati, 1958).

[22]Miles B. Cohen, *The System of Accentuation in the Hebrew
Bible* (Minneapolis: Milco Press, 1969).

[23]Yeiven, *Tiberian Masorah*, 157-274.

He has digested the work of Wickes for modern readers and has added extensive material on the interpretation of the accentuation, including the use of *Maqqeph* and *Ga'ya* (*Metheg*).

Subsequent to the KTAV reprint of Wickes' treatises, extensive work on the accents has been conducted by G. E. Weil and his colleagues at the *Centre Nationale de la Recherche Scientifique* (CNRS) in Nancy.[24] They made use of a computer to compile an exhaustive concordance of the accents in the Hebrew Bible and to construct tree diagrams of their interrelations. Their work has demonstrated that the use of the accents follows a strict system of rules. In addition to the extensive work of Yeiven and Weil, a few other scholars have investigated limited aspects of the accents.[25]

---

[24]G. E. Weil, P. Riviere, and M. Serfaty, *Concordance de la Cantilation du Pentateuque et des Cinq Migillot* (Paris-Nancy: CNRS, 1978); *Les Cantilations des Premiers Prophetes* (1981); *Les Cantilations des Livres Poetique* (1982); *Les Cantilations des Derniers Prophetes* (1982); *La Cantilation des Ouvrages Bibliques en Aramean* (1983).

[25]Nehemiah Allony, "The Book of Vocalization (Kitab Al Musawwitat) of Moses Ben Asher," *Leshonenu* (1983) 47(2):85-124; M. Aronoff, "Orthography and Linguistic Theory: The Syntactic Basis of Masoretic Hebrew Punctuation," *Language* (1985) 61:28-72; Mordecai Breuer, "Toward the Clarification of Problems in the Masoretic Accents," *Leshonenu* (1979) 43(4):243-53; "Toward the Clarification of Problems in Biblical Accents and Vocalization: The Ga'ya for Improvement of Reading," *Leshonenu* (1979) 44(1):3-11; "Clarifying Problems in the Accents and Vowel Signs of the Biblical Text," *Leshonenu* (1985) 48/49(2/3):118-31; M. B. Cohen, "Masoretic Accents as a Biblical Commentary," *Journal of the Ancient Near Eastern Society* (1972)4:2-11; A. Dotan, "The Minor Ga'ya," *Textus* (1964) 4:55-75; E. J. Revell, "The Oldest Evidence for the Hebrew Accent System," *Bulletin of the John*

In spite of the information available about the
accents, most expositors of the Hebrew Old Testament
regard them to be of little importance to a clear
understanding of the text. On the contrary, the
accents may be quite important to the student of
Scripture. Wickes correctly explained their
importance: "The accentuators thus did their best to
assist both reader and hearers in apprehending what
seemed to them the true meaning of the Sacred Text.
And this is for us the recommendation of their
system."[26] Indeed, he emphasized that

> their very name, טְעָמִים, points to the importance
> attached to then in this respect: they were so called
> because they were considered really to indicate the
> 'meanings'. And so, in the present day, there is not
> a work which touches on the subject of the accents but
> lays special stress on this their *interpunctional*
> value."[27]

Rylands Library (1971-72) 54:214-222; "The Oldest Accent List in
the *Diqduqe Hate'amim*," *Textus* (1973) 8:138-159; "Aristotle and
the Accents," *Journal of Semitic Studies*, (1974) 19:19-35; "The
Hebrew Accents and the Greek Ekphonetic Neumes," *Studies in
Eastern Chant* (1974) 4:140-70; "The Diacritical Dots and the
Development of the Arabic Alphabet," *Journal of Semitic Studies*
(1975) 20:178-80; "Biblical Punctuation and Chant in the Second
Temple Period," *JSL* (1976); "Pausal Forms and the Structure of
Biblical Poetry," *Vetus Testamentum* (1981) 31:186-199; David
Weisberg, "The Rare Accents of the Twenty-One Books," *Jewish
Quarterly Review* (April 1966) 56(4):315-36, (July 1966) 57(1):57-
70, (January 1967) 57(3):227-38; Eric Werner, "Trop and Tropus:
Etymology and History," *Hebrew Union College Annual* (1975)
46:289-96; H. Yalon, "Metiga," *Leshonenu* (1964-65) 29:24-26;
Israel Yeivin, "Some Manifestations of Milra' Tendency in Hebrew,"
Eretz-Israel (1958) 5:145-49; "A Unique Combination of Accents,"
Textus (1960) 1:209-10.

   [26] Wickes, I, 51.

   [27] Wickes, I, 3-4; emphasis his.

The accents complement the grammar and syntax of Hebrew, preserving the traditional understanding of the text, an understanding with roots in the deep recesses of antiquity. No serious expositor of Scripture should neglect such important keys to Biblical exposition. Mason and Bernard offered strict advice:

> the order of construction marked out by the accents should always be strictly adhered to; and no Commentator, however great his name and credit, who might construe in a manner at variance with the arrangement and connexion of a sentence as defined by the Accents, ought to be attended to: as indeed we are enjoined by that mighty master of Hebrew lore, *Aben Ezra*, in those significant words,--

כל פירוש שאינו על פי הנחת הטעמים לא תאבה לו ולא תשמע אליו

> Any interpretation which is not in accordance with the arrangement of the Accents, thou shalt not consent to it, nor listen to it.[18]

Although exceptions may be found to this exhortation, yet it is worthy of careful adherence. The essence of this exhortation is echoed by a current Hebrew grammarian, Bruce K. Waltke:

> So important is the accentuation of Hebrew grammar for understanding that medieval Jewish sources paid more attention to it than to establishing the correct pronunciation of words. . . . At present it is best to consider the accents as an early and relatively reliable witness to a correct interpretation of the text.[19]

- - - - - - - - - - - - - - - -

[18]Mason and Bernard, II, 235-36.

[19]Bruce K. Waltke, "The New International Version and Its Textual Principles in the Book of Psalms," *Journal of the Evangelical Theological Society* (March 1989) 32(1):25-26. See Bruce K. Waltke and M. O'Connor, *An Introduction to Biblical*

Antiquity of the Accents

The Masoretic vowel points preserve the oral tradition of the text and the accent marks preserve the tradition of cantillation or oral punctuation. Although these signs were not added to the consonantal text until about the eighth or ninth century A.D.,[30] there is evidence that these signs essentially represent an oral tradition that antedates that time by about a millennium. E. J. Revell suggested that the accentuational tradition may have been stabilized earlier than that of pronunciation.[31] He found evidence for the existence of the Hebrew accent system in the second century B.C.[32] The spacing of the words in an early manuscript of the LXX corresponds strikingly with the accents in the Hebrew Bible. Important data from Qumran also seems to support this view.

When the Masoretes developed a system of signs to represent the cantillation that had been orally transmitted to then from antiquity, they evidently developed a set of symbols that had a rather simple syntactic grammar of its own. This grammar defined the hierarchy and range of governance for each symbol. This system was designed to accommodate both the

----

Hebrew Syntax (Winona Lake, IN: Eisenbrauns, 1990); but even this excellent work treats the accents sparsely.

[30]Yeivin concluded "that both vowel and accent signs must have been introduced sometime between the close of the Talmud (c. 600) and 750" (*Tiberian Masorah*, 164).

[31]Revell, "Punctuation and Chant," 181.

[32]Revell, "The Oldest Evidence," 214-22.

musical and syntactical requirements of cantillation. The development of such a system was indeed ingenious.

Usually the simple syntactic grammar of accents was adequate to reflect the sense of the verses to which they were applied. But occasionally the linguistic complexity of a verse exceeded the capacity of the simple syntax of the accents. In these instances the accentuators had to improvise, making necessary compromises to adapt a simple accent grammar to a complex linguistic grammar. Also they had to improvise when the musical restraints of the accent grammar were in conflict with the linguistic syntax. These instances provide the student of accentuation with interesting problems of interpretation.

Four Purposes of Primary Accents

The accents in Biblical Hebrew serve four purposes: (1) phonetically they mark the syllable that receives the principal stress in pronunciation; (2) syntactically they indicate the degree of grammatical separation or connection between adjoining words and phrases much like punctuation marks in English; (3) musically they indicate the relative intonation of a word in cantillation; and (4) in addition, they often reflect the poetic structure of the text.

Marking Stress

Every Hebrew word or phonetic unit has a prominent syllable that receives stress in pronunciation. The prominently stressed syllable of a Hebrew word is marked by one of the accents. The accent mark usually is written above the first consonant of the stressed syllable or below it and immediately to the left of any

vowel there.[33] Most Hebrew words receive the prominent
stress on the last syllable (the ultima); a few are
stressed on the next-to-last syllable (the penultima).
The prominent stress never occurs earlier than the
penultima.   In a few cases the stress distinguishes
inflected forms that otherwise would be spelled exactly
the same.

Marking Syntactic Relationship

    Syntactically the Hebrew accents indicate the
degree of grammatical separation or connection between
adjoining words and phrases much like punctuation marks
in English.   There are two types of accents: (1)
disjunctive accents that divide words or phrases, and
(2) conjunctive accents that join words or phrases.   In
the reading of Hebrew Scripture,   the disjunctive
accents call for a pause following the words on which
they occur.   The duration of the pause depends on the
type of accent: the stronger disjunctive accents call
for longer pauses.   In addition, the two strongest
disjunctive accents frequently alter the pronunciation
of some words,   causing the stress to shift to the
penultima with a corresponding lengthening of the vowel
of the stressed syllable.   On the other hand,   a
conjunctive accent calls for the word on which it
occurs to be read with no pause between it and the word
that follows.[34] This syntactic function of the accents

----

    [33]A few accents are written on the first or last letter of
the word regardless of where the stress occurs. Those that appear
on the first letter of the word are called *prepositive*, and those
that appear on the last *postpositive*. For words marked with these
accents,   the stressed syllable must be determined by the
traditional place of stress associated with the inflected form of
the word.

is discussed in depth in the main body of this work.

Musical Cantillation

In addition to marking the stressed syllable and syntactic relationships, the marks of accentuation also indicate the relative intonation of a word in cantillation, that is, the public liturgical reading of the Hebrew Scriptures in the synagogue. Avigar Herzog described an elaborate system of cantillation.[33] Several different traditions have developed throughout the extended history of synagogue worship. Weil opposed the idea that the system of cantillation may be referred to as "musical." John J. Hughes summarized Weil's views on cantillation:

> According to Weil, the Masoretic chains of cantillation are mathematically governed, following "very rigid rules of production and succession," and have nothing to do with a musical system. Instead, they constitute a precise, rule-governed reading system that enables the reader "to give to his sentence an accent of meaning which is linked to the traditional reading."[34]

----

[32] The rules of the accents are not wholly governed by the syntax of the text, but also to some degree by musical considerations. This is true because only a limited number of conjunctive accents may precede a given disjunctive, and then the laws of governance demand another disjunctive regardless of where the syntactic division needs to occur. This is circumvented to some extent by the use of *Maqqeph*, but minor discrepancies occur. Also the syntactic laws of the accents are much simpler than those of the Hebrew language itself. Thus a certain amount of disharmony is expected.

[33] Avigor Herzog, "Masoretic Accents (Musical Rendition)," *Encyclopedia Judaica* (1971).

[34] John J. Hughes, *Bits, Bytes & Biblical Studies* (Grand Rapids: Zondervan, 1987), 518.

Weil reasoned that a system that would be primarily musical would require at least one note for each of the syllables of each word of the text. He is right in observing that the accents do not define a syllable-by-syllable melody for the text, but he is wrong in denying that the accents are devoid of any musical connotation.

In the first place, those who describe the musical character of the accents indicate that each accent signifies a sequence of tones, rather than a single tone. Thus a kind of melody is defined for each word, even though the number of tones of the melody ascribed to a word may not exactly match the number of syllables in the given word. The cantor must accommodate the melody to the syllables of the word, either by singing multiple tones on a single syllable (melisma) or multiple syllables with a single tone (chant).

In the second place, although it is true that the grammar rules of accentuation are well defined and mathematically governed, yet the rules are sufficiently flexible in certain areas as to accommodate musical variety.[17] In fact, this flexibility may be accounted for by phonetic and musical considerations. Where the grammar rules of accentuation admit options, the

---

[17]The low level disjunctive accents have flexibility in their grammatical structure, and flexible sequences of preceding conjunctive accents. Also the *Zaqeph* exhibits considerable flexibility; and the substitution of *Segolta* for *Zaqeph*, *Pashta* for *Rebia*, and the transformation of *Geresh* are for musical reasons. In the books of poetry even more flexibility exists. Frequently the choice of the conjunctive serving a given disjunctive is determined by musical considerations. The transformation of *Rebia Mugrash*, *Dechi*, and of *Legarmeh* are for musical reasons, as well as the substitution of *Great Shalsheleth* for *Rebia Mugrash*, and of *Little Rebia* for *Sinnor*.

choices are made nearly always on the basis of musical considerations, that is, on the rhythmic and phonetic nature of the context. The evidence supports the view that the accents provide a type of musical guide for chanting (cantillating) the reading of the text.

Yeivin stated that

> their primary function . . . is to represent the musical motifs to which the Biblical text was chanted in the public reading. This chant enhanced the beauty and solemnity of the reading, but because the purpose of the reading was to present the text clearly and intelligibly to the hearers, the chant is dependent on the text, and emphasizes the logical relationships of the words.[38]

Herzog reasoned that the liturgical reading of Scripture in the synagogue was quite early, and that "as to the musical element, the sources merely say that the Bible was to be read and studied only by melodic recitation (cf. Meg. 23a; Song R. 4:11)."[39] He further stated that

> the Tiberian system of accent signs and vowel signs and their functions was based on existing practices not only of the pronunciation and grammatical basis and syntactic structure of the text, but also of its musical rendition.[40]

Herzog was likely correct. Therefore the musical influence on the Hebrew accents should not be excluded even though they are observed to follow well-defined rules.

----

[38] Yeivin, *Tiberian Masorah*, 158.

[39] Herzog, 1098.

[40] Herzog, 1100.

Poetic Structure

Much of the Hebrew Old Testament is written with poetic structure, even those portions that are commonly regarded as prose. Wickes observed:

> It is important to notice the influence which *parallelism* has on the division of the verse. This main ornament of the Hebrew style characterizes all the poetical and (to a great extent) the prophetical parts of the twenty-one Books. It is also found in the simply narrative portions, for a poetic colouring often shews itself even there. The most conspicuous instances are where it is marked by the main dichotomy, but it appears hardly less frequently in the minor divisions of the verse.[41]

This has become increasingly evident as a result of recent studies in Hebrew poetry.[42] For example, Duane L. Christensen asserted that "much of Scripture as we know it was probably performed and sung in liturgical settings in ancient Israel, and thus the form of Scripture is essentially poetic."[43] Again he wrote that

> research in Deuteronomy over the course of the past several years suggests that the Hebrew text in its present form, as preserved by the Masoretes, is a musical composition. The canting tradition of the

----

[41]Wickes, II, 38-39; emphasis his.

[42]M. O'Connor, *Hebrew Verse Structure* (Winona Lake, IN: Eisenbrauns, 1980); Wilfred G. E. Watson, *Classical Hebrew Poetry*, JSOT Supplement 26 (Sheffield: JSOT Press, 1984); S. Haik-Vantoura, *La Musique de la Bible Révelée* (Paris: Dessain et Tolra, 1976); Duane L. Christensen, "Prose and Poetry in the Bible: The Narrative Poetics of Deuteronomy 1, 9-18," *ZAW* (1985) 97:179-189.

[43]Duane L. Christensen and M. Naruchi, "The Mosaic Authorship of the Pentateuch," *Journal of the Evangelical Theological Society* (December 1989) 32(4):467.

> synagogues preserves accurate memory of the original
> performance of the text during the period of the
> second temple in Jerusalem and perhaps earlier. . . .
>
> The book of Deuteronomy is poetry in its entirety.
> . . . Though it contains a lyric 'Song of Moses'
> (chap. 32), most of the book is in the form of
> didactic poetry of a lesser nature so far as
> heightened speech goes.[44]

Finally, in regard to the book of Jonah, which is commonly regarded to be a mixture of prose and poetry, he concluded:

> In light of the foregoing metrical reading of this
> delightful literary masterpiece, it is clear that the
> book of Jonah can be described as a narrative poem,
> written in metrical language in five parts which are
> integrally structured along two primary dimensions.[45]

It is not unusual for the use of the accents to be influenced by poetic structure as well as grammatical syntax. In good poetry, grammatical syntax and poetic structure exhibit considerable harmony. Where such harmony fails, it should not be surprising to find the accents being influenced at times by the rhetorical demands of the poetic structure.

Two Systems of Accentuation

Two sets of accent marks are used in the Hebrew Bible: (1) those used in the twenty-one so-called

----

[44]Christensen and Naruchi, 469-70.

[45]Duane L. Christensen, "Narrative Poetics and the Interpretation of the Book of Jonah," *Directions in Biblical Hebrew Poetry*, ed. Elaine R. Follis, *JSOT* Supplement (1987) 40:45.

prose books of the Hebrew canon; and (2) those used in
the so-called books of poetry (Psalms, Job, and
Proverbs) also referred to as the Books of Truth, based
on the acronym אֱמֶת (truth) constructed from the first
letters of their Hebrew names אִיּוֹב--Job, מִשְׁלֵי--
Proverbs, and תְּהִלִּים--Psalms.⁴⁴   Part One of this work
deals with the set of accents as used in the
Pentateuch. Although this part deals only with the
Pentateuch, it is reasonable to assume that the rules
that explain the use of the accents in the Pentateuch
explain the use of the accents in the remaining prose
books. Part Two deals with those used in the books of
poetry.

For each system of accentuation a set of rules is
provided which have been exhaustively tested and
tabulated by means of a computer. The rules define the
structural syntax of the Hebrew accents using a
generative phrase-structure grammar as a model. Each
set of accents has its own rules and associated
grammar--similar in structure but different in content.
The grammars have proven to be simple and consistent.
They confirm the general conclusions of Weil that the
accents follow a strict system of rules, and they
demonstrate that the rules are consistent with a
generative phrase-structure model. This work differs
from those of Yeiven and Weil in that it deals
primarily with the structural syntax of the accents and
their rules, not primarily with the reasons behind the
rules and their interpretation.

----

⁴⁴Yeivin noted that the accents in the prose sections of Job
(1:1-3:2; 42:7-17) belong to those of the prose books (*Tiberian
Masorah*, 157-8), but the prose verses in 32:1-6a belong to those
of the books of poetry.

PART I

THE SYNTAX OF THE HEBREW ACCENTS
USED IN THE PENTATEUCH

CHAPTER 1

The Prose Accents Marks

As previously stated, two sets of accent marks are used in the Hebrew Bible: (1) those used in the twenty-one so-called prose books of the Hebrew canon; and (2) those used in the so-called books of poetry (Psalms, Job, and Proverbs). Part I of this work deals with the set of accents as used in the Pentateuch. A set of rules of accentuation is provided which have been exhaustively tested and tabulated by means of a computer. The rules define the structural syntax of the Hebrew accents using a generative phrase-structure grammar as a model. It is expected that the rules that explain the use of the accents in the Pentateuch also explain the use of the accents in the remaining prose books.

List of Prose Accents

The following is a list of the accents used in the twenty-one so-called prose books. They are listed and numbered according to the list provided as a companion to BHK.[1] Tables 1-3 provide a numerical summary of the

----

[1] *Erläuterung der Accente zu Kittels Biblia Hebraica,* **Privileg. Bibelanstalt,** Stuttgart. Some authorities have used

accents as used in the Pentateuch.

Disjunctive Accents

Name	Example

(0) Soph Pasuq (סוֹף פָּסוּק)........................דָּבָר׃*

(1) Silluq (סִלּוּק)....................................דָּבָֽר

(2) Athnach (אַתְנַח)..................................דָּבָ֑ר

(3) Segolta (סְגוֹלְתָּא) (postpositive)...............דָּבָ֒ר

(4) Shalsheleth (שַׁלְשֶׁלֶת)..........................דָּבָ֓ר ׀

(5) Little Zaqeph (זָקֵף קָטָן).......................דְּבָ֔ר

(6) Great Zaqeph (זָקֵף גָּדוֹל).....................דְּבָ֕ר

(7) Rebia (רְבִיעַ)....................................דְּבָ֗ר

(8) Tiphcha (טִפְחָא)..................................דָּבָ֖ר

(9) Zarqa (זַרְקָא) (postpositive)..................דָּבָ֘ר

(10) Pashta (פַּשְׁטָא) (postpositive).................דָּבָ֙ר

(11) Yethib (יְתִיב) (prepositive)..................דָּבָ֚ר

(12) Tebir (תְּבִיר)...................................דָּבָ֛ר

(13) Geresh (גֶּרֶשׁ)...................................דָּבָ֜ר

----

different names for some of the accents. These are not regarded
as important for this work. Consult Wickes for more detail.

  *Contrary to accepted authorities, I treat *Soph Pasuq* as a
member of the set of disjunctive accents, because it fits into the
syntax rules that govern their use. It is true that *Soph Pasuq*
does not mark the stressed syllable of a word, but it does mark
the end a verse segment—that segment consisting of the entire
verse.   The consistency of the rules of hierarchic governance
demonstrates that *Silluq* closes the last major segment of a verse,
and not the verse as a whole. This is not the case, however, in
the poetic books, where *Silluq* governs the whole verse.

Name   Example

(14) Garshaim (גַּרְשַׁיִם)................................. דָּבָ֞ר

(15) Pazer (פָּזֵר)...................................... דָּבָ֡ר

(16) Great Pazer (פָּזֵר גָּדוֹל)......................... דָּבָ֟ר

(17) Great Telisha (תְּלִישָׁא גְדוֹלָה) (prepositive)...... ֠דָּבָר

(18) Legarmeh (לְגַרְמֵהּ)................................. דָּבָ֣ר ׀

Conjunctive Accents
     Name   Example

(19) Munach (מוּנַח)................................. דָּבָ֣ר

(20) Mahpak (מַהְפַּךְ)................................. דָּבָ֤ר

(21) Mereka (מֵרְכָא)................................. דָּבָ֥ר

(22) Double Mereka (מֵרְכָא כְּפוּלָה)................... דָּבָ֦ר

(23) Darga (דַּרְגָּא)................................. דָּבָ֧ר

(24) Azla (אַזְלָא)................................. דָּבָ֨ר

(25) Little Telisha (תְּלִישָׁא קְטַנָּה) (postpositive)... דָּבָ֩ר

(26) Galgal (גַּלְגַּל)................................. דָּבָ֪ר

(27) Mayela (מָאיְלָא)[3]........................... וַיְהִ֜י־נָ֯א

(28) Paseq (פָּסֵק)[4]................................. דָּבָ֯ר ׀

----

[3] *Mayela* is really a *Tiphcha-Metheg*. See the discussion under *Metheg* and *Tiphcha*.

[4] *Paseq* is not on the standard list of accents, but it must be included in any discussion of them. It is not a conjunctive accent as its position in the list implies; nor does it mark a stressed syllable as do most of the other accents. But it does call for a slight pause in imitation of a disjunctive accent.

TABLE 1
Numerical Summary of the Disjunctive Accents

	Gen	Ex	Lev	Num	Deut	Total
Soph Pasuq	1533	1213	859	1288	959	5852
Silluq	1533	1213	859	1288	959	5852
Athnach	1466	1145	813	1151	908	5483
Segolta	72	79	55	96	66	368
Shalsheleth	3	0	1	0	0	4
Little Zaqeph	1879	1474	987	1359	1293	6992
Great Zaqeph	175	99	56	125	69	524
Rebia	610	504	312	497	507	2430
Tiphcha	2968	2350	1667	2435	1865	11285
Zarqa	73	80	56	96	66	371
Pashta	1428	1130	777	1055	1039	5429
Yethib	79	90	50	72	65	356
Tebir	623	585	417	576	477	2678
Geresh	244	228	175	223	242	1112
Garshaim	113	99	76	114	108	510
Pazer	29	29	27	36	33	154
Great Pazer	0	0	0	1	0	1
Great Telisha	51	42	56	50	67	266
Legarmeh	60	62	45	60	56	283
Total	12939	10422	7288	10522	8779	49950

TABLE 2
Numerical Summary of the Conjunctive Accents

	Gen	Ex	Lev	Num	Deut	Total
Munach	2271	1835	1270	1748	1653	8777
Mahpak	798	655	452	568	569	3042
Mereka	2415	1879	1371	1857	1595	9117
Double Mereka	1	1	1	2	0	5
Darga	253	221	171	237	209	1091
Azla	247	373	307	393	413	1733
Little Telisha	92	87	71	88	113	451
Galgal	0	0	0	1	0	1
Paseq	29	12	8	20	20	89
Total	6106	5063	3651	4914	4572	24306

TABLE 3
Numerical Summary of Secondary Accents[s]

	Gen	Ex	Lev	Num	Deut	Total
Metheg (Left)	906	797	551	808	793	3855
Metheg (Right)	241	80	40	38	57	456
Metheg (Ultima)	15	2	1	9	7	34
Munach-Metheg	72	86	38	80	88	364
Azla-Metheg	30	31	27	42	24	154
Tiphcha-Metheg	1	0	1	2	0	4
Mereka-Metheg	1	1	1	1	1	5
Mahpak-Metheg	0	0	0	0	0	0[6]
Total	1266	997	659	980	970	4872

----

[s] These statistics of the secondary accents are based on the coding in the computer diskette text supplied by the Facility for Computer Analysis of Texts (FCAT) at the University of Pennsylvania. Unfortunately the *Metheg* was frequently confused for a *Silluq* and I had to automatically convert it to a *Metheg* by the rule: "Any *Silluq* not immediately before *Soph Pasuq* must be converted to *Metheg*." This leaves the statistics with some uncertainty. The accuracy of the coding of the remaining details of the text is much more reliable, having been carefully collated beforehand by others.

[6] *Mahpak-Metheg* is not used in the Pentateuch.

CHAPTER 2

The Prose Laws Of Accentuation

The use of the accents in the Hebrew Bible is governed by strict well-behaved rules. They have their own laws of grammar and syntax, which in turn are in harmony with the grammar and syntax of Biblical Hebrew.

The Laws of Hierarchic Governance

The early authorities recognized a hierarchic order among the disjunctive accents, referring to the various ranks in terms of European nobility.[1] Lee categorized the accents according to the following hierarchic order:[2]

        Emperors:...*Silluq, Athnach*
        Kings:......*Segolta, Zaqeph* (both), *Tiphcha, Rebia*
        Dukes:......*Zarqa, Pashta, Tebir, Geresh* (both)
        Counts:.....*Pazer, Great Telisha*
        Servants:...All conjunctives

On the other hand, Mason and Bernard arranged them in the following ranks:[3]

----

[1]First introduced by Samuel Bohlius in his *Scrutinium sensus Scripturae Sacrae ex accentibus* (1636); Wickes I, ix, 11.

[2]Lee, p. 386; by "both" he meant *Little Zaqeph* and *Great Zaqeph*, and *Geresh* and *Garshaim* (double *Geresh*).

```
Emperors:......Silluq, Athnach
Kings:.........Segolta, Zaqeph (both), Tiphcha
Princes:.......Rebia, Zarqa, Pashta, Tebir, Yethib,
               Shalsheleth
Officers:......Pazer (both), Great Telisha,
               Geresh (both), Paseq
Servants:......All conjunctives
```

Wickes noted this earlier arrangement of the accents in a hierarchic order, but he rejected such categories and terms of nobility.[4] Evident differences in the classification of the accents demonstrate the lack of agreement among the authorities. My own research supports the existence of hierarchic order among the accents, but with the following hierarchic ranks:[5]

Hierarchy	Disjunctive Accents
I	*Soph Pasuq*
II	*Silluq, Athnach*
III	*Tiphcha, Zaqeph, Segolta*
IV	*Tebir, Pashta, Zarqa, Rebia*
V	*Geresh, Pazer, Great Telisha*

In addition, the disjunctive accents observe the

----

[3]Mason and Bernard, II, pp. 232-34.

[4]Wickes, I, 11;   he held to an individual hierarchy for each accent.

[5]Yeivin follows the same ranking except that he has only four "grades" not including *Soph Pasuq* (*Tiberian Masorah*, 159).   He preferred the term "grade" rather than "hierarchy" because the disjunctive character of the "grades" is relative, not absolute. Although, from the point of view of the syntax of the language, the disjunctive force of an accent is relative;   yet, within a verse as far as the syntax laws of the accents themselves are concerned, the hierarchy is absolute.

following rules of governance:

(1) A disjunctive accent governs the domain of a segment of a verse. It stands at the end of the segment it governs. The domain of the segment extends from the given accent forward toward the beginning of the verse until it reaches an accent of equal or greater hierarchic rank, or until it reaches the beginning of the verse.

(2) The domain of a given disjunctive accent may include lesser segments (if any) governed by disjunctive accents immediately subordinate to the given accent.

(3) The domain of a disjunctive accent may consist of the one word (or word-unit) on which the accent appears, in which case the domain is regarded as empty. It may include one lesser segment governed by the immediately subordinate disjunctive accent defined as the "near" subordinate of the given accent, in which case the lesser segment is referred to as "the near subordinate segment," and the domain is regarded as fractional. Finally, it may include a near subordinate segment and, in addition, one or more lesser segments each governed by the immediately subordinate disjunctive accent defined as the "remote" subordinate of the given accent,* in which

----

*The term "remote" is used with respect to the given disjunctive accent and in the direction toward the beginning of the verse. Thus a "near" subordinate segment is adjacent to the word-unit of the given accent, and a "remote" subordinate

case the additional lesser segments are referred to as "the remote subordinate segments," and the domain is regarded as full. Thus the domain of a disjunctive accent may be:

    (a) empty, containing only the word-unit bearing the given accent, with no subordinate segments;

    (b) fractional, containing only a near subordinate segment;

    (c) full, containing a near and one or more remote subordinate segments.

(4) Rules (2) and (3) apply to the governance of hierarchies I-III. The governance of hierarchy IV is similar but has a little more freedom, and accents in hierarchy V govern only empty segments.

(5) The defined order of subordination among the disjunctive accents is as follows:[7]

Hierarchy	Disjunctive	Defined Subordinate Near	Defined Subordinate Remote
I	Soph Pasuq	Silluq	Athnach[8]
II	Silluq	Tiphcha	Zaqeph
	Athnach	Tiphcha	Zaqeph/(Segolta)[9]
III	Tiphcha	Tebir	Rebia
	Little Zaqeph	Pashta	Rebia
	Segolta	Zarqa	Rebia

----

segment is at a distance from the word-unit of the given accent in the direction of the beginning of the verse. There can be no remote subordinate segment without at least an empty near subordinate segment.

[7] Minor deviations from this rule are discussed in the later commentary on the individual accents.

(Continued)

Hierarchy	Disjunctive	Defined Subordinate Near	Remote
IV	*Tebir*	*Geresh*	*Pazer/Telisha*
	Pashta	*Geresh*	*Pazer/Telisha*
	Zarqa	*Geresh*	*Pazer/Telisha*
	Rebia[10]	*Geresh*	*Pazer/Telisha*
V	*Geresh*	Empty	
	Pazer	Empty	
	Telisha	Empty	

The distinguishing characteristic of each hierarchic rank is that it embraces the segments of the next lower rank in its domain. Thus in hierarchy II, both *Silluq* and *Athnach* have *Tiphcha* as the near subordinate segment in their domains, and they have *Zaqeph* as the principal remote segment. In hierarchy III, *Tiphcha*, *Little Zaqeph*, and *Segolta* have *Rebia* in their domains as the remote subordinate segment, and each has a unique near segment from hierarchy IV. In hierarchy IV, *Tebir*, *Pashta*, *Zarqa*, and *Rebia* have their subordinate segments from hierarchy V, all of which have empty domains.

It is interesting to note the increasing number of accents in the succeeding lower hierarchies: Hierarchy I has only one, Hierarchy II has two, Hierarchy III has three, and Hierarchy IV has four. Only in Hierarchy V,

----

*Only one *Athnach* segment is permitted.

*In the domain of *Athnach*, a *Segolta* segment may replace an initial *Zaqeph* segment under certain conditions.

[10] *Rebia* may be preceded by a *Legarmeh* segment, and on rare occasions so may *Pashta* and *Geresh*.

which has only three, does the correspondence cease.
Of course this does not include the alternate
substitutes which have no independent syntactic role.

An accent does not appear in a verse without the
governance of one of the accents to which it is
subordinate. Thus a *Tiphcha* never appears without a
following *Athnach* or *Silluq*; a *Zarqa* never appears
without a following *Segolta*; a *Tebir* never without a
following *Tiphcha*; a *Rebia* never without a following
Tiphcha, *Zaqeph*, or *Segolta*; and so forth.
Furthermore, a remote segment never appears in a verse
without its corresponding near segment. Thus *Athnach*
never appears without a following *Silluq*; a *Zaqeph*
never without a following *Tiphcha*; a *Rebia* never
without a following *Tebir, Pashta*, or *Zarqa*.

The Law of Substitution

Some of the disjunctive accents do not appear in
the laws of hierarchic governance, but serve the role
of designated substitutes for some of the accents in
those laws. Except for *Segolta*, in most cases
substitution takes place for musical reasons, that is,
when the regular segment is empty and the associated
disjunctive accent has no preceding conjunctives. More
specific conditions for substitution are given in the
commentaries on the individual accents. The following
is a list of the substitute segments and the segments
which they replace:

<u>Regular Segment</u>   <u>Substitute Segment</u>

Little Zaqeph..........*Great Zaqeph*
Little Zaqeph..........*Segolta*
Segolta...............*Shalsheleth*

(Continued)

Regular Segment	Substitute Segment
Pashta................	Yethib
Rebia.................	Pashta
Geresh................	Garshaim
Geresh................	Virtual Geresh
Little Pazer..........	Great Pazer
Little Pazer..........	Great Telisha

The Law of Conjunctives

A sequence of words closely related grammatically and syntactically are joined together by conjunctive accents; that is, the first and intermediate words in the sequence have conjunctive accents, and the last word has a disjunctive accent. As far as the governance of the disjunctive accents is concerned, such a conjoined sequence of words functions as a single word (or word-unit); that is, the presence of conjunctive accents has little or no effect on the syntax of the disjunctive accents.[11]

On the other hand, a given disjunctive accent determines the number and kind of conjunctive accents that may appear on the conjoined words preceding it. The following is a list of the number and kind of conjunctive accents that may precede each of the disjunctives:[12]

----

[11]Conjunctive accents have influence on the operation of some of the rules of substitution.

[12]Minor deviations from these general rules are discussed in the later commentary on the individual accents.

Disjunctive Accent	Number and Kind of Permitted Conjunctive Accents[13]
Soph Pasuq.............	None
Silluq..................	0-1 *Mereka*
Athnach.................	0-2 *Munach*
Tiphcha.................	0-1 *Mereka*
Little Zaqeph..........	0-2 *Munach*
Great Zaqeph...........	None
Segolta.................	0-2 *Munach*
Shalsheleth............	None
Rebia...................	0-3 *Munach, Darga, Munach*
Pashta..................	0-2 *Mahpak/Mereka* and *Azla/Munach*
Yethib..................	None
Tebir...................	0-2 *Darga/Mereka* and *Azla/Munach*
Zarqa...................	0-2 *Munach/Mereka* and *Azla/Munach*
Geresh..................	0-5 *Azla/Munach, Little Telisha, Munach*
Garshaim................	0-1 *Munach*
Little Pazer...........	0-6 *Munach*
Great Pazer............	2-6 *Galgal, Munach*
Great Telisha..........	0-5 *Munach*
Legarmeh................	0-2 *Mereka, Azla*

For those disjunctive accents that admit more than one type of conjunctive before them, an ordered rank exists among the admitted conjunctives. In Hebrew order, the ranks are as follows:

Number of Conjunctives	Order of the Conjunctive Ranks
1	Disjunctive + I
2	Disjunctive + I + II
3	Disjunctive + I + II + III
4	Disjunctive + I + II + III + III
5+	Disjunctive + I + II + III + III...+ (III)

----

[13] In this chart the conjunctive accents are listed in Hebrew order according to their rank as discussed in the next paragraph. The slash separates alternatives.

A conjunctive in ordered rank I stands immediately before its governing disjunctive. A conjunctive in ordered rank II stands immediately before its companion in rank I, and a conjunctive in rank III stands immediately before its companion in rank II. A conjunctive in rank III may be repeated when there are more than three conjunctives. Except for *Great Pazer*, the service of disjunctive accents by their admissible conjunctives is optional. But if conjunctives are used, they must appear in their ordered ranks; those of lower ordered rank may not be used without their following companions of higher order.

Apart from a few exceptions discussed in the later commentary, the conjunctive accents generally have the same ordered rank for every disjunctive accent which they may lawfully serve. The most common ordered rank of the conjunctive accents is as follows:

Ordered Rank	Conjunctives in the Rank[14]
I	*Munach, Mahpak, Mereka, Darga, Azla, Galgal*
II	*Darga, Azla, Little Telisha*
III	*Munach*

Several additional observations are of interest. The disjunctive accents of highest hierarchic rank admit the least number of preceding conjunctives. Rank I admits none. Ranks II and III admit a sequence of no more than two of the same kind of conjunctive. Those in Rank IV, and *Geresh* in Rank V, admit sequences of

----

[14] Alternates are not included in the list.

specific conjunctives in ordered ranks;   whereas the
others in   Rank V admit longer sequences of only one
kind of conjunctive.

Mereka serves almost exclusively as the regular or
alternate rank I conjunctive for accents governing near
subordinate segments,   never repeating.   *Munach* serves
as the sole or rank I conjunctive for most accents
governing remote subordinate segments;   it serves as
the musical alternate for rank II *Azla*;   and it serves
as the only conjunctive in ordered rank III, frequently
repeating.   Table 4 defines the ordered rank of the
conjunctives with   respect   to   their   associated
disjunctive.

TABLE 4
Ordered Ranks of the Conjunctives

Disjunctive	Ordered Rank				
	I		II		III
Accent	Regular	Altern.	Regular	Altern.	
Rebia	Munach	--	Darga	--	Munach
Tebir	Darga	Mereka	Azla[15]	Munach	--
Pashta	Mahpak	Mereka	Azla	Munach	--
Zarqa	Munach	Mereka	Azla	Munach	--
Geresh	Azla	--	L.Tel.	--	Munach
Great Pazer	Galgal	--	--		Munach

----

[15]In some cases *Tebir*, *Pashta*, and *Zarqa* appear to have
additional conjunctives, but Wickes (II, 110) correctly attributed

The Law of Transformation

Wickes documented the musical restraints that govern the proximity of certain accents. In the prose books, for musical reasons, *Geresh* cannot stand very close to any of the disjunctives that govern it without being transformed into a *Virtual Geresh* which has a conjunctive standing in its place.[16] In such cases the transformed *Geresh* functions musically as a conjunctive, while continuing to function syntactically as a disjunctive. A similar musical restraint causes *Rebia* to transform into *Pashta* under certain conditions.[17] Similar transformations occur with the accents in the books of poetry.

The Law of Continuous Dichotomy

Regarding the hierarchic governance of disjunctive accents, Wickes formulated the Law of Continuous Dichotomy.[18] Basically the law states that every verse has at least one division (caesura). The disjunctive accents first divide a verse into two dichotomous segments; then these two segments are each divided

----

this to the presence of *Virtual Geresh*, that is, the trans-formation of *Geresh* the presence of which is preserved by its residual conjunctives.

[16]Wickes, II, 100-1.

[17]Wickes, II, 78-79.

[18]Wickes, II, 29-58; he attributed the origin of the theory to C. Florinus in his *Doctrina de Accentuatione divina* (1667), see I, 38, n.1.

into two lesser segments, and so forth, until
dichotomous division can no longer take place.
Dichotomous division occurs where the grammar and
syntax of Hebrew admit the natural separation of
clauses and phrases. Division ceases where grammar and
syntax call for close, inseparable relations between
contiguous words, in which case conjunctive accents are
used.

In regard to the books of poetry, Wickes noted
that the process of division

> proceeds to bisect each minor clause, into which the
> half of the verse has been divided, *supposing three
> words, at least, remain in it;* and so on
> continuously, with every new clause that is formed, so
> long as the conditions just named be fulfilled.[19]

He referred to this process as the Law of Continuous
Dichotomy. This law he also imposed on the prose
books, with an easing of the requirement to divide
three-word clauses in the case of some accents.

However, strictly speaking, this should not be
regarded as a "law." Instead, it should be understood
as the natural consequence of the disjunctive accents
being limited to the service of only one conjunctive--a
limitation imposed by the syntactic grammar of the
accents themselves, not by the syntax of the Hebrew
language. In the books of poetry a disjunctive accent
may be served, at the most, by only one conjunctive.[20]

----

[19]Wickes, I, 38; emphasis his.

[20]See the discussion of the law of conjunctives in Part Two
on the poetic books.

Consequently, in a clause of three words, division must occur whether logic or Hebrew syntax require it or not. The same is true in the prose books for those disjunctives that may be served by only one conjunctive. This restraint is eased only for those disjunctives that may be served by more than one conjunctive, and then only to the degree permitted by the maximum allowable number of conjunctives.

The first major division is made with *Athnach*, the second with *Little Zaqeph* (or one of its admissible substitutes), the third with *Rebia*, and after that by a more varied use of the weak disjunctives. According to Wickes, this dichotomy "served to mark the logical and syntactical interpunction, . . . [and] it constitutes one of the marked and distinguishing features of the system of Hebrew accentuation."[21] But he regarded the fact that it was carried out to the minutest detail to be attributed to something else: "The object aimed at was that which is the essential characteristic of the accentuation--*musical effect.*"[22]

Wickes provided an extremely valuable commentary on the principles involved in determining the place in a verse where division may be expected to occur. Usually division occurs between complementary elements of the verse, or between parallel clauses or phrases of equal function. Division occurs on the basis of equality of rank not on the basis of the length of the segments. Thus one segment may be long and the other

----

[21]Wickes, II, 29.

[22]Wickes, II, 30; emphasis his.

short.   The   following   is a   brief   summary   of   the
syntactic   circumstances under which he indicated   that
division may be expected to occur:[23]

Segment A	Segment B
Clause................Clause
Named subject.........Predicate
Pronoun + Verb........Object
Object................Pronoun + Verb
Adverbial Phrase......Clause
Vocative..............Clause
Phrase................Phrase

He   also noted the common syntactic   relationships
that   usually   require   conjunctive   accents.   The
following is a list of these relationships:

   (1) Two nouns in apposition;

   (2) Two   nouns joined by *Waw* conjunctive forming a
      compound part of speech;

   (3) A substantive and its modifier, such as:

      (a) a   substantive   with   an   attributive
         adjective,

      (b) a substantive with a relative pronoun,

      (c) a substantive with an adverbial modifier;

   (4) A   construct   noun   with   its   *nomen rectum*;

   (5) Two   verbs   in   the   same   grammatical
      construction.

Conjunctives are usually used to join the above
constructions,   but when the constructions are too long
for   the   allowable number of conjunctives,   then   mild
disjunctives are required.

----

[23]Wickes,   II,   30-58.   Yeivin provided   further   valuable
discussion on this subject (*Tiberian Masorah*, 172-76).

Wickes noted that "the interpunctional value of the accents is *relative*, not absolute."[24] He also indicated that the usually expected dichotomy may have been violated for musical or rhetorical purposes.[25] Wickes' law of dichotomy is of great value, but it has several basic flaws.

Unnatural Binary Restraint

First of all it imposes an unnecessary and unnatural binary restraint on the syntax of Hebrew. No natural language is limited to binary rules of grammar and syntax. In addition to pairs, complementary and parallel elements of a language may appear in triplets and quadruplets, or in fact any multiple within the natural limits of language. Hebrew is no different. Wickes noted this problem, but attempted to justify this binary restraint: "In certain cases, indeed, the same accent is *repeated* in the division of the clause; but, from the very nature of the continuous dichotomy, *it loses in disjunctive value* each time of repetition."[26] But this must be certainly doubted in many cases. The *Athnach* domain may include three subordinate segments (*Tiphcha, Zaqeph,* and *Segolta*) all of which are of approximately equal syntactic function. The domains of *Tebir, Zarqa, Pashta,* and *Rebia* may include three subordinate segments (*Geresh, Great*

----

[24]Wickes, II, 58; emphasis his.

[25]Wickes, II, 32-35.

[26]Wickes, II, 31; emphasis his. Yeivin agreed with Wickes on this point (*Tiberian Masorah,* 170).

Telisha, and *Little Pazer*) all of which are of
approximately equal syntactic function; and *Rebia* may
have a fourth (*Legarmeh*). Therefore it seems better to
set aside the binary restraint, and admit triplets,
quadruplets and more when they occur naturally in the
text.

Wickes first developed this strict law of
dichotomy in his treatise on the accents of the books
of poetry. He then arbitrarily imposed the law on the
prose books in his second treatise. I have attempted
to show how inadequate the law is for the books of
poetry in the discussion contained in Part II. It is
just as inadequate to force such an unnatural binary
restraint on the prose books.

Obscure Near Segment

Second, Wickes seems to have overlooked the fact
that the near subordinate segment of a dichotomy is
closed by a disjunctive accent of the same hierarchic
rank as that of the accent that closes the remote
segment. Thus a near *Tiphcha* segment always follows a
remote *Zaqeph* segment (if any) or its substitute; a
remote *Rebia* segment is always followed by a near
Tebir, *Pashta*, or *Zarqa* segment, depending on whether
the *Rebia* is in a *Tiphcha*, *Zaqeph*, or *Segolta* segment,
respectively; a *Geresh* segment always follows a remote
Pazer (if any) or *Great Telisha* (if any). By analogy,
a remote *Athnach* segment is always followed by a near
Silluq segment. In other words, a companion near
subordinate segment must always follow a remote
subordinate segment.

Thus the dichotomy is not indicated by a single

disjunctive accent that appears between two segments; but it is indicated by two accents of equal rank, one closing the near segment and the other closing the remote segment(s). Although Wickes defined the rules of dichotomy for the near segments, he seems to have obscured the parallel role of the near segment and the equal rank of its accent.[27] Yet recognizing this phenomenon greatly simplifies the syntax of the accents.

The role of the near disjunctive accents is obscured by the fact that (apart from *Silluq*) the near disjunctives cannot rest on the last word of the segments which they govern. For example, even though a *Tiphcha* segment ends with the word on which *Silluq* rests, because two accents cannot appear on the same word, the *Tiphcha* of necessity must rest on the first or second word before *Silluq*, depending on the presence of a conjunctive serving *Silluq*; and similarly before *Athnach*. The same is true about *Tebir* before *Tiphcha*, *Pashta* before *Zaqeph*, *Zarqa* before *Segolta*, and *Geresh* before its governing disjunctives.[28] As a result, in very short segments these near disjunctive accents may be forced to rest (1) on a word which syntactically should have a conjunctive, (2) at a minor division within the domain of the disjunctive itself, or (3) in

--- --- --- --- --- --- --- ---

[27]Wickes did recognize the similarity of the dichotomy of the *Tiphcha* and *Zaqeph* segments (II, 89), the similarity of *Segolta* with *Zaqeph* (II, 87-88), and the similarity of the *Rebia* segment with the *Zarqa*, *Pashta*, *Tebir* segments (II, 99-111). But he seems not to have clearly noted their parallel roles.

[28]Once the placement of a near disjunctive is determined, it governs its segment from that location.

place of its companion remote accent. In the first condition Wickes regarded the accent as functioning as merely a "foretone" of the disjunctive following it; in the second condition he regarded the accent to mark the minor division only; and in the third he regarded it as marking the major division.

But this understanding involves several contradictions. On the one hand, the dichotomy of the near disjunctives is comparable to that of their companion remote disjunctives, suggesting that the near and remote accents are of of equal rank and governance. On the other hand, the near disjunctive often must rest on a word which syntactically requires no division or only weak division, suggesting that the accent is not disjunctive at all, or at least much weaker than its disjunctive rank requires.

If the near disjunctives really had such vacillating values, and the dichotomy really were marked only by remote disjunctives, then the confusion could have been resolved (if the ancient accentuators had wanted to) by using in their stead conjunctives or minor disjunctives of lower rank where required, and by letting the remote disjunctives alone mark the end of segments--that is, by doing away with near disjunctives altogether. But the rules of governance, which evidently were formulated by the ancient accentuators themselves, require the presence of a near disjunctive whenever the larger segment in which they occur has a companion remote subordinate segment, regardless of the divisions (if any) that may occur in the near subordinate segment.

Therefore, from the point of view of the grammar

and syntax of the accents, it is better to understand
the near disjunctives to always have their full
disjunctive force, but postponed to the end of the
segment of which they are a part. It is due to the
accidents of musical requirements that they rest on
words that otherwise would have a conjunctive or lesser
disjunctive accent. This latter consideration has
significance for interpreting the accents, but not for
their syntax.

Criteria of Division

     Wickes defined the criteria for the choice of a
disjunctive accent on the basis of the number of words
(or sometimes syllables) between a given disjunctive
accent and the place where the next major division
occurs. For example, concerning the dichotomy of
Silluq he wrote that "with the main dichotomy on the
fifth word and further, Athnach *alone* can be
employed."[29] Yet he himself recorded a few exceptions
to this rule, all of which conform to the laws of
hierarchic governance outlined herein, and which need
not be explained, as he did, as exceptions in need of
correction.[30] But he based his laws on the behavior of
the accents in short segments--the very place where the
near disjunctives appear to have vacillating values.
On the contrary, the long segments should provide the
basis for the laws of hierarchic governance.

     A better criteria for the choice of a disjunctive

----

[29]Wickes, II, 64; emphasis his.

[30]See Ezr 2:35; Neh 7:17, 38; 1 Chr 7:13; 23:12; 2 Chr 1:18.

accent within a given segment should be based on the
depth of further division within the segment and the
relative intensity of the major division of the
segment.[1] For example, an *Athnach* segment that has
three depths of division in at least one of its
subordinate segments must have of necessity a *Zaqeph*
(or *Segolta*) remote subordinate segment and a *Tiphcha*
as the near subordinate segment, regardless of the
number of words between the *Athnach* and the place of
major division. If not enough words intervene to
accommodate *Tiphcha*, then *Tiphcha* must replace the
expected *Zaqeph*, and the governance of the *Tiphcha*
prevails; there is no alternative. This gives the
full segment the surface appearance of a fractional
one; and *Tiphcha*, which indicates the presence of an
empty near subordinate segment, also marks the end of
its companion remote segment. A *Silluq* segment has a
similar restraint.

Whereas, an *Athnach* segment that has no more than
two depths of division in any of its subordinate
segments may be divided as above; or because of
musical or rhetorical preference, it may be fractional
having only a near subordinate *Tiphcha* segment divided
into a *Tebir* segment and a *Rebia* segment, one or both
of which are divided once more. In this latter case,
both *Tiphcha* and *Tebir* are required regardless of the
number of words between *Athnach* and the place of major
division. If not enough words intervene to accommodate
both, then *Tebir* must replace the expected *Rebia*; this

----

[1]Where the laws of hierarchic governance admit flexibility,
musical preference may have influenced a given choice.

gives the full *Tiphcha* segment the surface appearance
of a fractional one. But if not enough words intervene
to accommodate even the *Tiphcha*, then this option is
not admitted--*Tiphcha* must stand in place of *Rebia*. A
Silluq segment has similar flexibility and restraints.

On the other hand, an *Athnach* segment that has
only one further depth of division may be divided as
above; or because of musical or rhetorical preference,
it may be fractional having only a near *Tiphcha*
segment, itself fractional having only a near *Tebir*
segment divided into a *Geresh* and *Pazer* segments. In
this latter case, *Tiphcha*, *Tebir*, and *Geresh* are
required regardless of the number of words between
Athnach and the major division. If not enough words
intervene to accommodate all three, then *Geresh* must
replace the expected *Pazer*; this gives the full *Tebir*
segment the surface appearance of a fractional one.
But if not enough words intervene to accommodate both
Tiphcha and *Tebir*, then this option is not admitted--
Tiphcha must stand in place of *Tebir*. A *Silluq* segment
has similar flexibility and restraints.

These same principles apply to the division of
segments of lower hierarchic ranks, except that the
flexibility diminishes in each successively lower rank.
The principles better explain the behavior of near
disjunctives in the context of short segments. The
application of the principles to the individual accents
is explained in the commentary section that follows.

Complexity

The complexity of Wickes' laws of the accents led
me to search for a simpler scheme, one that could be

programmed on a computer and tested exhaustively. The Law of Conjunctives, the Law of Hierarchical Governance, and the Law of Substitution provide such a scheme. The chapters that follow contain an exhaustive commentary of each accent as used in the Pentateuch, showing the laws in more refined detail and discussing observed deviations and problems.

CHAPTER 3
The Prose Accent In Hierarchy I

This chapter and those that follow discuss each of the Hebrew accents, giving an exhaustive account of their conformity to the laws of the conjunctives, hierarchic governance and substitution, as they are used in the Pentateuch.[1]   Any deviation from these laws is noted, examples are given, problems are discussed, and a count is given of the number of times each alternative is used. The accents are discussed in the order of their hierarchic rank rather than the order in which they are presented on the BHK list. This facilitates clarity. This present chapter discusses the accent in Hierarchy I.

The most dominant hierarchy contains only one accent, *Soph Pasuq*.   The name *Soph Pasuq* means "end of

----

[1] The text of the Hebrew Bible used for this research was supplied on computer diskettes by the Facility for Computer Analysis of Texts (FCAT) at the University of Pennsylvania. The text was that of *Biblia Hebraica Stuttgartensia*, edited by K. Elliger and W. Rudolph (Stuttgart: Deutsche Bibelgesellschaft, 1967/77); copyright held by the German Bible Society, in cooperation with the United Bible Society. Minor corrections were made to the text of the diskettes where it did not conform to the text of BHS, or where the accents in BHS did not conform with the consensus of other printed Hebrew Bibles and the clear expectation of the commonly accepted accent rules.

verse." The accent mark consists of two prominent dots
(:) following the last word of a verse.[2]   It is one of
the few accents that does not mark the stressed
syllable of a word, and has no musical designation
except to signify a major pause.

The domain of *Soph Pasuq* is like that of all other
disjunctives in that it governs a near subordinate
segment (*Silluq*) and a remote subordinate segment
(*Athnach*).   Yet it is unique from the others in that
its domain obviously may not be empty, that is, the
near subordinate segment is mandatory. It also is
unique in that its remote subordinate segment may not
repeat.   Thus its law of governance is rigid and
inflexible.

Authorities have not regarded it as part of the
system of accentuation, but as an independent
punctuation mark. However, its use fits into the
overall pattern of hierarchic governance as the most

----

[2] In Lev 18:17 BHS lacks *Soph Pasuq*, but it is present in BHK,
Bomberg (B), and *Miqra'oth Gedoloth* (MG). This is an evident
defect in BHS or its exemplar, Leningrad B19A (L).

In BHS and BHK in the Book of Numbers, the location of the
division between chapters 25 and 26 does not coincide with the
Hebrew accents. The last verse of chapter 25 (25:19) and 26:1
form only one verse as far as the accents are concerned.   25:19
ends with *Athnach* (with no *Soph Pasuq*), whereas 26:1 consists of
the *Silluq* segment, with *Soph Pasuq* at the end of the verse. On
the other hand, B and MG have *Soph Pasuq* at the end of 25:19. If
BHS has the correct accentuation, then 25:19 would be the only
example of a verse without a *Silluq* segment in the Pentateuch.
Most versions incorporate 25:19 into 26:1 as though they were one
verse, in harmony with the accents.

BHS also lacks *Soph Pasuq* at the end of Ex 20:3, 4, 8, 9, and
10; but it has a footnote indicating that L differs from most mss
and editions in this regard. So also at Deut 5:12 without a note.
These places occur in the records of the Decalog where the
Masoretes provided two sets of accents, to be discussed in a later
section.

dominant   disjunctive   governing   the   two   principal
segments   of   a verse: a *Silluq* segment as   the   near
subordinate   segment,   and an *Athnach* segment   as   the
remote subordinate segment.   The domain of *Soph   Pasuq*
is[3]

(Rule 1)   SOP = $\left\{ \begin{array}{l} \text{Sop + SIL} \\ \text{Sop + SIL + ATH} \end{array} \right\}$

where "SOP"   represents the domain of   a   *Soph   Pasuq*
segment,   that   is,   the entire   verse;   and   "Sop"
represents the word-unit bearing the accent *Soph Pasuq*,
that is,   the   last word-unit in the   verse.   "SIL"
represents   the domain of the *Silluq* near   subordinate
segment,   and "ATH" represents the domain of an *Athnach*
remote subordinate segment.   SOP is never empty.   SIL
is mandatory,   but may be empty;   it is never   omitted
and never repeated.[4]

A verse must have at least a SIL segment,   because
obviously SOP cannot be empty.   If the main   syntactic
division of the verse is strong, then the verse usually
has   both   a SIL and an ATH segment (#1).[5]   If   either

----

[3]The   order of the symbols in the syntax rules follows Hebrew
order.

[4]The   syntax   rules   are written in the form of   a   generative
phrase-structure grammar.   Symbols written in all capital letters
(i.e.,   SIL) represent verse segments governed by a disjunctive
accent;   those written with an initial capital letter (i.e., Ath)
represent   a   word-unit bearing the designated accent.   Those
written   with all lower case letters (i.e.,   ath)   represents a
single   phonetic-unit bearing the designated accent;   only these
last   symbols are terminal symbols.   Brackets enclose the options
of a rule.   Parentheses enclose an element that may be repeated.

[5]The notation "(#1)" refers to example #1 in subsequent text,
and so throughout the book.   Accents in the examples are   usually

major segment of the verse has at least one subordinate
segment with minor divisions that extend to three
depths (that is, it involves segments in Hierarchy V)
then the remote segment must be ATH; otherwise, the
near SIL segment may define the division of the verse
(#2). If the SIL segment is empty, then *Athnach* must
appear on the first or second word-unit before *Silluq*
(#3), depending on the presence of a conjunctive
serving *Silluq*; otherwise it obviously appears earlier
in the verse. Table 5 provides a numerical summary of
the structures of *Soph Pasuq*.

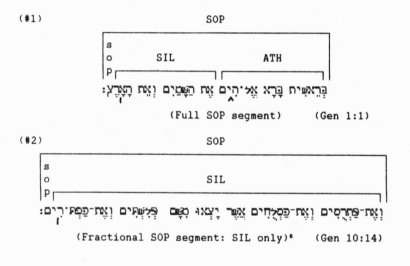

(#1)   SOP

(Full SOP segment)   (Gen 1:1)

(#2)   SOP

(Fractional SOP segment: SIL only)*   (Gen 10:14)

- - - - - - - - - - - - - - - - - -

limited to those accents under discussion and to the higher
ranking accents that govern them. Others are omitted for the sake
of clarity, especially the conjunctives and subordinate
disjunctives not of significance in the current discussion.

*Note that Gen 10:14 has no principal verb, but consists
only of accusative phrases; thus the major syntactic division is
weak, requiring only a *Silluq* segment.

(#3)

```
                          SOP
        ┌─────────────────────────────────────┐
      s │ SIL            ATH                   │
      o │  ┌─────┐  ┌────────────────────┐     │
      p │  │ Sil │  │                    │     │
        │  └─────┘  └────────────────────┘     │
        └─────────────────────────────────────┘
```

וַיֹּ֥אמֶר אֱלֹהִים יְהִי א֑וֹר וַיְהִי־אֽוֹר׃

(Full SOP with empty SIL)   (Gen 1:3)

TABLE 5
Numerical Summary of the Structures of
Soph Pasuq

	Gen	Ex	Lev	Num	Deut	Total
Empty	0	0	0	0	0	0
SIL only	67	68	46	137	51	369
SIL + ATH	1466	1145	813	1151	908	5483
Total	1533	1213	859	1288	959	5852

CHAPTER 4
The Prose Accents In Hierarchy II

The second most dominant hierarchy contains two accents, *Silluq* and *Athnach*. These two accents have several common characteristics. Their domains serve as subordinate segments in the domain of *Soph Pasuq*, and they have similar governance over the accents in Hierarchy III.

Both accents govern a *Tiphcha* segment as the near subordinate, and a *Zaqeph* segment as the remote subordinate. The domain of *Athnach* differs from that of *Silluq* only in that *Athnach* admits the substitution of a *Segolta* segment for an initial *Zaqeph* segment.

The laws of governance are rather strict, allowing only moderate flexibility. The domain of each may be empty; however, if it is not, then the near subordinate segment (*Tiphcha*) is mandatory, but does not admit repetition. The remote subordinate segment (*Zaqeph*), if any, may be repeated as the need for division requires; and in the case of the domain of *Athnach*, substitution of *Segolta* may occur.

Silluq

The name *Silluq* means "separation." The accent mark consists of a small vertical bar placed below the first consonant of the stressed syllable of the last word of the verse and to the left of any vowel there. Except in the anomalous cases,[1] it is the unfailing companion of *Soph Pasuq*.[2] It has no substitute segment.

Silluq evokes the pausal forms[3] of the words upon which it appears. It governs the near subordinate segment in the domain of *Soph Pasuq*. Its companion remote segment (if any) is *Athnach*. The domain of *Silluq* is

(Rule 2a) $$SIL = \begin{Bmatrix} Sil \\ Sil + TIP \\ Sil + TIP + (ZAQ) \end{Bmatrix}$$

where "Sil" represents the word-unit bearing the accent *Silluq*, "TIP" represents the domain of a *Tiphcha* near subordinate segment,[4] and "ZAQ" represents the

----

[1] In Ex 10:1 BHS and BHK erroneously lack a *Silluq* on the last word of the verse; whereas B and MG correctly have it. The same is true for Deut 2:9. These are possible defects in L.

In Num 27:9 BHS is missing a *Silluq* at the end of the verse, with no explanatory note. However, BHK, B, and MG correctly have *Silluq*. This is likely a defect in BHS. The same is true for Deut 12:2 and 23:12.

[2] Wickes (II, 61) regarded *Silluq* to govern the whole verse, but the parallel structure of its domain with that of *Athnach* (II, 69) seems to deny that possibility.

[3] Pausal forms involve tone lengthening of short vowels that would ordinarily remain short under stress, or a shift of the stress from the ultima to the penultima with a corresponding tone lengthening of a vowel that would otherwise reduce to *Shewa*. (See Ges. sect. 29; also Yeivin, *Tiberian Masorah*, 170).

[4] Wickes (II, 62) regarded *Tiphcha* to merely mark the

domain of a *Little Zaqeph* remote subordinate segment.
SIL may be empty, having only Sil (#1); it may be
fractional, having only Sil + TIP (#2); or it may be
full, having Sil + TIP + ZAQ (#3). A TIP segment must
intervene between Sil and ZAQ (if any). The
parentheses mean that ZAQ may repeat (#4, #5).[5] The
large brackets indicate optional alternatives for the
rule.

If the main syntactic division of the segment is
strong, then SIL usually has both TIP and ZAQ
subordinate segments. If either major segment of SIL
has at least one subordinate segment with minor
divisions that extend to two depths (that is, it
involves segments in Hierarchy V) then the remote
segment must be ZAQ; otherwise, the near TIP segment
may define the dichotomy of SIL. If the TIP segment is
empty, then *Zaqeph* must appear on the first or second
word-unit before *Tiphcha* (#3, #4), depending on the
presence of a conjunctive serving *Tiphcha*.

If the major syntactic division of SIL occurs on
the first word-unit before Sil, then TIP replaces ZAQ.
This is necessary because the syntax of the accents
demands that *Tiphcha* precede *Silluq* if SIL is not
empty. In this special case there is a virtual near

"foretone" of *Silluq* at times, but the segment between *Tiphcha* and
Zaqeph often is of parallel syntactic function, as his own
examples demonstrate. The complete domain of TIP includes as the
last element of its segment the word-unit bearing *Silluq*. That
word-unit terminates both the larger segment SIL and its near
subordinate segment TIP. Because two accents cannot appear on the
same word, *Tiphcha* must appear on the first word-unit before the
one bearing *Silluq*, even though its domain includes the latter.

[5] Wickes (II, 66) noted two places where ZAQ repeated four
times--2 Sam 17:9 and 2 Kings 1:3.

subordinate TIP consisting of the word-unit bearing
Sil, and an actual TIP standing as a substitute for ZAQ
(#2).   The syntax of the accents is in disharmony with
the syntax of the Hebrew language in cases of this
sort.   Such disharmony may result in interpretive
problems.   Table 6 provides a numerical summary of the
structures of *Silluq*.

(#1)

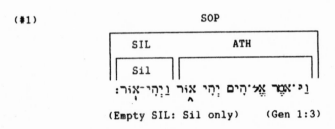

(Empty SIL: Sil only)   (Gen 1:3)

(#2)

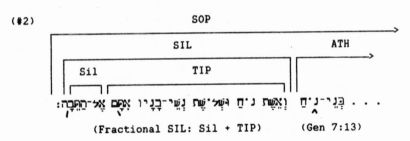

(Fractional SIL: Sil + TIP)   (Gen 7:13)

(#3)

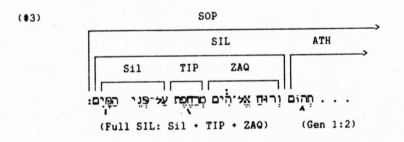

(Full SIL: Sil + TIP + ZAQ)   (Gen 1:2)

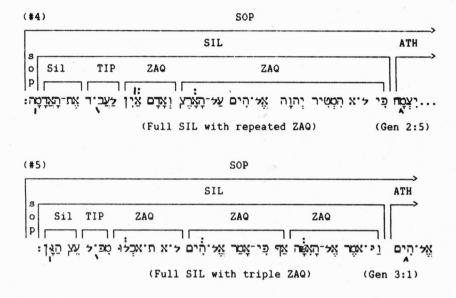

(#4)   SOP

(Full SIL with repeated ZAQ)   (Gen 2:5)

(#5)   SOP

(Full SIL with triple ZAQ)   (Gen 3:1)

TABLE 6
Numerical Summary of the Structures of
Silluq

	Gen	Ex	Lev	Num	Deut	Total
Empty	22	6	3	3	1	35
TIP only	759	614	513	703	415	3004
TIP + ZAQ	634	503	307	519	446	2409
TIP + 2-ZAQ	113	88	36	63	91	391
TIP + 3-ZAQ	5	2	0	0	6	13
Total	1533	1213	859	1288	959	5852

The accent may have only one conjunctive serving
it, and that must always be *Mereka* (mer). Table 7
provides a numerical summary of the conjunctives that
serve *Silluq*. In Hebrew order the rule is

(Rule 2b)   Sil = sil + [mer]

:יֶץ־רֶאָֽהָ וְאֵ֥ת) (Gen 1:1)

TABLE 7
Numerical Summary of Conjunctives
with *Silluq*

	Gen	Ex	Lev	Num	Deut	Total
sil only	890	752	487	774	578	3481
sil + mer	643	461	372	514	381	2371
Exceptions	0	0	0	0	0	0
Total	1533	1213	859	1288	959	5852

Athnach

The name *Athnach* means "rest." The accent mark
consists of two strokes joined at the top to form an
inverted "V" (ᴧ). It is placed below the first
consonant of the stressed syllable and to the left of
any vowel there. *Athnach*, like *Silluq*, evokes the
pausal form of a word. It governs the first principal
segment of a verse, the remote subordinate segment in
the domain of *Soph Pasuq*. An *Athnach* segment is never
repeated,* never occurs without its companion *Silluq*
segment, is seldom omitted (see under *Soph Pasuq*), and
has no substitute segment. The domain of *Athnach* is
like that of *Silluq* except that it admits an initial

----

*In Num 23:3 BHS has two *Athnachs*; whereas BHK, B, and MG
have only one. BHS has (ᴧ) *Athnach* where the others have *Mahpak*
(<). Likewise in Deut 33:25 BHS has two *Athnachs*; whereas BHK, B,
and MG have *Tiphcha* for the second one. These are probably
misprints in BHS.

Segolta segment:[7]

$$
\text{(Rule 3a)} \qquad \text{ATH} = \left[\begin{array}{l} \text{Ath} \\ \text{Ath + TIP} \\ \text{Ath + TIP + (ZAQ)} \\ \text{Ath + TIP + SEG} \\ \text{Ath + TIP + (ZAQ) + [SEG]} \end{array} \right]
$$

where "Ath" represents the word-unit bearing the accent *Athnach*; "TIP" represents the domain of a *Tiphcha* near subordinate segment; "ZAQ" represents the domain of a *Zaqeph* remote subordinate segment; and "SEG" represents the domain of a *Segolta* segment. ATH is rarely empty, having only one word-unit Ath (#1); it may be fractional, having Ath + TIP only (#2); or it may be full, having Ath + TIP + ZAQ (#3). A TIP segment must intervene between Ath and ZAQ or SEG (if any).[8] ZAQ may repeat (#4), and the most remote ZAQ may have a *Segolta* segment as a substitute (#5, #6).[9]

If the main syntactic division of the segment is strong, then ATH usually has both TIP and ZAQ and/or SEG subordinate segments. If either major segment of ATH has at least one subordinate segment with minor

- - - - - - - - - - - - - - - - - -

[7] Wickes (II, 69) recognized the similarity of the domains of *Athnach* and *Silluq*, yet regarded *Silluq* to govern the whole verse (II, 61). Such inconsistencies are avoided by the present rules.

[8] In Lev 25:20 BHS and BHK have *Mahpak*, on the word *no'kal*, leaving no *Tiphcha* between the *Athnach* and the *Zaqeph*; but B and MG correctly have *Tiphcha* instead of *Mahpak*. The complete domain of TIP includes the word-unit bearing the *Athnach* for the same reasons mentioned under the discussion of the *Silluq* segment.

[9] Wickes (II, 70) recorded two instances of three ZAQs with a SEG (Num 16:28; Jer 52:30), and two instances of four ZAQs with a SEG (2 Kings 1:6; Ezek 48:10). Note that *Great Zaqeph* functions as a substitute for *Zaqeph* in #4.

divisions that extend to two depths (that is, it involves segments in Hierarchy V) then the remote segment must be ZAQ (or SEG); otherwise, the near TIP segment may define the dichotomy of ATH. If the TIP segment is empty, then *Zaqeph* must appear on the first or second word before *Tiphcha*, depending on the presence of a conjunctive serving *Tiphcha*; otherwise it obviously appears earlier in the segment.

If the major syntactic division of ATH occurs on the first word-unit before Ath, then TIP replaces ZAQ. This is necessary because the syntax of the accents demands that Tip precede Ath if ATH is not empty. In this special case there is a virtual near subordinate TIP consisting of the word-unit bearing Ath, and an actual TIP standing as a substitute for ZAQ (#2). This is another instance of where the syntax of the accents is in disharmony with the syntax of the Hebrew language. Table 8 provides a numerical summary of the structures of the *Athnach* segment.

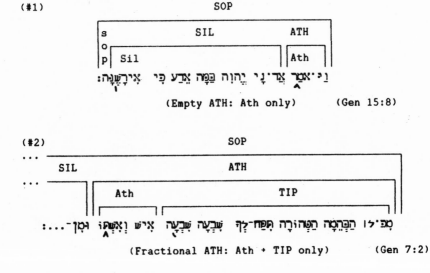

(#1)   SOP

(Empty ATH: Ath only)   (Gen 15:8)

(#2)   SOP

(Fractional ATH: Ath + TIP only)   (Gen 7:2)

(#3)

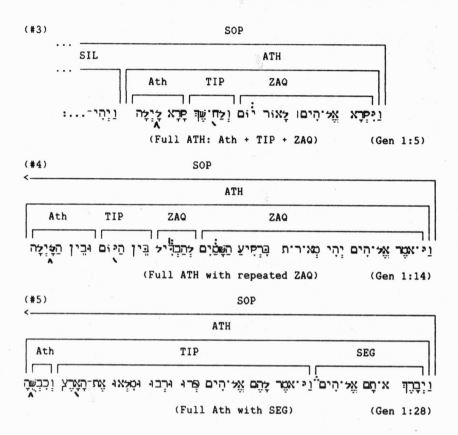

(#4)

(#5)

(#6)

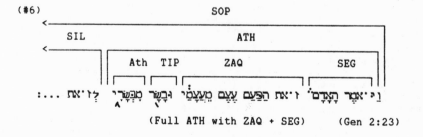

Athnach may have up to two conjunctives preceding it, and they must always be *Munach*. Table 9 provides a numerical summary of the conjunctives serving *athnach*. In Hebrew order, the rule is

(Rule 3b)   Ath = ath + [mun]⁰⁻²

פִּי סוֹב פַּתֶר   (Gen 40:16)

TABLE 8
Numerical Summary of the Structures of
Athnach

	Gen	Ex	Lev	Num	Deut	Total
Empty	9	2	2	0	1	14
TIP only	493	417	258	426	305	1899
TIP + ZAQ	685	491	383	527	426	2512
TIP + 2-ZAQ	198	152	113	99	108	670
TIP + 3-ZAQ	5	4	1	3	2	15
TIP + 4-ZAQ	1	0	0	0	0	1
TIP + SEG	11	13	9	12	8	53
TIP +ZAQ +SEG	49	51	42	65	48	255
TIP + 2-ZAQ +SEG	15	15	5	17	10	62
TIP + 3-ZAQ +SEG	0	0	0	2	0	2
Total	1466	1145	813	1151	908	5483

TABLE 9
Numerical Summary of Conjunctives
with *Athnach*

	Gen	Ex	Lev	Num	Deut	Total
ath only	867	620	467	650	540	3144
ath + mun	598	522	345	500	368	2333
ath + mun + mun	1	3	0	1	0	5[10]
Exceptions	0	0	1	0	0	1[11]
Total	1466	1145	813	1151	908	5183

----

[10] Gen 40:16;   Ex 2:12;   3:4;   12:39;   Num 22:36.   See also 1 Sam 17:39; 28:13;   2 Sam 12:19; 1 Kings 2:37; 21:16; 2 Kings 1:4; 11:1;   Isa 48:11;   54:4; 59:16;   60:1; Ezek 8:6 (Qere);   Amos 3:8 (Wickes, II, 70).   In every instance both words bearing *Munach* are monosyllables that could be joined by *Maqqeph* (cf. B and MG). It is likely that they should be so joined, and that the rule should limit *Athnach* to only one conjunctive.

[11] In Lev 25:20 BHS and BHK have ath + mun + mah, a very rare exception, but B and MG correctly have *Tiphcha* instead of *Mahpak*.

CHAPTER 5

The Prose Accents In Hierarchy III

The third most dominant hierarchy contains three accents and their lawful substitutes, *Tiphcha*, *Little Zaqeph* (or *Great Zaqeph*), and *Segolta* (or *Shalsheleth*). These three accents have several common characteristics. Their domains serve as subordinate segments in the domain of Hierarchy II accents, and they have similar governance over the accents in Hierarchy IV.[1]

All three govern a *Rebia* segment as the remote subordinate, and each governs its own unique near subordinate segment. *Tiphcha* governs *Tebir* as its near subordinate segment, *Zaqeph* governs *Pashta*, and *Segolta* governs *Zarqa*.

The laws of governance in Hierarchy III are much like those in the upper hierarchies. The domains of the accents in Hierarchy III may be empty; but, if not, the near subordinate segment is mandatory, and technically it does not admit repetition.[2] The remote

----

[1] The substitutes govern only empty domains.

[2] Apparent repetition may occur due to admissible substitutions for a *Rebia* segment. See the next note.

subordinate segment (*Rebia*), if any, may be repeated as the need for division requires. Substitution for *Rebia* may occur due to musical restraints or the need for variety.[3]

Tiphcha

The name *Tiphcha* means "disturbance." The accent mark consists of a single diagonal stroke with its top inclined to the left similar to the English back-slash(\); in some printed editions it has a slight downward curvature. It is placed below the first consonant of the stressed syllable and to the left of any vowel there. *Tiphcha* evokes a pausal form when it marks the main syntactic division of a verse.[4] A *Tiphcha* segment serves as the near subordinate segment in the domain of *Silluq* and *Athnach*. Its companion remote segment (if any) is *Zaqeph* or one of its admissible substitutes. A *Tiphcha* segment never is repeated.[5] *Tiphcha* is the most frequently used accent in the prose books, being used 11,286 times in the Pentateuch alone. In Hebrew order, the domain of *Tiphcha* is

----

[3]Due to musical restraints a *Rebia* may be replaced by a *Pashta* occasionally, or on rare occasions by a *Tebir* or *Zarqa*. Such substitution creates the surface appearance of repeated near segments.

[4]This occurs in Num 9:1; Deut 5:32; 6:22; Josh 13:16; Jer 8:1; 13:13; 29:2; 52:18; Ezek 41:17; Neh 5:17; 1 Chr 28:1; 2 Chr 20:22; 24:9; 34:20 (Wickes, II, 61).

[5]In Num 11:25 BHS has two *Tiphchas* in an *Athnach* segment; whereas BHK B and MG correctly have *Mereka* in place of the first one. BHS is possibly defective here.

$$
\text{(Rule 4a)} \qquad \text{TIP} = \begin{bmatrix} \text{Tip} \\ \text{Tip + TEB} \\ \text{Tip + TEB + (REB)} \end{bmatrix}
$$

where "Tip" represents the word-unit bearing the accent *Tiphcha*,[6] "TEB" represents the domain of the near subordinate segment *Tebir*, and "REB" represents the domain of the remote subordinate segment *Rebia*. TIP is very often empty, having only one word-unit Tip (#1, #2); it is frequently fractional, having only Tip + TEB (#2, #3); and it is occasionally full, having Tip + TEB + REB (#3). A TEB segment must intervene between Tip and REB (if any). REB is rarely repeated.[7] For musical reasons a *Pashta* segment may substitute for REB (#4); I refer to such uses of a *Pashta* segment as "*Pashta-B*" (PASHB). Also for musical reasons a *Tebir* segment may substitute for REB (#5);[8] I refer to such

----

[6] In Deut 24:10 BHS is erroneously missing a *Tiphcha* on the word before *Athnach*; a footnote indicates that L is lacking the accent contrary to most MSS and Edd. BHK, B, and MG correctly have *Tiphcha*.
   In Lev 25:20 BHS and BHK erroneously have a *Mahpak* on the word *no'kal* before *Athnach*; whereas B and MG correctly have *Tiphcha*. L is possibly defective there.
   In Deut 13:19 BHS and BHK erroneously have a *Mereka* on the word before *Athnach* instead of *Tiphcha*; whereas B and MG correctly have *Tiphcha*. L is possibly defective there.
   In Ex 4:10 BHS is lacking a *Tiphcha* on the word *dabberka*, whereas BHK, B and MG correctly have it. A footnote in BHS indicates that L is defective there.

[7] Two *Rebia* segments occur in a *Tiphcha* segment in Ex 7:19, Num 28:14, and 35:5. Wickes (II, 78) recorded three *Rebia* segments in 1 Kings 3:11 and 1 Chr 13:2.

[8] Two *Tebir* segments occur in a *Tiphcha* segment in Gen 8:17; 13:18; Ex 3:1; Num 14:40; Deut 3:27; 4:38; 6:10; 8:2; 26:2; 30:20. Wickes correctly suggested that TEB replaces REB under

uses of a *Tebir* segment as *Tebir-B* (TEBB).[9]

If the main syntactic division of the segment is strong, then TIP usually has both TEB and REB as subordinate segments. If either major segment of TIP has at least one subordinate segment with a minor division then the remote segment must be REB; otherwise, the near TEB segment may define the dichotomy of TIP. If the TEB segment is empty, then *Rebia* must appear on the first, second or third word before *Tebir*, depending on the number of conjunctives serving *Tebir*.

If the major syntactic division of TIP occurs on the first word-unit before Tip, then TEB replaces REB. This is necessary because the syntax of the accents demands that a *Tebir* precede *Tiphcha* if TIP is not empty. In this special case there is a virtual near subordinate TEB consisting of the word-unit bearing Tip, and an actual TEB standing as a substitute for REB (#2a).[10] This is another instance where the syntax of

----

certain musical conditions (II, 90-91), thus accounting for an occasional apparent repetition of TEB.

[9]According to Yeivin, "one *revia* can follow another only if three or more words occur between them. Where this is not the case, *pashta* is used instead of the first *revia* before *tifha*.. . . This use of *pashta* is only possible, however, if it is separated from *tevir* by two or more words. If this in not the case, *tevir* and not *pashta* is used instead of the first *revia* before *tifha*, so that . . . *tifha* is preceded by two *tevirs*" (*Tiberian Masorah*, 192). He listed three places where two *Tebirs* occur without a preceding *Rebia* (Eccl 4:8; 6:2; Josh 20:4), but BHS does not have two *Tebirs* in the Eccl passages. Wickes (II, 90) noted three instances where only one word intervenes between *Tebir* and *Pashta-B* (Num 7:87; Judg 16:23; 2 Chr 18:23) for which he proposed emendations.

[10]As discussed previously, the domain of *Tiphcha* actually includes the Sil or Ath following it; but of necessity it must

the accents is in disharmony with the syntax of the
Hebrew language. Table 10 provides a numerical summary
of the structures of the *Tiphcha* segment.

(#1)

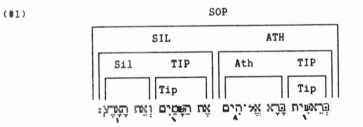

(Empty TIP twice: Tip only)   (Gen 1:1)

(#2)

(Empty TIP and fractional TIP: Tip + TEB)   (Gen 1:8)

(#3)

(Fractional TIP and full TIP: Tip + TEB + REB)   (Gen 2:4)

----

stand on the first word-unit before either. However, as far as
the governance of its own subordinate segments is concerned, the
governance is reckoned from the word on which *Tiphcha* stands.
This principle is true for all near subordinate segments.

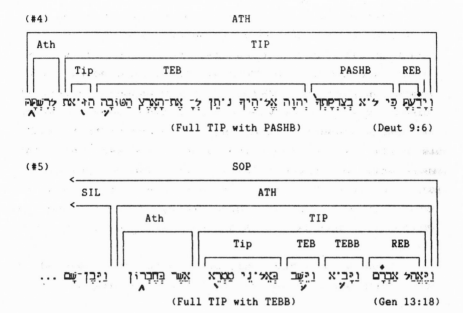

(#4)

(Full TIP with PASHB)   (Deut 9:6)

(#5)

(Full TIP with TEBB)   (Gen 13:18)

TABLE 10
Numerical Summary of the Structures of
Tiphcha

	Gen	Ex	Lev	Num	Deut	Total
Empty	2347	1766	1250	1861	1394	8618
TEB only	522	491	342	456	356	2167
TEB + REB	96	90	74	115	106	481
TEB + 2-REB	0	1	0	2	0	3[11]
TEB + PASHB + REB	0	0	1	1	3	5[12]
TEB+REB+PASHB+REB	1	1	0	0	0	2[13]
TEB + TEBB + REB	2	1	0	1	6	10[14]
Total	2968	2350	1667	2436	1865	11286

Tiphcha is used to mark a secondary stress on rare occasions where *Metheg* would be expected.[13] In this function it is called *Mayela*, but it really is like other accents such as *Munach*, *Azla*, and *Mereka* that stand in place of a *Metheg*. The phenomenon occurs at times by attraction when a disjunctive accent governs an empty segment; the conjunctive accent that would naturally serve the given accent is drawn into the word-unit to replace *Metheg*. Here a disjunctive accent is drawn into the same function by analogy; *Tiphcha* is drawn into a word-unit governed by *Silluq* to replace *Metheg*, because *Tiphcha* naturally precedes this accent.

Tiphcha may have only one conjunctive preceding it, and that must be *Mereka*;[14] but on rare occasions

- - - - - - - - - - - - - - - - - -

[11] Ex 2:19; Num 28:14; 35:5.

[12] Lev 8:26; Num 7:87; Deut 9:6; 20:20; 28:14.

[13] Gen 38:12; Ex 36:3.

[14] Gen 8:17; 13:18; Ex 3:1; Num 14:40; Deut 3:27; 4:38; 6:10; 8:2; 26:2; 30:20.

[15] See Lev 21:4 and Num 15:21; according to Wickes (II, 67) this occurs five times in the OT, these two in the Pentateuch and Isa 8:17; Hos 11:6; and 1 Chr 2:53. In all but the last, the word immediately preceding the *Silluq* has *Athnach*; and in the last, it has *Zaqeph*; this phenomenon occasionally draws a *Tiphcha* to replace *Metheg* because *Tiphcha* naturally intervenes between *Silluq* and *Athnach* or *Zaqeph*. But see Lev 13:18 and 18:20 (and others) where this did not happen. Wickes (II, 73) recorded eleven places where this also occurs in the same word with *Athnach*: Gen 8:18; Num 28:26; 2 Kings 9:2; Jer 2:31; Ezek 7:25; 10:13; 11:18; Ruth 1:10; Dan 4:9, 18; 2 Chr 20:8.

[16] In Ex 31:9 BHS and BHK erroneously have *Munach* + *Tiphcha*; whereas B and MG have mer + tip as expected. In Deut 13:15 BHS and BHK erroneously have *Darga* + *Darga* + *Tiphcha*; whereas B and

Darga + *Double Mereka* + *Tiphcha*[17] is found.   Table 11
provides   a numerical summary of the conjunctives   that
serve *Tiphcha*.   In Hebrew order the rule is

$$\text{(Rule 4b)} \qquad \text{Tip} = \begin{Bmatrix} \text{tip} \\ \text{tip + mer} \\ \text{tip + mer2 + dar} \end{Bmatrix}$$

וַיַּגֶּשׁ־לוֹ וַיֵּ֖רְ   (Gen 27:25)

TABLE 11
Numerical Summary of Conjunctives
with *Tiphcha*

	Gen	Ex	Lev	Num	Deut	Total
tip only	1387	1111	801	1281	809	5389
tip + mer	1580	1237	865	1153	1055	5890
tip + mer2 + dar	1	1	1	2	0	5
Exceptions	0	1	0	0	1	2[18]
Total	2968	2350	1667	2436	1865	11286

Little Zaqeph

The name *Little Zaqeph* means "small upright."   The
accent   mark consists of two dots   arranged   vertically

MG have *Darga* + *Tebir* + *Tiphcha* which conforms to the laws of
hierarchic governance.   A footnote in BHS calls attention to this
deviation.

[17]See Gen 27:25;   Ex 5:15; Lev 10:1; Num 14:3; 32:42. Wickes
noted that this occurs nine other times in the OT (II, 91):   1
Kings 10:3;   20:29; Ezek 14:4; Hab 1:3; Zech 3:2;   Ezra 7:25;   Neh
3:38; 2 Chr 9:2; 20:30.

[18]Ex 31:9; Deut 13:15.

like a small colon (:). The accent is placed above the
first consonant of the stressed syllable. A *Little*
Zaqeph segment is the remote subordinate segment in the
domains of *Silluq* and *Athnach,* and subject to
replacement by its lawful substitutes. Its companion
near segment is *Tiphcha* which is never lacking when a
Zaqeph segment (or its substitute) is present. It is
often repeated twice in the domain of *Silluq* or
Athnach, and occasionally three times.[19] The domain of
Little Zaqeph is the most complex and flexible of all
the other accents; it is

$$(\text{Rule 5a}) \qquad \text{ZAQ} = \begin{Bmatrix} \text{Zaq or GZaq} \\ \text{Zaq + PASH} \\ \text{Zaq + PASH + (REB)} \end{Bmatrix}$$

where "Zaq" represents the word-unit bearing the accent
Little Zaqeph,[20] and "GZaq" represents a word-unit
bearing the accent *Great Zaqeph,* the lawful substitute
for Zaq. "PASH" represents the domain of the near

----

[19]In the *Silluq* domain ZAQ repeats three times in thirteen
places in the Pentateuch (Gen 3:1; 9:16; 27:42; 35:1; 44:16; Ex
18:3; 32:1, 8; Deut 4:21; 15:4; 19:14; 30:16; 31:16), and often it
repeats two times (Gen 1:16; 2:5, 9; 3:1, 17; etc.).   In the
Athnach domain ZAQ repeats three times in eighteen places (Gen
1:11; 9:23; 12:7; 19:8; 26:24; Ex 6:8; 32:2; 33:8; 35:5; Lev 4:21;
Num 7:5; 16:28; 18:28; 35:6; 36:3; Deut 1:22; 19:10; 30:10), and
often it repeats two times (Gen 1:7, 14, 18, 20; 2:19; etc.);
once it repeats four times (Gen 35:22).

[20]In Gen 35:19   BHS and BHK erroneously have a *Rebia* on the
word *'Ephratha;*   whereas B and MG correctly have a *Little Zaqeph.*
This is possibly a defect in L.
     In Ex 28:1 BHS erroneously has a *Little Zaqeph* on the word
'itto; whereas BHK, B, and MG correctly have a *Rebia.*   BHS has
no footnote, so it is possibly a misprint.

subordinate segment *Pashta* or its lawful substitute *Yethib*, and "REB" represents the domain of the remote subordinate segment *Rebia*. ZAQ may be empty, having only Zaq or GZaq (#1); it may be fractional, having only Zaq + PASH (#2); or it may be full, having Zaq + PASH + REB (#3). A PASH segment must intervene between Zaq and REB (if any), and may not repeat. REB may repeat (#4); and, as in the *Tiphcha* segment, for musical reasons a *Pashta-B* segment may substitute for REB (#5, #6); this may create the surface appearance of a repeated PASH.[21]

If the main syntactic division of the segment ZAQ is strong, then ZAQ usually has both PASH and REB as subordinate segments. If either major segment of ZAQ has at least one subordinate segment with a minor division then the remote segment must be REB; otherwise the near PASH segment may define the dichotomy of ZAQ. If the PASH segment is empty, then *Rebia* must appear on the first, second, or third word before *Pashta*, depending on the number of conjunctives serving the *Pashta*.

If one of the major syntactic divisions of ZAQ occurs on the first word before the *Zaqeph*, then PASH replaces the expected REB. This is necessary because

----

[21]According to Yeivin, "one *revia* can follow another only if there are at least three words between them. If this is not the case, then *pashta* is used in place of the *revia* closer to *zaqef*. . . . *Pashta* is not repeated under other conditions" (*Tiberian Masorah*, 187).

Wickes (II, 78) noted only two instances where three *Rebia* segments stand without transformation (1 Kings 3:11 and 1 Chr 13:2). He recorded (II, 80) three instances where four *Rebia* segments are due with transformation (2 Sam 14:7; 1 Kings 2:24; 1 Chr 13:2) and one instance where five are due (Ezra 7:25).

the syntax of the accents demands that a *Pashta* precede
Zaqeph if ZAQ is not empty.   In this special case there
is a virtual near subordinate PASH consisting of the
word-unit bearing Zaq, and an actual PASH standing as a
substitute · for REB (#2).   This is another instance of
where the syntax of the accents is not in harmony with
the syntax of the Hebrew language.   Table 12 provides a
numerical summary of the structures of the *Little
Zaqeph* segment.

(#1)

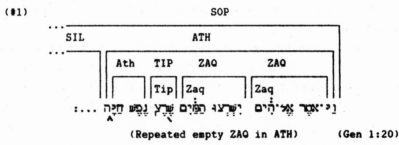

(Repeated empty ZAQ in ATH)   (Gen 1:20)

(#2)

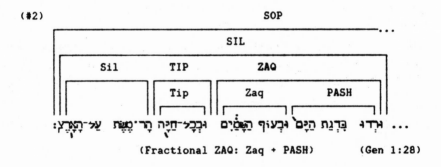

(Fractional ZAQ: Zaq + PASH)   (Gen 1:28)

(#3)

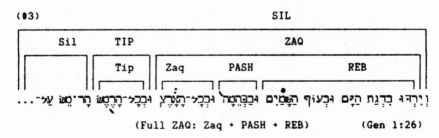

(Full ZAQ: Zaq + PASH + REB)   (Gen 1:26)

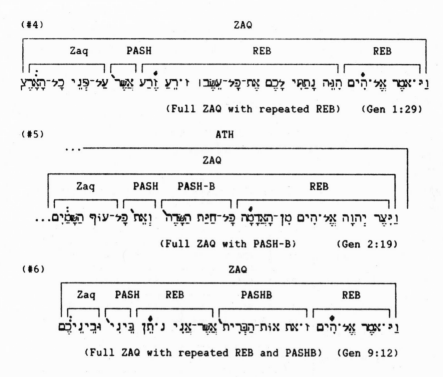

(#4)

(Full ZAQ with repeated REB)   (Gen 1:29)

(#5)

(Full ZAQ with PASH-B)   (Gen 2:19)

(#6)

(Full ZAQ with repeated REB and PASHB)   (Gen 9:12)

Little Zaqeph may have up to two conjunctives preceding it, and they must always be *Munach*. According to Yeivin, *Zaqeph* is served by two *Munachs* only when *Zaqeph* is preceded by *Pashta* or its substitute *Yethib*.[11]   This is consistently true in the

----

[11]Yeivin, *Tiberian Masorah*, 182. As for rank II *Munach*, Wickes (II, 77) noted that about 80% of the time it rests on אֵת. In the Pentateuch this is the case. The remaining instances involve short particles (such as אֵת, הִנֵּה, יֵשׁ, לֹא), compound numbers, or other short words that could (and probably should) be joined by *Maqqeph* (cf. B and MG). If that is consistently the case, perhaps the rule should limit *Zaqeph* to only one *Munach*, and regard the remote one as standing in place of *Maqqeph*. Note a similar condition with *Athnach* (p. 63).

Pentateuch.   Table 13   provides a numerical summary of
the   conjunctives that serve *Zaqeph*.   In Hebrew order,
the rule is

(Rule 5b)   Zaq = zaq + [mun]$^{0-2}$

אֲשֶׁר נָתַתָּה עִמָּדִי   (Gen 3:12)

TABLE 12
Numerical Summary of the Structures of
Little Zaqeph

	Gen	Ex	Lev	Num	Deut	Total
Empty	604	386	240	378	300	1908
PASH only	970	805	591	764	708	3838
PASH + REB	421	345	189	319	310	1584
PASH + 2-REB	3	1	0	3	6	13[13]
PASH + PASHB + REB	52	33	21	20	38	164
PASH+REB+PASHB+REB	4	3	2	0	0	8[14]
PASH+PASH-B +2-REB	0	0	1	0	0	1[15]
Total	2054	1573	1043	1484	1362	7516

----

   [13]Gen 1:29;   15:13;   30:32; Ex 16:8; Num 17:5; 19:2;   22:30;
Deut 1:1, 28; 4:9, 19; 13:6; 17:8.

   [14]Gen 9:12;   15:5;   17:19; 27:37; Ex 4:18; 29:22;   32:1;   Lev
7:21.

   [15]Lev 22:3.

TABLE 13
Numerical Summary of Conjunctives
with *Little Zaqeph*

	Gen	Ex	Lev	Num	Deut	Total
zaq only	727	662	433	641	539	3002
zaq + mun	1137	795	549	708	746	3935
zaq + mun + mun	14	16	5	10	8	53
Exceptions	1	1	0	0	0	2[16]
Total	1879	1474	987	1359	1293	6992

Great Zaqeph

The name *Great Zaqeph* means "great upright." The
accent mark consists of the two dots of *Little Zaqeph*
with a vertical bar immediately to the left of the
dots. The accent is placed above the first consonant
of the stressed syllable. A *Great Zaqeph* is the
substitute accent for the *Little Zaqeph* when the
following conditions exist:

(1) the ZAQ segment is empty, and

(2) the empty segment consists of only one word
(i.e., no conjunctives),[17] and

(3) the one word is short, usually without a
Metheg.[18]

----

[16] In Ex 38:12 BHS and BHK erroneously have a *Mereka* before
Zaqeph, but B and MG correctly have *Munach*. This is possibly a
defect in L. In Gen 18:18 BHS and BHK erroneously have the words
wenibreku bo with *Azla* and *Little Zaqeph* respectively; whereas B
and MG correctly have *wenibreku-bo* with *Azla-Metheg* and *Little
Zaqeph*, the difference being the *Maqqeph*.

[17] Twice BHS erroneously has *Munach* before a *Great Zaqeph* (Lev
14:29; Deut 10:3), but in both cases BHK, B, and MG correctly have
Little Zaqeph. These are possibly misprints in BHS.

Table 14   provides a numerical summary of the structure
of the *Great Zaqeph* segment.

(#1)   וַיֹּ֗אמֶר אֶת־קֹלְךָ֥ שָׁמַ֖עְתִּי בַּגָּ֑ן וָאִירָ֛א כִּי־עֵירֹ֥ם אָנֹ֖כִי וָאֵחָבֵֽא׃
                                                        (Gen 3:10)

(#2)   וַאֵלֶּד עָדָ֖ה אֶת־יָבָ֑ל ה֣וּא הָיָ֔ה אֲבִ֕י יֹ֥שֵׁב אֹ֖הֶל וּמִקְנֶֽה׃
                                                        (Gen 4:20)

TABLE 14
Numerical Summary of the Structure of
Great Zaqeph

	Gen	Ex	Lev	Num	Deut	Total
GZaq	175	99	56	125	69	524

According to the accentuation in BHS there are a
few places where substitution did not occur as
expected.   Most of these are explained as possible
textual problems in BHS:

(1) Gen 22:2;   35:1;   45:14; Ex 25:20, 34; 26:17;
    29:23; 34:1; 36:22; 37:9, 16; Lev 9:19;   Num
    3:36;   4:27, 32;   6:10; 8:8; 10:14, 22, 25;
    18:29; 20:12; 32:33; Deut 10:2; 12:1; 17:8, 9;
    30:1; 31:5; 32:46; so BHS and BHK, but B and
    MG have an associated *Azla-Metheg*.

(2) Lev 15:12;   Num 10:18; so BHS, but BHK, B, and
    MG have an associated *Azla-Metheg*.

(3) Lev 19:37; so BHS and BHK, but B and MG have
    an associated *Metheg*.

----

[18]There are a few exceptions where *Great Zaqeph* is preceded
by *Metheg*. This occurs in Gen 5:6, 18, 28, 32; 8:6; 11:16; 37:23;
Ex 11:1; 16:6, 12; 28:21; Lev 27:32: Num 1:7; 16:30; Deut 4:22;
19:1; 26:5; 33:2. Wickes (II, 83) stated that *Munach* and *Methiga*
(*Azla*) may not replace *Metheg* in the same word with *Great Zaqeph*;
this is true in the Pentateuch.

(4) Deut 2:36; so BHS and BHK, but B and MG have
Great Zaqeph.

Segolta

The name *Segolta* means "cluster." The accent mark
consists of three dots forming a triangle like an
inverted *Segol.* The accent is postpositive, so it
appears above the left corner of the last letter of the
word regardless of which syllable is stressed. A
Segolta segment may substitute for an initial, non-
empty *Little Zaqeph* segment in the domain of *Athnach.*
As a result, it always has a *Tiphcha* segment as a
companion near segment, and may have a parallel
intervening *Zaqeph* segment. The substitution is not
mandatory, and I have found no satisfactory
explanation of the conditions under which substitution
was made. Perhaps the possibility of substitution
provides a degree of flexibility for some musical
variety in cantillation.[19] A *Segolta* segment never
repeats, and an empty *Segolta* segment has *Shalsheleth*
as a substitute. The domain of *Segolta* is

(Rule 6a) $$\text{SEG} = \begin{cases} \text{Shal} \\ \text{Seg + ZAR} \\ \text{Seg + ZAR + (REB)} \end{cases}$$

where "Shal" represents the alternate substitute
Shalsheleth, "Seg" represents the word-unit bearing

----

[19] Wickes (II, 72) regarded the substitution to be made purely
for musical reasons. He recorded (II, 85) one instance where a
Segolta segment erroneously replaces an *Athnach* segment (Ezra
7:13).

the *Segolta* accent, "ZAR" represents the domain of a
near subordinate segment *Zarqa*, and "REB" represents
the domain of a remote subordinate segment *Rebia*. If
SEG is empty, then *Shalsheleth* is its mandatory
substitute. ZAR is never lacking before *Segolta*. SEG
may be fractional, having only the ZAR segment (#1,
#4), or it may be full, having both ZAR and REB (#1,
#2). ZAR is never repeated, and REB is repeated
rarely. For musical reasons ZAR may substitute for a
repeated REB (#3); this creates the surface appearance
of a repeated ZAR. I refer to such uses of ZAR as
Zarqa-B (ZARB). Also for musical reasons *Pashta-B* may
substitute for a repeated REB.[10]

If the main syntactic division of the segment SEG
is strong, then SEG usually has both ZAR and REB as
subordinate segments. If either major segment of SEG
has at least one subordinate segment with a minor
division then the remote segment must be REB;
otherwise the near ZAR segment may define the dichotomy
of SEG. If the ZAR segment is empty, then *Rebia* must
appear on the first, second, or third word before
Zarqa, depending on the number of conjunctives serving
the *Zarqa*.

If one of the major syntactic divisions of SEG

----

[10]According to Yeivin, "one *revia* can follow another only if
they are separated by three or more words. Where this is not the
case, the first *revia* before *segolta* is replaced by *pashta*. . . .
Even this transformation can occur only where the *pashta* is
separated from the following *zarqa* by two or more words. Where
this is not the case, the first *revia* before *segolta* is replaced
by *zarqa* (instead of by *pashta*), so that . . . *segolta* is preceded
by two *zarqas*" (*Tiberian Masorah*, 189-90). He recorded one place
where three *zarqas* appear before *Segolta* (2 Kings 1:16), and two
places where *Zarqa* repeats without a preceding *Rebia* (1 Sam 2:15;
Isa 45:1). Note further that Isa 45:1 lacks *Segolta* after *Zarqa*.

occurs on the first word before the *Segolta*, then ZAR
replaces the expected REB. This is necessary because
the syntax of the accents demands that a *Zarqa* must
precede *Segolta* if SEG is not empty. In this special
case there is a virtual near subordinate ZAR consisting
of the word-unit bearing Seg, and an actual ZAR
standing as a substitute for REB (#1). This is another
instance where the syntax of the accents is in
disharmony with the syntax of the Hebrew language.

A *Segolta* segment may appear as the sole remote
segment in the domain of *Athnach* (#4), that is, SEG may
be used without a subsequent ZAQ. This occurs eleven
times in Genesis, thirteen times in Exodus, nine times
in Leviticus, twelve times in Numbers, and eight times
in Deuteronomy.[31] Table 15 provides a numerical
summary of the structures of the *Segolta* segment.

(#1)   ATH

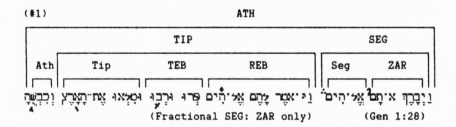

(Fractional SEG: ZAR only)   (Gen 1:28)

----

[31]See Gen 1:28;   17:20;   26:28;   27:33; 30:40, 41;   31:32;
41:45;   42:21;   43:34; 47:17; Ex 3:15; 8:17; 12:4; 16:29; 17:6;
25:33;   30:12; 31:15; 35:2, 35; 36:6;   37:19;   39:5; Lev 5:7,   11;
6:3; 7:18; 11:35; 14:21; 17:5; 25:30; 28:2; Num 11:17;   16:5;
18:11, 19, 26; 22:22; 27:3, 11; 30:6, 13; 35:2;   36:8; Deut 1:7;
2:24; 5:31; 19:6, 9; 22:3; 27:4; 31:14.

TABLE 15
Numerical Summary of the Structures of
Segolta

	Gen	Ex	Lev	Num	Deut	Total
Empty (= Shal)	3	0	1	0	0	4
ZAR only	49	56	32	65	34	236
ZAR + REB	22	22	22	31	31	128
ZAR + ZARB + REB	1	1	1	0	0	3[32]
ZAR + PASHB + REB	0	0	0	0	1	1[33]
Total	75	79	56	96	66	372

(#2)   ZAQ   SEG

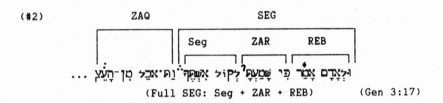

(Full SEG: Seg + ZAR + REB)   (Gen 3:17)

(#3)   TIP   SEG

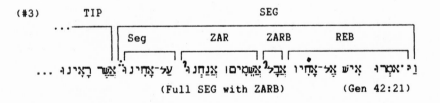

(Full SEG with ZARB)   (Gen 42:21)

----

[32] Gen 42:21; Ex 12:29; and Lev 17:5.

[33] Deut 12:18.

(#4)   ATH

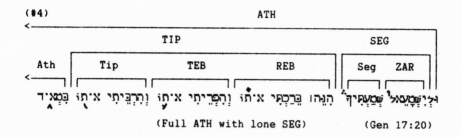

(Full ATH with lone SEG)   (Gen 17:20)

Segolta may have up to two conjunctives before it,
both of which must be *Munach*. Table 16 provides a
numerical summary of the conjunctives that serve
Segolta. In Hebrew order the rule is

(Rule 6b)   Seg = seg + [mun]$^{0-2}$

כִּי עָשִׂיתָ זֹּאת (Gen 3:14)

TABLE 16
Numerical Summary of Conjunctives
with *Segolta*

	Gen	Ex	Lev	Num	Deut	Total
seg only	33	38	18	44	30	163
seg + mun	35	37	35	51	29	187
seg + mun + mun	4	4	2	1	7	18[34]
Total	72	79	55	96	66	368

----

[34]Gen 3:14; 22:9; 26:28; 36:39; Ex 16:29; 28:27; 35:35;
39:20; Lev 4:31; 8:31; Num 5:27; Deut 6:2; 9:21, 28; 12:1, 21;
14:23; 27:2. As is the case of *Zaqeph*, the Rank II *Munach* may
merely replace *Maqqeph* in every case, although the evidence is not
as strong (cf. B and MG).

Shalsheleth

The name *Shalsheleth* means "triplet" or "chain." The accent mark consists of a vertical, three-stepped zigzag line placed above the first consonant of the stressed syllable, together with a vertical stroke like a *Paseq* immediately following the word. The *Shalsheleth* segment is a mandatory substitute for an initial, empty, one-word *Segolta* segment in the domain of *Athnach*. Thus the accent only appears on the first word of a verse. Obviously the domain of *Shalsheleth* is always empty, and it admits no conjunctives. Although *Shalsheleth* is commonly regarded as a substitute for an empty *Segolta* segment, nothing prevents it from being regarded as a rare substitute for an initial *Great Zaqeph* which could have stood in its place in every instance.

Shalsheleth is a rare accent. It occurs only seven times in the Hebrew Bible, four times in the Pentateuch and three times in the other prose books.[33]

----

[33] See Gen 19:16; 24:12; 39:8; Lev 8:23; Isa 13:8; Am 1:2; Ezr 5:15. Wickes (II, 85) suggested that the accent was used (instead of *Segolta* or *Zaqeph*) to attach some special meaning to the passage. Weisberg agreed, stating, "It is my feeling that the question of why the rare accents were introduced may be answered by the assumption that these accents . . . are devices introduced by the Masoretes to connect certain Biblical words with homiletical interpretations" (*JQR* 56(4):333). He regarded *Shalsheleth* to signify some element of hesitation, reticence, repetition, or vacillation (*JQR* 56(4):334).

CHAPTER 6
The Prose Accents In Hierarchy IV

The fourth most dominant hierarchy contains four accents and their lawful substitutes, *Tebir*, *Pashta* (or *Yethib*), *Zarqa*, and *Rebia*. These four accents have many common characteristics. Their domains serve as subordinate segments in the domains of the accents in Hierarchy III, and they have almost the same governance over the accents in Hierarchy V.

The laws of governance are most flexible in this hierarchy, being more strongly affected by rhythmic and musical influences. The syntactic divisions are weak and suitable to variation of expression without significant effect on meaning. Their domains are frequently empty, not subject to further division. But if not empty, the near subordinate segment (*Geresh*) is always present, although present only virtually in some cases.[1]

The most common remote subordinate segment is

----

[1]For musical reasons *Geresh* usually transforms when it is due on the first word before *Tebir*, *Pashta*, or *Zarqa* (but not before *Rebia*), being replaced by the rank I conjunctive of the associated disjunctive accent, and leaving only its residual conjunctives (if any) as evidence of its presence. I regard this phenomenon as a real occurrence of *Geresh* in this work, and refer to it as *Virtual-Geresh*.

Pazer which may repeat. Musical restrictions require *Great Telisha* to replace *Pazer* at times;[2] and musical flexibility permits *Geresh* and *Great Telisha* to reverse positions on rare occasions. *Rebia* admits a *Legarmeh* (or two) between it and *Geresh* (if any).

Tebir

The name *Tebir* means "broken." The accent mark consists of a single diagonal stroke with its top inclined to the right similar to the English slash (/); in some printed editions it has a slight downward curvature. Above the stroke at its middle is a single dot. The accent mark is placed below the first consonant of the stressed syllable and immediately to the left of any vowel there. A *Tebir* segment functions as the near subordinate segment in the domain of *Tiphcha*. Its companion remote segment (if any) is *Rebia*. It never repeats[3] and has no substitute. It most often is empty, but when not so it has a domain of

----

[2]For musical reasons *Great Telisha* usually replaces *Pazer* when it would occur on the first or second word (phonetic-unit) before *Geresh*, but not so earlier in the segment. Wickes noted that *Great Telisha* must not precede the conjunctive accent *Little Telisha* without an intervening disjunctive accent (Wickes, II, 104). The only place where *Great Telisha* could precede *Little Telisha* is on the third word before *Geresh* or *Virtual-Geresh* or earlier. In BHS and BHK *Great Telisha* precedes *Little Telisha* in 2 Sam 14:32, whereas B and MG have *Pazer* as expected. In BHS *Great Telisha* and *Little Telisha* occur on the same word (!) in Est 6:13, whereas BHK, B, and MG have only *Little Telisha*.

[3]A *Tebir-B* segment may stand in place of a *Rebia* segment for musical reasons, giving the surface appearance of a repeated *Tebir*. See the discussion under *Tiphcha* and under *Rebia*.

flexible structure like *Pashta,*   *Zarqa* and *Rebia.* The
domain of *Tebir* is

(Rule 7a)   TEB = $\left\{\begin{array}{l}\text{Teb}\\\text{Teb + GER}\\\text{Teb + GER + (PAZ)}\end{array}\right\}$

where "Teb" represents the word-unit bearing the *Tebir*
accent,   "GER" represents the domain of a   near
subordinate segment *Geresh* or its lawful substitute
Garshaim or *Virtual-Geresh,* "PAZ" represents the domain
of a *Pazer* segment or its substitute   *Great   Telisha*
(GTEL).   TEB may be empty (#1), or fractional with Teb
+ GER only (#2). GER does not repeat.[4]   Teb may be
full with Teb + GER + PAZ (#3).   PAZ may   repeat.[5]
For musical reasons,   *Great Telisha* usually substitutes
for *Pazer* when it would occur on the first or second
word before *Geresh* (#4).   On rare occasions *Geresh* and
Great Telisha may interchange positions.   Table 17
provides a numerical summary of the structures of TEB.

(#1)   SIL   ATH

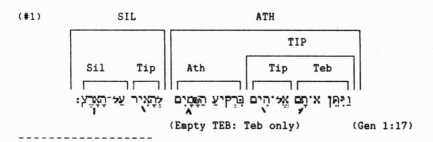

(Empty TEB: Teb only)   (Gen 1:17)

----

[4] In Num 3:39 a *Virtual-Geresh* follows *Geresh* in an unusual
situation.   Note that the words "and Aaron"   are   marked with
Niqqudim.   Note a similar situation in Deut 20:14.   Wickes (II,
104) proposed corrections for these exceptions.

[5] Wickes (II, 106) recorded six instances with three *Pazers*
(Ezra 8:16; Neh 8:4;   11:7; 12:41; 1 Chr 3:24; 28:1), one with
five *Pazers* (2 Chr 17:8), and one with eight *Pazers* (1 Chr 15:1).

(#2)

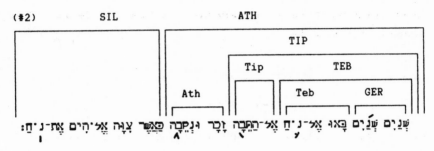

(Fractional TEB with Teb + GER only)   (Gen 7:9)

(#3)

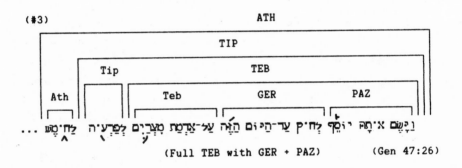

(Full TEB with GER + PAZ)   (Gen 47:26)

(#4)

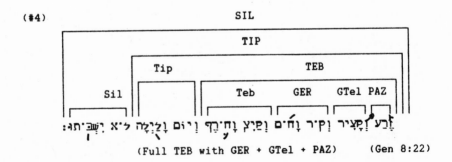

(Full TEB with GER + GTel + PAZ)   (Gen 8:22)

TABLE 17
Numerical Summary of the Structures of
Tebir

	Gen	Ex	Lev	Num	Deut	Total
Empty	546	515	365	506	407	2339
GER only	54	47	30	44	48	223
GER + GTel	13	22	14	13	16	78
GER + PAZ	4	1	7	5	3	20
GER + GTel + PAZ	3	0	1	6	1	11[6]
GER + 2-PAZ	1	0	0	1	0	2[7]
GTel + GER	1	0	0	0	1	2[8]
GTel + GER + PAZ	1	0	0	0	0	1[9]
Exceptions	0	0	0	1	1	2[10]
Total	623	585	417	576	477	2678

Tebir may have up to two preceding conjunctive accents arranged by ordered rank:[11] *Darga* is of rank I with *Mereka* as its alternate,[12] *Azla* is of rank II with *Munach* as its alternative.[13] This produces the

----

[6]Gen 7:2; 8:22; 45:23; Lev 21:12; Num 29:18, 21, 24, 27, 30, 33; Deut 6:22.

[7]Gen 27:33; Num 9:5.   [8]Gen 13:1; Deut 26:12.

[9]Gen 21:14.

[10]Num 3:39; Deut 20:14--both are V-Ger following Ger.

[11]See discussion under the Law of Conjunctives.

[12]According to Yeivin (*Tiberian Masorah*, 201-2), *Darga* usually is used where the *Tebir* and *Darga* would be separated by *Paseq* or more than one syllable, otherwise *Mereka* is used.

following possible sequences in Hebrew order:

```
teb + dar
teb + dar + mun
teb + dar + azl
teb + mer
teb + mer + mun
teb + mer + azl
```

Table 18   a summary of the conjunctives   used   with
Tebir. In Hebrew order the rule is:

(Rule 7b)   Teb = $\left\{ \begin{array}{l} \text{teb} \\ \text{teb} + \left[\begin{array}{l} \text{dar} \\ \text{mer} \end{array} \right] + [\left[\begin{array}{l} \text{azl} \\ \text{mun} \end{array} \right]] \end{array} \right\}$

TABLE 18
Numerical Summary of Conjunctives
with *Tebir*

	Gen	Ex	Lev	Num	Deut	Total
teb only	228	229	149	208	180	994
teb + dar	176	169	118	173	132	768
teb + dar + mun	13	5	10	6	2	36
teb + dar + azl	44	39	39	47	52	221
teb + mer	135	113	70	105	82	505
teb + mer + mun	1	6	7	7	7	28
teb + mer + azl	25	24	24	30	21	124
Exceptions	1	0	0	0	0	1[14]
Total	623	585	417	576	476	2677

----

[14] According to Yeivin (*Tiberian Masorah*, 204) *Munach* is used
when the accent would fall on the first letter of the word,
otherwise *Azla* is used.

Pashta

The   name   *Pashta* means "extending."   The   accent
mark consists of a diagonal line with its top   inclined
to the left like and English back-slash (\);   in some
printed   editions   it   has   an   upward   curvature.   The
accent   is   postpositive,   being   placed   above   the   left
corner of the last letter of a word regardless of which
syllable is stressed.   If the stress does not occur on
the ultima,   a   *Pashta* is also placed above the   first
consonant of the stressed syllable.   When *Pashta* occurs
on   a   monosyllabic word,   it may be confused with   the
conjunctive accent *Azla* which is similar in appearance.
However,   *Pashta* is postpositive whereas *Azla* is   not;
and their syntactic environments differ such that   they
may clearly be distinguished.

A *Pashta* segment functions as the near subordinate
segment in the domain of *Little Zaqeph*.   Its companion
remote segment (if any) is *Rebia*.   It may replace *Rebia*
under certain musical conditions, and has *Yethib* as its
lawful substitute.   It is most often empty,   but has a
domain of flexible structure like that of *Tebir*,   *Zarqa*
and *Rebia*.   The domain of *Pashta* is

(Rule 8a)   PASH = $\begin{cases} \text{Pash/yeth} \\ \text{Pash + GER} \\ \text{Pash + GER + (PAZ)} \end{cases}$

----

[14] In Gen 1:12   BHS and BHK have '*etz* '*ôseh perî* with *Darga* +
Mereka + *Tebir* respectively,   contrary to expectation;   whereas B
and MG have '*etz* '*ôseh-perî* with *Darga* + *Metheg* + *Tebir*,
according to expectation.   The difference is that B   and MG have a
Maqqeph that   designates   '*ôseh* as a   construct   form   capable   of
receiving *Metheg*.
In Deut 5:7,   *Munach* serves *Tebir*,   but the verse has double
accents,   and has *Mereka-Metheg* in the word-unit bearing *Tebir*.

where "Pash" represents the word-unit bearing the
accent *Pashta;*[15] "yeth" represents *Yethib,* the lawful
substitute of Pash; "GER" represents the near
subordinate segment *Geresh* or its lawful substitute
Garshaim or *Virtual-Geresh,* "PAZ" represents a *Pazer*
segment or its substitutes *Great Telisha* (GTEL) or
Great Pazer (GPAZ). PASH may be empty (#1), or
fractional with Pash + GER only (#2). GER does not
repeat. PASH may be full with Pash + GER + PAZ (#3).
PAZ may repeat.[16] *Great Telisha* usually substitutes
for *Pazer* when it would occur on the first or second
word before *Geresh* (#4). On rare occasions *Geresh* and
Great Telisha may interchange positions. Table 19
provides a numerical summary of the structures of PASH.

(#1)

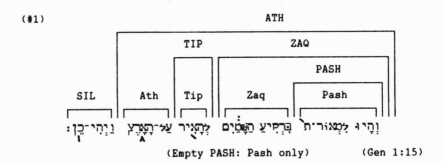

(Empty PASH: Pash only)   (Gen 1:15)

----

[15]Wickes (II, 120) noted three occurrences where a rare
Legarmeh precedes *Pashta* (Lev 10:6; 21:10; Ruth 1:2).

[16]Wickes (II, 106) recorded two instances of three *Pazers*
(Dan 3:7; Neh 13:15), four with four *Pazers* (Josh 7:24; Ezek
43:11; Dan 3:2; 1 Chr 15:24), one with five *Pazers* (Neh 12:36),
and one with six *Pazers* (Neh 8:7).

(#2)   ZAQ

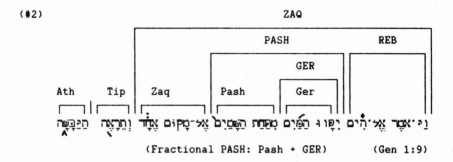

(Fractional PASH: Pash + GER)   (Gen 1:9)

(#3)   ZAQ

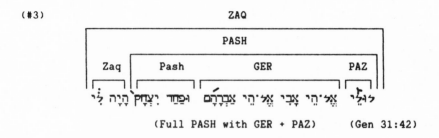

(Full PASH with GER + PAZ)   (Gen 31:42)

(#4)   ZAQ   ZAQ

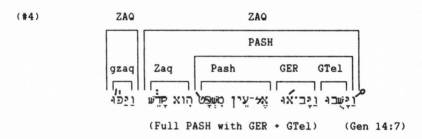

(Full PASH with GER + GTel)   (Gen 14:7)

For musical reasons *Pashta* sometimes substitutes for *Rebia*. In this work I refer to this use of *Pashta* as *Pashta-B*. Wickes stated:

> It is a musical law that when R'bhîa is to be repeated, *there must be three words or more* (i.e. a sufficient melody) *between the two R'bhîas*. Where this is not the case, the second R'bhîa is *transformed* and Pashta put in its stead.[17]

TABLE 19
Numerical Summary of the Structures of
Pashta

	Gen	Ex	Lev	Num	Deut	Total
Empty	1326	1074	705	992	941	5038
Ger only	96	92	67	86	90	431
Ger + GTel	20	13	19	19	24	95
Ger + Paz	5	7	8	9	4	33
Ger + GTel + Paz	2	0	2	0	1	5[18]
GTel + Ger	1	0	2	0	0	3[19]
GTel + Ger + Paz	0	0	0	0	1	1[20]
Exceptions	0	1	0	0	1	2[21]
Total	1450	1187	803	1106	1062	5608

----

[17] Wickes, II, 78; emphasis his.

[18] Gen 22:2; 50:17; Lev 14:13; 20:17; Deut 5:14.

[19] Gen 1:12; Lev 4:7; 13:57. A similar unusual sequence of
accents occurs in Isa 9:5;   Yeivin made special note of this
passage stating "פלא has *telisha* immediately after *geresh* before
pashta, a most surprising combination, intended,   for whatever
reason, to separate פלא from יועץ" (*Tiberian Masorah*, 225).

[20] Deut 17:5.

[21] In Ex 5:8 a *Virtual-Geresh* follows a *Geresh* in an unusual
situation. Wickes (II, 105) suggested a correction for this
exception. In Deut 12:30 BHS erroneously has *Azla* on the word
lē'mōr which produces a false repetition of *Geresh*;   whereas BHK,
B, and MG correctly have *Rebia* on the word.   This is possibly a
misprint in BHS.

He   further   stated   that   "*two Pashtas* often   come
together.   But   then   the   first   is   always   due   to
transformation, and *R'bhia must precede.*"[22]

When   this transformation would be required before
Tebir,   a   *Tebir-B* is sometimes used,   and when before a
Zarqa,   a   *Zarqa-B* is sometimes used.   Usually *Pashta-B*
is empty, but occasionally it undergoes division.   The
syntactic   structures of *Pashta-B* are the same as those
of *Pashta*.   Table 20   provides a numerical summary   of
the structures of *Pashta-B*.

Pashta may   have up to two preceding conjunctive
accents arranged   by ordered rank:[23]   *Mahpak* is of rank
I with *Mereka* as its alternate,[24] *Azla* is of rank   II

TABLE 20
Numerical Summary of the Structures of
Pashta-B

	Gen	Ex	Lev	Num	Deut	Total
Empty	53	31	22	18	36	160
Ger only	4	5	1	2	5	17
Ger + GTel	0	1	1	1	1	4[25]
Exceptions	0	0	0	0	0	0
Total	57	37	24	21	42	181

----

[22]Wickes, II, 79; emphasis his.

[23]See discussion under the Law of Conjunctives.

[24]According to Wickes (II, 107),   mer is used when no
syllable (and no *Paseq*) intervenes, and mah when the interval is
one or more syllables.

[25]Ex 32:12; Lev 8:26; Num 22:5; Deut 9:6.

with *Munach* as its alternative.[16]   This produces   the
following possible sequences in Hebrew order:

pash + mah
pash + mah + mun
pash + mah + azl
pash + mer
pash + mer + mun
pash + mer + azl

Table   21   provides   a   numerical   summary   of   the
conjunctives used before *Pashta*.   In Hebrew order the
rule is:

(Rule 8b)   Pash = $\left\{ \begin{array}{l} \text{pash} \\ \text{pash} + \left[\begin{array}{l} \text{mah} \\ \text{mer} \end{array} \right] \end{array} \right\} + [\left\{ \begin{array}{l} \text{mun} \\ \text{azl} \end{array} \right\}]$

TABLE 21
Numerical Summary of Conjunctives
with *Pashta*

	Gen	Ex	Lev	Num	Deut	Total
pash only	605	452	299	452	431	2239
pash + mah	647	537	367	452	432	2435
pash + mah + mun	25	23	19	17	36	120
pash + mah + azl	126	94	66	98	101	485
pash + mer	18	18	18	22	23	99
pash + mer + mun	1	3	0	4	1	9
pash + mer + azl	6	6	8	9	13	42
Exceptions	0	1	0	1	2	4[37]
Total	1428	1134	777	1055	1039	5433

----

[16] According to Yeivin (*Tiberian Masorah*, 196-97), *Munach* is
used when the accent falls on the first letter of the word,   and
Azla otherwise, with one exception in Est 9:15.

Yethib

The name *Yethib* means "resting." The accent mark consists of two diagonal strokes joined at the left to form a sideward "V" (<). The accent is prepositive, being placed below and to the right of the first letter of a word regardless of which syllable is stressed. *Yethib* is the substitute accent for *Pashta* under the following conditions:

(1) the *Pashta* segment is empty, consisting of only one word with no conjunctives, and

(2) the word is short, having no secondary accent such as *Metheg*, and usually stressed on the first syllable.

Consequently, *Yethib* has an empty domain and admits no preceding conjunctives.

On one-syllable words *Yethib* and *Mahpak* may be confused. But the above rules should distinguish them in most cases. *Mahpak* serves only as the conjunctive of ordered rank I for *Pashta*, and may be preceded by the other lawful conjunctives serving *Pashta*. On the other hand, *Yethib* may stand only where empty *Pashta* itself could stand, without preceding conjunctives.[18]

----

[17] In Ex 10:13   BHS and BHK have *nihag ruach qadim* with *Mahpak*, *Mereka*, and *Pashta* respectively, which is contrary to expectation; whereas B and MG have *nihag ruach-qadim* with *Mahpak*, *Metheg*, and *Pashta*, which conform with the laws of hierarchic governance.   The difference is that B and MG have the *Maqqeph*.

In Num 17:23   BHS and BHK have *wayyose' perach* with *Mahpak*, *Mereka*, and *Pashta*, contrary to expectation, particularly with two accents on one word.   On the other hand B and MG have *Mahpak*, *Metheg*, and *Pashta* which conform to the laws of hierarchic governance.   The *Metheg* marks secondary stress on the ultima, a rare but lawful practice.

In Deut 11:25 and 32:39   BHS erroneously has *Munach* before *Pashta*; whereas BHK, B, and MG correctly have *Mahpak*.   These are possibly misprints in BHS.

Table   22   provides a numerical summary of the use   of
Yethib.

TABLE 22
Numerical Summary of the Use of *Yethib*

	Gen	Ex	Lev	Num	Deut	Total
yet	79	90	50	72	65	356

Zarqa

The   name   *Zarqa* means "scattering."   The   accent
mark consists of a vertical stroke with its   top   bent
sharply   toward   the left to form the appearance   of   a
walking cane;   in some printed editions it   has   the
appearance of a backwards English "S"   reclining on its
back   (~).   The accent is postpositive,   being   placed
above   the   left corner of the last letter of   a   word
regardless of which syllable is stressed.[28]   A   *Zarqa*
segment   functions   as the near subordinate segment   in
the   domain of *Segolta.*[30]   Its companion remote segment

----

[28]Wickes (II,   106-7) noted that the Masoretes made a list of
passages where the ambiguous sign was to be cantillated as *Yethib.*
These included Lev 5:2 and Deut 1:4 in the Pentateuch, which in my
opinion seem more suitable as *Mahpak.*   Yeivin noted that two
Yethibs in succession occur nowhere in the Hebrew Bible   (*Tiberian
Masorah,* 199).

[29]On very rare occasions a second *Zarqa* may appear above the
stressed syllable.   See 2 Sam 3:8 where this occurs in BHS but not
BHK, B, or MG;   see also 2 Chr 19:2   where it occurs in BHS and
BHK, but not B and MG.

[30]Yeivin noted one place where *Zarqa* is not followed by
Segolta (Isa 45:1).   This verse exhibits two irregularities: (1)
two *zarqas* occur with no preceding *Rebia,* and (2) two *Munachs*
serve a *Rebia.*   It has been suggested that the expected *Segolta*
was replaced by *Munach* for exegetical reasons (*Tiberian Masorah,*
205).   See also Wickes II, 136.

(if any) is *Rebia*. It is never repeated,[11] never
omitted, and has no substitute. It is usually empty;
but when not so, it has a flexible domain similar to
that of *Tebir*, *Pashta*, and *Rebia*. The domain of *Zarqa*
is

$$(Rule\ 9a) \qquad ZAR = \begin{cases} Zar \\ Zar + GER \\ Zar + GER + (PAZ) \end{cases}$$

where "Zar" represents the word-unit bearing the accent
Zarqa, "GER" represents the near subordinate segment
Geresh or its lawful substitute *Garshaim* or *Virtual-
Geresh*, "PAZ" represents a *Pazer* segment or its lawful
substitute, a *Great Telisha* segment (GTEL). ZAR is
often empty, consisting of Zar only (#1); it may be
fractional, consisting of Zar + GER (#2); or it may be
full, consisting of Zar + GER + PAZ (#4). PAZ may
repeat. *Great Telisha* usually substitutes for *Pazer*
when it would occur on the first or second word before
Geresh (#3). Table 23 provides a numerical summary
of the structures of a ZAR segment.

(#1)   SEG

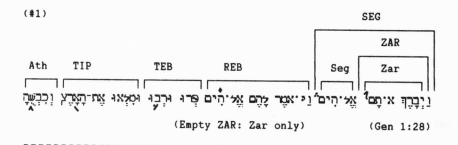

(Empty ZAR: Zar only)   (Gen 1:28)

----

[11]A ZARB segment may stand in place of a REB segment for
musical reasons, giving the surface appearance of a repeated
Zarqa. See the discussion under *Segolta* and under *Rebia*.

(#2)

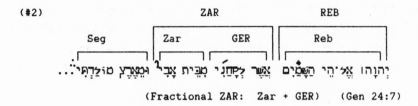

(Fractional ZAR: Zar + GER)   (Gen 24:7)

(#3)

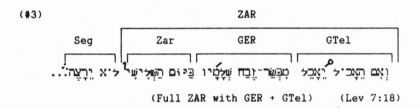

(Full ZAR with GER + GTel)   (Lev 7:18)

(#4)

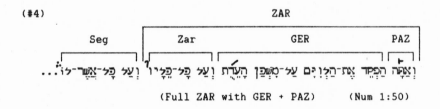

(Full ZAR with GER + PAZ)   (Num 1:50)

Zarqa may have up to two preceding conjunctive
accents arranged by ordered rank:[32] *Munach* is of rank I
with *Mereka* as its alternate,[33] *Azla* is of rank II with
Munach as its alternate.[34] This produces the following

----

[32]See discussion under the Law of Conjunctives.

[33]The rule for using the *Mereka* is not clear.   Yeivin listed
only ten instances (*Tiberian Masorah*, 205).

[34]*Munach* usually is used where the accent falls on the first
letter of a word, otherwise *Azla* is used (Yeivin,   *Tiberian
Masorah*, 205-8).

possible sequences in Hebrew order:

zar + mun

zar + mun + mun

zar + mun + azl

zar + mer

zar + mer + mun

zar + mer + azl

TABLE 23
Numerical Summary of the Structures of
Zarqa

	Gen	Ex	Lev	Num	Deut	Total
Empty	57	70	47	79	50	303
Ger only	11	8	3	12	9	43
Ger + GTel	4	2	6	4	7	23
Ger + Paz	0	0	0	1	0	1[35]
Ger + GTel + Paz	1	0	0	0	0	1[36]
Total	73	80	56	96	66	371

Table 24 provides a numerical summary of the conjunctives used with *Zarqa*. In Hebrew order the rule is:

$$\text{(Rule 9b)} \qquad \text{Zar} = \begin{bmatrix} \text{zar} \\ \text{zar} + \begin{bmatrix} \text{mun} \\ \text{mer} \end{bmatrix} \\ \text{zar} + \begin{bmatrix} \text{mun} \\ \text{mer} \end{bmatrix} + \begin{bmatrix} \text{mun} \\ \text{azl} \end{bmatrix} \end{bmatrix}$$

----

[35] Num 1:50.   [36] Gen 36:6.

TABLE 24
Numerical Summary of Conjunctives
with *Zarqa*

	Gen	Ex	Lev	Num	Deut	Total
zar only	19	19	21	16	21	96
zar + mun	41	43	21	61	27	193
zar + mun + mun	0	2	3	2	2	9
zar + mun + azl	9	10	8	5	7	39
zar + mer	1	2	1	0	0	4
zar + mer + mun	0	0	0	0	0	0
zar + mer + azl	3	4	2	12	9	30
Exceptions	0	0	0	0	0	0
Total	73	80	56	96	66	371

Rebia

The name *Rebia* means "quarter." The accent mark consists of a prominent diamond-shaped dot placed above the first consonant of the stressed syllable of a word. A *Rebia* segment functions as the remote subordinate segment in the domains of *Tiphcha*, *Little Zaqeph*, and *Segolta*. Its mandatory companion near segments are *Tebir* (in the domain of *Tiphcha*), *Pashta* (in the domain of *Little Zaqeph*), and *Zarqa* (in the domain of *Segolta*). It may be repeated (see under the above-mentioned domains); and it has *Pashta-B*, *Tebir-B*, and *Zarqa-B* as possible substitutes. It often is empty; but when not so, it has a flexible domain similar to *Tebir*, *Pashta*, and *Zarqa*, except for the added role of an optional *Legarmeh* segment. The domain of *Rebia* is

$$\text{(Rule 10a)} \quad \text{REB} = \begin{cases} \text{PASHB / TEBB / ZARB} \\ \text{Reb} \\ \text{Reb + LEG} \\ \text{Reb + [LEG] + GER} \\ \text{Reb + [LEG] + GER + (PAZ)} \end{cases}$$

where "Reb" represents the word-unit bearing the accent *Rebia*, "LEG" represents an optional *Legarmeh* segment, "GER" represents the near subordinate segment *Geresh* or its lawful substitute *Garshaim* (but not *Virtual-Geresh*), "PAZ" represents a *Pazer* segment, or its lawful substitutes, a *Great Telisha* segment (GTEL) or a *Great Pazer* segment (GPAZ). REB is often empty, consisting of Reb only (#1); it may be fractional, consisting of Reb + GER (#2); or it may be full, consisting of Reb + GER + PAZ (#4). PAZ may repeat.[37] *Great Telisha* usually substitutes for *Pazer* when it would occur on the first or second word before *Geresh* (#3, #5). The optional LEG segment[38] before Reb is peculiar to the *Rebia* segment and distinguishes its structure from that of its companion segments TEB,

----

[37] *Pazer* occurs twice in a *Rebia* segment in Ex 4:9 and 22:8. Wickes (II, 97) recorded an example of where PAZ occurs five times in REB (1 Chr 16:5).

[38] On rare occasions Leg repeats before Reb, but this may be due to the structure of the LEG segment itself. See the later discussion under *Legarmeh*. It occurs twice in the domain of *Rebia* seven times in the Pentateuch: Gen 7:23; 19:14; Lev 10:9; Num 4:26; 31:30; 32:33; Deut 31:16. Wickes (II, 95) seems to imply that Leg does not appear on the first word before Reb, but he stated that in such cases Leg really stands in place of *Paseq*. Apart from the cases where Leg stands alone in the segment, GER is present in a non-empty segment.

PASH, and ZAR. Table 25 provides a numerical summary
of the structures of a REB segment.

(#1)

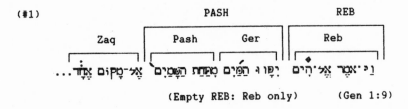

(Empty REB: Reb only)   (Gen 1:9)

(#2)

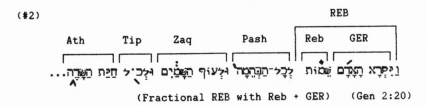

(Fractional REB with Reb + GER)   (Gen 2:20)

(#3)

(Full REB with GER + GTel)   (Gen 8:13)

(#4)

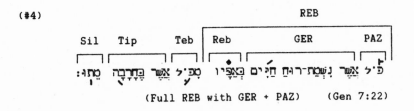

(Full REB with GER + PAZ)   (Gen 7:22)

(#5)

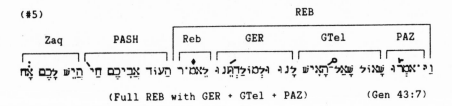

(Full REB with GER + GTel + PAZ)   (Gen 43:7)

TABLE 25
Numerical Summary of the Structures of
Rebia

	Gen	Ex	Lev	Num	Deut	Total
Empty	383	300	164	269	286	1402
Ger only	161	123	92	156	136	668
Ger + Paz	10	15	7	10	18	60
Ger + 2-Paz	0	1	0	1	0	2[39]
Ger + GTel	2	1	8	7	11	29
Ger + GTel + Paz	1	1	0	0	2	4[40]
Ger + GTel + 2-Paz	0	1	0	0	0	1[41]
Leg only	35	36	12	37	21	141
Leg + Ger	14	24	23	12	28	101
2-Leg + Ger	2	0	1	3	1	7[42]
Leg + Ger + GTel	2	1	3	0	0	6[43]
Leg + Ger + Paz	0	1	2	2	3	8[44]
Leg+Ger+GTel+Paz	0	0	0	0	1	1[45]
Total	610	504	312	497	507	2430

----

[39] Ex 4:9; Num 11:26.

[40] Gen 43:7; Ex 13:5; Deut 5:14; 25:19.

[41] Ex 22:8.

[42] Gen 7:23; 19:14; Lev 10:9; Num 4:26; 31:30; 32:33; Deut 31:16.

[43] Gen 1:30; 17:8; Ex 29:22; Lev 13:3, 59; 14:51.

[44] Ex 7:19; Lev 5:4; 11:26; Num 3:38; 11:32; Deut 16:16; 22:6; 27:3.

Rebia may have up to three conjunctives preceding it, arranged by ordered rank:[46] *Munach* is of rank I, *Darga* of rank II, and *Munach* of rank III,[47] producing the following possible patterns:

>   reb + mun
>   reb + mun + dar
>   reb + mun + dar + mun

Table 26 provides a numerical summary of the conjunctives used with *Rebia*. In Hebrew order the rule is

(Rule 10b)   Reb = $\left\{\begin{array}{l}\text{reb} \\ \text{reb + mun} \\ \text{reb + mun + dar + [mun]}\end{array}\right.$

אֲשֶׁר יִשְׁרְתוּ עָלָיו בָּהֶם (Num 4:14)

----

[45]Deut 13:7.

[46]See discussion under the Law of Conjunctives.

[47]According to Yeivin, *Rebia* has a Rank III conjunctive only eight times in the Hebrew Bible: Num 4:14; 2 Sam 21:2; 1 Kings 19:21; 2 Kings 20:3; Isa 5:25; 38:3; Eccl 4:8; Ezra 6:12 (*Tiberian Masorah*, 192-3). In most cases the rank III mun may merely replace *Maqqeph*.

TABLE 26
Numerical Summary of Conjunctives
with *Rebia*

	Gen	Ex	Lev	Num	Deut	Total
reb only	284	214	114	231	215	1058
reb + mun	308	282	195	257	271	1313
reb + mun + dar	18	8	3	8	21	58
reb + mun + dar + mun	0	0	0	1	0	1**
Exceptions	0	0	0	0	0	0
Total	610	504	312	497	507	2430

**Num 4:14.

CHAPTER 7
The Prose Accents In Hierarchy V

The least dominant hierarchy contains four accents and their lawful substitutes, *Geresh* (or *Double Geresh*), *Pazer* (or *Great Pazer*), *Great Telisha*, and *Legarmeh*. These four accents govern empty domains, that is, no further division is permitted; they are served only by their lawful conjunctives.

Geresh

The name *Geresh* means "expulsion." The accent mark consists of a diagonal stroke with its top inclined to the right like and English slash (/); in some printed editions it has an upward curvature. It appears above the first consonant of the stressed syllable of a word, but only in certain contexts. It is used on words with the stress on the penultima or with a preceding *Azla*; otherwise its substitute *Garshaim* is used. A *Geresh* segment functions as a near subordinate segment in the domains of *Tebir*, *Pashta*, *Zarqa*, and *Rebia*. *Geresh* is never repeated;[1]

----

[1] Note exceptions in Ex 5:8; Num 3:39 and Deut 20:14. As previously discussed, Wickes (II, 104-5) proposed corrections for these exceptions.

and has an empty domain.[2]   In Hebrew order the rule is

(Rule 11a)   GER = $\left\{\begin{array}{c}\text{Ger2} \\ \text{Ger}\end{array}\right\}$

where "Ger" represents a word-unit bearing the accent
Geresh and "Ger2" represents a word-unit bearing its
alternate *Garshaim* (Double *Geresh*).

Due to musical reasons, *Geresh* is prone to
transformation;   that is, it vanishes, being replaced
by a conjunctive accent, and leaves evidence of its
presence only by the conjunctives that serve it (if
any). Wickes wrote that

> Géresh . . . does not always maintain its position.
> When due on the first word before Pashta, T'bhîr, or
> Zarqa, it is almost invariably transformed to a
> servus. . . . What is observable is that Great
> T'lîsha and Pazer are often found *subordinated to this
> servus* (which stands for Géresh) just as if Géresh
> itself were present.[3]

What is said of *Geresh* applies also to *Garshaim*.   I
refer to such a "transformed" *Geresh* as *Virtual-Geresh*,
and treat it as a real occurrence of disjunctive
division in the rules. When such a transformation
occurs, the servus (conjunctive accent) to which *Geresh*

----

[2] On rare occasions *Geresh* governs a *Legarmeh*, but this seems
inconsistent with the other uses of *Legarmeh* and with the nature
of the domain of *Geresh*. Wickes (II, 118) suggested that *Legarmeh*
substitutes for *Great Telisha* at times.   It occurs before *Geresh*
in eleven places in the Hebrew Bible: Gen 28:9; 1 Sam 14:3, 47; 2
Sam 13:32; 2 Kings 18:17; Jer 4:19; 38:11; 40:11; Ezek 9:2; Hag
2:12; 2 Chr 26:15.   Once *Virtual Geresh* governs *Legarmeh* (Isa
36:2).

[3] Wickes II, 117-8; emphasis his.

is transformed is the normal rank I conjunctive that
serves the disjunctive before which *Geresh* would stand
--that is, before *Tebir* a *Geresh* is transformed to a
Darga (or its substitute *Mereka*), before *Pashta* it is
transformed to *Mahpak* (or its substitute *Mereka*), and
before *Zarqa* it is transformed to *Munach* (or its
substitute *Mereka*). *Geresh* does not transform
before *Rebia*. If the transformed *Geresh* had any
conjunctives serving it, they remain to serve the
Virtual-Geresh as though *Geresh* itself were present,
and their presence is evidence of the existence of
Virtual-Geresh. But the transformation takes place
even when the *Geresh* would have no conjunctives serving
it.

Apart from some rare exceptions, *Geresh* (or its
lawful substitutes) follows the expectations of the
laws of governance for a near subordinate segment: it
never repeats, and is never lacking after its companion
remote subordinate segments *Pazer* or *Great Telisha*.[4]
Table 27 provides a numerical summary of the use of
Geresh and *Virtual-Geresh*.

Geresh may have up to five[5] conjunctives preceding
it, arranged according to ordered ranks:[6]　　*Azla* is of

----

[4] In Deut 12:30, on the word לְשָׁמְרִי, BHS erroneously has *Azla*
which produces a false repetition of *Geresh*; whereas BHK, B, and
MG correctly have *Rebia* on the word. This is possibly a misprint
in BHS.
　　In Ex 5:8; Num 3:39 and Deut 20:14 *Virtual-Geresh* follows
Geresh contrary to expectation. In these places Wickes (II, 104-
5) proposed corrections to the text. In Gen 1:12; 13:1; 21:14;
Lev 4:7; 13:57; Deut 17:5 GER and GTel reverse their natural
order.

[5] So Wickes (II, 112), but only up to four occur in the
Pentateuch.

TABLE 27
Numerical Summary of Use of *Geresh*

	Gen	Ex	Lev	Num	Deut	Total
Geresh	244	228	175	223	242	1112
Virtual-Geresh	56	41	46	59	65	267
Total	300	269	221	282	307	1379

rank I with *Munach* as its alternative,[7] *Little Telisha*
of rank II, and *Munach* of rank III.   This produces the
following possible sequences:

```
ger + mun
ger + azl
ger + azl + ltel
ger + azl + ltel + mun
ger + azl + ltel + mun + mun
ger + azl + ltel + mun + mun + mun
```

Table   28   provides   a   numerical   summary   of   the
conjunctives   used with *Geresh*.   In Hebrew   order   the
rule is

(Rule 11b)   Ger = $\left\{\begin{array}{l} \text{ger + [mun]} \\ \text{ger + azl} \\ \text{ger + azl + ltel + [mun]}^{0-3} \end{array}\right\}$

קַ֞ם סַפֵּ֧ק וּנְטֵה־יָדְךָ֛ עַל־מֵימֵ֥י מִצְרַ֖יִם   (Ex 7:19)

----

[6]See discussion under the Law of Conjunctives.

[7]Wickes (II, 112) noted that the conjunctive is *Munach* when
on the first letter of the word, and *Azla* otherwise;   but *Munach*
is not used when *Little Telisha* precedes, because for musical
reasons *Little Telisha* must be followed by *Azla*.

TABLE 28
Numerical Summary of Conjunctives
with *Geresh*⁸

	Gen	Ex	Lev	Num	Deut	Total
ger only	29	32	14	29	30	134
ger + mun	2	1	1	2	3	9
ger + azl	149	125	99	133	125	631
ger + azl + ltel	53	57	45	47	66	268
ger+azl+ltel+mun	11	12	16	12	15	66
ger+azl+ltel+mun+mun	0	1	0	0	2	3
Exceptions	0	0	0	0	1	1⁹
Total	244	228	175	223	242	1112

Garshaim

The name *Garshaim* means "double expulsion." The accent mark consists of two *Geresh* marks side by side, as the dual form of the name implies. It appears above the first consonant of the stressed syllable of a word but only in certain contexts. It is used as a substitute for *Geresh* on words with the stress on the ultima and without a preceding *Azla*. *Garshaim* is not repeated, and has an empty domain.

Garshaim may have one preceding conjunctive and that must be *Munach*. Table 29 provides a numerical

----

⁸The table does not include the data for *Virtual-Geresh*.

⁹In Deut 12:30 BHS has the word לְמֹאֵר with *Azla*, creating the erroneous sequence Azl + Azl + Ger; whereas BHK, B, and MG have *Rebia* that results in the lawful sequence Azl + Reb + Ger. This is possibly a defect in BHS.

summary of the use of conjunctives with *Garshaim*.   In
Hebrew order the rule is

(Rule 12)   Ger2 = ger2 + [mun]

                          אֶ֯ פְּרִ֜י   (Gen 1:11)

TABLE 29
Numerical Summary of Conjunctives
with *Garshaim*

	Gen	Ex	Lev	Num	Deut	Total
ger2 only	104	89	68	91	97	449
ger2 + mun	9	10	8	23	11	61
Total	113	99	76	114	108	510

Pazer

       The   name *Pazer* means "scattering."   The   accent
mark   consists   of a vertical stroke with a   horizontal
arm   midway   on   the   right (├─);   in   some   printed
editions the arm is bent upward at the elbow (┘).   It
is   placed   above the first consonant of   the   stressed
syllable of the word.   A *Pazer* segment functions as the
remote   subordinate   segment in the   domain   of   *Tebir*,
Pashta, Zarqa, and *Rebia*.   It has *Great Pazer* and *Great
Telisha* as its lawful alternates.

       Great Telisha nearly always replaces *Pazer* when it
would occur on the first or second word (phonetic-unit)
before   *Geresh*,   but it fails to do so at times if   the
first or second word is long, having numerous syllables
or   words   joined   by *Maqqeph*.[10]   It fails   in   a   few

instances even when *Pazer* occurs on the first word before *Geresh.*[11]   *Great Pazer* replaces *Pazer* under special conditions discussed under that accent.   A *Pazer* segment may repeat as often as required.[12]

Pazer has an empty domain. In Hebrew order the rule is

$$\text{(Rule 13)} \qquad \text{PAZ} = \left\{ \begin{array}{l} \text{GTel or GPaz} \\ \text{Paz} \end{array} \right\}$$

where "Paz" represents a word-unit bearing the accent *Pazer*, "GTel" represents a word-unit bearing the substitute accent *Great Telisha*, and "GPaz" represents a word-unit bearing the substitute accent *Great Pazer*.

Pazer may have up to six preceding conjunctives, all *Munach,*[13] but only up to four occur in the Pentateuch. Table 30 provides a numerical summary of the conjunctives used with *Pazer*. In Hebrew order the rule is

----

[10]This occurs in Gen 32:33; Ex 4:31; 12:27; 34:4; Lev 13:58; Num 18:7; Deut 16:16; Josh 4:8; 22:9, 31; Judg 7:25; 1 Sam 20:2 (but note K and Q); 1 Kings 16:7; Est 4:11; Jer 38:7, 12; 39:16; Ezek 32:25; 46:9; and Dan 5:23.

[11]*Pazer* occurs on the first word before *Geresh* in Deut 22:6; Josh 18:28; 1 Sam 30:14; Jer 28:14; and 44:18. It occurs on the first word before *Garshaim* in Gen 10:13; 1 Sam 17:23; 1 Kings 19:11; 2 Kings 8:29; 1 Chr 1:1; 24:4; 27:25; 2Chr 3:3; 20:26; 22:6; Neh 12:36 (note five PAZ); Eccl 8:11; Isa 16:9; Dan 2:28; Est 1:17; 6:13.

[12]*Pazer* is seldom repeated, but it occurs twice in a *Tebir* segment in Gen 27:33 and Num 9:5; it occurs twice in a *Rebia* segment in Ex 4:9; 22:8; and Num 11:26. Wickes (II, 113) noted an instance where it repeats eight times in a *Tebir* segment (1 Chr 15:18).

[13]Wickes, II, 114.

(Rule 13b)   Paz = paz + (mun)$^{0-6}$

הַיְּטָא נָדָב וַאֲבִיהוּ לִפְנֵי יְהוָה (Num 3:4)

TABLE 30
Numerical Summary of Conjunctives
With *Pazer*

	Gen	Ex	Lev	Num	Deut	Total
paz only	22	23	18	14	18	95
paz+mun	4	5	4	13	9	35
paz+mun+mun	2	1	5	7	5	20
paz+mun+mun+mun	1	0	0	1	1	3
paz+mun+mun+mun+mun	0	0	0	1	0	1
Total	29	29	27	36	33	154

Great Telisha

The name *Great Telisha* means "great drawing out."
The accent mark consists of a diagonal stroke with its
top inclined to the right and with a small circle on
its top. The accent is prepositive and appears above
the upper right-hand corner of the first letter of the
word. A *Great Telisha* segment functions as the lawful
substitute for a *Pazer* segment, the remote subordinate
segment in the domain of *Tebir*, *Pashta*, *Zarqa*, and
Rebia.[14] It has an empty domain and never repeats.

----

[14] In rare instances *Great Telisha* interchanges position with
its companion near subordinate segment *Geresh* (Gen 1:12; 13:1;
21:14; Lev 4:7; 13:57; Deut 17:5; Josh 2:1; 21:6; 23:4; 1 Sam
17:51; 2 Sam 18:29; 1 Kings 16:21; 2 Chr 35:12; Ezra 5:3; 8:17;
Neh 3:15; Isa 9:5; Ezek 3:15; Dan 9:25; Amos 8:13) and with its
alternate *Garshaim* (Deut 26:12; Neh 5:18).

Great Telisha nearly always replaces *Pazer* when it would stand on the first or second word (phonetic-unit) before *Geresh*. This accounts for the observation of Wickes that *Great Telisha* cannot precede *Little Telisha* without an intervening disjunctive,[15] because *Little Telisha*, the rank II conjunctive serving *Geresh*, must stand (if at all) on the second word before *Geresh*. This observation must be supplemented by the fact that *Great Telisha* never precedes *Pazer*. See the previous discussion under *Pazer*.

Great Telisha may have up to five preceding conjunctives, all *Munach*.[16] Table 31 provides a numerical summary of the conjunctives used with *Great Telisha*. In Hebrew order the rule is

(Rule 14) $\text{GTel} = \left\{ \begin{array}{l} \text{gtel} \\ \text{gtel} + (\text{mun})^{0-3} \end{array} \right\}$

וְרָאָה הַכֹּהֵן אֶת־הַנֶּגַע בְּעוֹר־הַבָּשָׂר   (Lev 13:3)

Great Pazer

The name *Great Pazer* means "great scattering." The accent mark consists of two diagonal strokes joined at the bottom like and English "V" with a small circle on top of each branch, thus the alternate name *Qarne Para* meaning "horns of a cow." Its form suggests that it may be a *Double Telisha*. The accent is placed above

----

[15]Wickes, II, 115; he noted an exception in 2 Sam 14:32 which he regarded as a mistake.

[16]A maximum of only three conjunctives precede it in the Pentateuch. Wickes (II, 115) listed four instances where four *Munachs* occur before *Great Telisha* (Judg 18:7; 2 Sam 8:10; Neh 4:1; 6:1), and two instances of five (Jer 41:1; Ezek 47:12); however, BHS has four only in Neh 6:1.

TABLE 31
Numerical Summary of Conjunctives
With *Great Telisha*

	Gen	Ex	Lev	Num	Deut	Total
gtel only	40	28	44	36	41	189
gtel+mun	11	12	8	11	15	57
gtel+mun+mun	0	2	3	1	8	14
gtel+mun+mun+mun	0	0	1	2	3	6
Exceptions	0	0	0	0	0	0
Total	51	42	56	50	67	266

the first consonant of the stressed syllable of the
word.   It never repeats, and has an empty domain.
Great Pazer functions as a rare substitute for *Pazer*,
but I have found no explanation of the circumstances
under which substitution takes place.   It occurs only
sixteen times in the Hebrew Bible[17] and only once in
the Pentateuch.

Great Pazer must have two preceding conjunctives,
and may have up to six; the rank II must be *Munach* and
the rank I *Galgal*[18] as follows:

----

[17] It occurs in Num 35:5; Josh 19:51; 2 Sam 4:2; 2 Kings 10:5;
Jer 13:13; 38:25; Ezek 48:21; Est 7:9; Ezra 6:9; Neh 1:6; 5:13;
13:5, 15; 1Chr 28:1; 2Chr 24:5 35:7. Wickes (II, 114) pointed out
that it occurs eight times before *Rebia* and eight times before
Pashta.   He also suggested that *Great Pazer* was used to call
attention to something noteworthy in the text.   Weisberg
suggested that this accent was introduced to "mark a *midrash
halaka,* (interpretation involving a legal point in Jewish law)"
(*JQR* 56(4):334).

[18] Wickes, II, 114.

gpaz + gal + mun

In Num 35:5 it has only two conjunctives in that order; this is the only occurrence of *Galgal* in the Pentateuch.   In Hebrew order the rule is

(Rule 15)   GPaz = gpaz + gal + [(mun)][1-5]

בְּאַמָּה֩   אַלְפַּ֤יִם   (Num 35:5)

Legarmeh

The name *Legarmeh* means "break" or "to itself." The accent mark combines two marks. The first consists of a vertical and a horizontal stroke joined to form a right angle with the corner at the lower right like a reversed English "L" (⌐) like *Munach*;   it is placed below the first letter of the stressed syllable of the word and immediately to the left of any vowel there. The second is a vertical stroke (|) immediately following the word.   Together they resemble the combination of *Munach* followed by *Paseq* (discussed later).   A *Legarmeh* segment functions as a subordinate segment in the domain of *Rebia,* and of *Pashta* (seldom)[19] and *Geresh* (rarely).   It seldom repeats,[20] and has an empty domain.

Legarmeh may have up to two conjunctives before it, in ordered rank.   Ordered rank I is *Mereka,*[21]   and

----

[19]Yeivin (*Tiberian Masorah,* 215) listed three instances of *Legarmeh* before *Pashta* (Lev 10:6;   21:10;   Ruth 1:2);   he also listed two instances before *Pazer* (Dan 3:2; Neh 8:7), and one before *Tebir* (Isa 36:2).

[20]It occurs twice in the domain of *Rebia* seven times in the Pentateuch: Gen 7:23; 19:14; Lev 10:9; Num 4:26; 31:30; 32:33; Deut 31:16.

rank II is *Azla*.[22]   Other apparent conjunctives are
explained in the later discussion on *Pseudo-Legarmeh*.
Table 32 provides a numerical summary of the
conjunctives used with *Legarmeh*. In Hebrew order the
rule is

(Rule 16) $\text{Leg} = \begin{bmatrix} \text{leg} \\ \text{leg + mer} \\ \text{leg + mer + azl} \end{bmatrix}$

בָּאֵי הֵל יַעֲקֹב| (Gen 31:33)

TABLE 32
Numerical Summary of Conjunctives
with *Legarmeh*

	Gen	Ex	Lev	Num	Deut	Total
leg only	59	61	41	60	53	274
leg + mer	1	1	4	0	3	9
Total	60	62	45	60	56	283

Paseq

The name *Paseq* means "cutting off" or
"interrupter." The accent mark consists of a vertical
stroke (|) immediately following a word, or, perhaps
more accurately, immediately preceding the word to

----

[21]*Mereka* appears as the conjunctive of *Legarmeh* in Gen 31:33;
Ex 14:10; Lev 10:6; 13:52, 59; 21:10; Deut 6:10; 13:6; and 27:3.

[22]Wickes (II, 120) noted only three instances of *Azla* serving
Legarmeh as Rank II: 1 Kings 14:21; Eccl 6:2; 2 Chr 12:13. In
one instance (1 Sam 27:1) *Munach* occurs, and in one instance (Ezek
8:6) *Mereka* occurs. Yeivin noted that *Munach* serves when the
stress is on the first syllable, *Mereka* on the second syllable,
and *Azla* otherwise (*Tiberian Masorah*, 216).

which it refers.   *Paseq* is an auxiliary accent in that
it does not affect the laws of hierarchic governance;[23]
the   syntax   of Hebrew accents completely   ignores   the
presence   of   *Paseq*.   However,   *Paseq*   does   affect
cantillation in that it requires a short pause   between
the words it separates,   without affecting the   melody.
Paseq has   no domain;   it governs no   words   with   or
without   accents,   and consequently is not   served   by
conjunctives.

Wickes[24]   suggested that *Paseq* provides the final
touch,   adding   yet one more pause where   the   maximum
division   has   already occurred.   He   recognized   two
classes of *Paseq*:[25]

(1) The ordinary *Paseq* with four functions:

(a) The   *Paseq* of distinction,   used to avoid
confusion (cf. Gen 18:15)

(b) The *Paseq* of emphasis (cf. Ex 15:18)

(c) The *Paseq* of the homonym (cf. Gen 22:11)

(d) The *Paseq* of euphony,   to avoid mispronun-
ciation in awkward places

(2) The extraordinary *Paseq* with two functions:

(a) It appears before *Pashta, Tebir,* and *Zarqa*

(b) It   marks an auxiliary disjunctive in   the
domains   of   *Geresh,*   *Pazer,*   and   *Great
Telisha.*

----

[23]Yeivin noted that *Paseq* does affect the rules of phonetics,
and does affect the choice of conjunctives before some accents, as
with *Tebir* and *Zarqa* (*Tiberian Masorah,* 216).

[24]Wickes,   II, 120.   Praetorius suggested that *Paseq* may be a
relic of a mark indicating an abbreviation in the text (*ZAW* (1899)
53:683-692).

[25]Wickes, II, 122-25.

It is interesting to note that *Paseq* always immediately precedes a disjunctive accent and intervenes between it and the normal conjunctives that serve it (if any), at least in the Pentateuch. Table 33 provides a numerical summary of the use of *Paseq*.

TABLE 33
Numerical Summary of the Use of *Paseq*[2 6]

Before:	Gen	Ex	Lev	Num	Deut	Total
Silluq	0	3	0	1	1	5
Athnach	6	0	0	1	0	7
Segolta	1	1	0	0	1	3
Little Zaqeph	0	1	0	0	0	1
Tiphcha	1	2	1	1	1	6
Zarqa	5	2	2	4	4	17
Pashta	5	1	1	1	3	11
Tebir	9	1	0	4	2	16
Geresh	0	0	2	1	2	5
Pazer	2	0	1	6	3	12
Little Telisha	0	1	1	1	3	6
Total	29	12	8	20	20	89

[2 6]Before *Silluq*:   Ex 16:5;   17:15;   23:17;   Num 5:22;   Deut 6:4.   Before *Athnach*: Gen 18:15, 21;   22:11, 14; 39:10; 46:2;   Num 3:2.   Before *Segolta*: Gen 26:28; Ex 35:35; Deut 9:21.   Before *Zaqeph*: Ex 34:6. Before *Tiphcha*: Gen 18:15; Ex 15:18;   34:23; Lev 13:45; Num 21:1; Deut 7:26.   Before *Zarqa*: Gen 3:14;   30:20; 37:22;   42:21; 43:11; Ex 17:6; 34:6; Lev 10:12; 11:35;   Num 6:20; 11:25;   22:20;   30:13; Deut 3:20; 9:4; 28:25, 68.   Before *Pashta*: Gen 1:5, 10, 27;   21:17; 46:2; Ex 30:34; Lev 10:3; Num 6:26;   Deut

Pseudo-Legarmeh

Whenever *Paseq* follows a word accented with
Munach, it is possible to confuse such a configuration
of accents with *Legarmeh*. This confusion could happen
before any disjunctive accent that admits *Munach* as a
preceding conjunctive. Several criteria distinguish
true *Legarmeh* from its counterpart, *Munach* + *Paseq*
(which I have labeled *Pseudo-Legarmeh*):[17]

(1) *Legarmeh* only appears before *Rebia* and
occasionally before *Pashta* and *Geresh*;[18]

(2) *Legarmeh* occasionally has its own preceding
conjunctive *Mereka*;

(3) *Legarmeh* never intervenes between a disjunctive accent and its lawful conjunctives;[19]

4:32; 8:15; 27:9. Before *Tebir*: Gen 2:21, 22; 12:17; 14:15;
17:13; 18:15; 30:8; 42:13, 22; Ex 13:18; Num 6:25; 15:31;
17:28; 35:16; Deut 6:22; 7:26. Before *Geresh*: Lev 10:6; 11:32;
Num 3:38; Deut 17:8; 29:12. Before *Pazer*: Gen 1:21; 21:14; Lev
23:20; Num 9:10; 11:26 (twice); 16:7; 17:21; 32:33; Deut 7:1;
16:16; 22:6. Before *Little Telisha*: Ex 14:21; Lev 5:12; Num
32:29; Deut 25:19; 28:12, 20. Wickes (II, 127) listed two in Ex
20:4 and two in Deut 5:8 where double accents occur. He listed
two in Num 16:7, but BHS has only one, and one in Num 3:4 not in
BHS.

[17]They occur in Gen 1:21; 18:15, 21; 22:11, 14; 37:22;
39:10; 42:21; 43:11; 46:2; Ex 34:6; Num 3:2; 9:10; 11:26; 32:29;
Deut 7:1; 22:6; 25:19.

[18]*Legarmeh* cannot be distinguished from *Pseudo-Legarmeh* in
this context because these accents are naturally served by *Munach*.
Wickes (II, 119) stated that *Legarmeh* stands in place of *Paseq*
whenever it would be due before *Rebia*; this is due to musical
considerations.

[19]This is true because *Legarmeh* is a true disjunctive,
whereas *Paseq* is not. For example, see Lev 10:6 and 21:10 where
Legarmeh precedes the conjunctive *Mahpak* before *Pashta*; and see

(4) *Paseq* always immediately precedes a disjunctive accent and intervenes between the disjunctive and its preceding conjunctives (if any), at least in the Pentateuch.

Gen 28:9 where *Legarmeh* precedes the conjunctive *Azla* before *Geresh*.

CHAPTER 8

The Prose Conjunctive Accents

There are eight conjunctive accents some of which
serve a number of different disjunctives, and some of
which are dedicated to the service of only one. Some
serve only in ordered sets of conjunctives, and others
function as musical alternatives.

Munach

The name *Munach* means "sustained." The accent
mark consists of a vertical and a horizontal stroke
joined to form a right angle with the corner at the
lower right like a reversed English "L" (⌐); it is
placed below the first letter of the stressed syllable
of the word and immediately to the left of any vowel
there.

Munach is the most versatile of the conjunctive
accents. It serves as the sole conjunctive for six
disjunctives as follows:[1]

----

[1] In the case of *Athnach*, *Zaqeph*, and *Segolta*, the Rank II
Munach may be understood as a replacement for *Maqqeph*.

Disjunctive	Number Permitted
Athnach	0-2
Little Zaqeph	0-2
Segolta	0-2
Garshaim	0-1
Great Telisha	0-5
Pazer	0-6

It is interesting to note that all the accents served by *Munach* in this manner govern the domains of remote subordinate segments (except for *Garshaim*).

In addition, *Munach* serves in ordered rank I for *Rebia*, *Zarqa*, and occasionally for *Geresh*. It serves in ordered rank II for *Great Pazer*, *Tebir*, *Pashta*, and *Zarqa*. It serves in ordered rank III for *Rebia*, and *Geresh*. It also serves as an alternative for *Azla* when *Azla* would be due on the first letter of a word. Table 34 provides a numerical summary of the use of *Munach* serving in the rank I position before various disjunctives. Table 35 is a summary of its use in the rank II position, and Table 36 is for the rank III position.

Finally, *Munach* is frequently used as a substitute for *Metheg* to mark a secondary stress. Such a "*Munach-Metheg*" appears 364 times in BHS in the Pentateuch. With few exceptions[2] it appears on a word bearing a

----

[2] In Gen 36:13 BHS has two *Munachs* on the word *'elle'*, whereas BHK, B, and MG have only one, functioning as a conjunctive; BHS has a footnote indicating that L differs from most MSS and printed editions here. In Gen 45:5, Ex 20:10 and 32:31 a *Munach-Metheg* appears before *Rebia* and in Gen 50:17 it appears before *Pazer*; these rare exceptions are supported by BHS, BHK, B, and MG, but Masoretic notes (in some editions) point out the two accents on one word in Gen 50:17 and Ex 32:31. In Deut 5:15 it appears

TABLE 34
Numerical Summary *Munach*
Serving in the Rank I Position

Serving:	Gen	Ex	Lev	Num	Deut	Total
Athnach	598	522	345	500	368	2333
Segolta	35	37	35	51	29	187
Little Zaqeph	1137	795	549	708	746	3935
Rebia	326	290	198	265	292	1371
Zarqa	50	55	33	68	36	242
Geresh	2	1	1	2	3	9
Garshaim	9	10	8	23	11	61
Pazer	7	6	9	21	15	58
Great Telisha	11	14	12	14	26	77
Total	2175	1730	1190	1652	1526	8273

Little Zaqeph (without preceding conjunctives) that governs an empty segment. For musical reasons in this context, a *Munach*, which would normally serve *Zaqeph*, is drawn by attraction to replace an expected *Metheg* in the word. The transformation does not occur on the first syllable of a word, or with *Heavy Metheg* known as *Ga'ya*.[3] Table 37 provides a numerical summary of the

----

before *Mahpak* before *Pashta*. Wickes (II, 73) noted two instances where *Munach-Metheg* stands before *Athnach* (2 Sam 12:25; 1 Chr 5:20). In all these exceptions, *Munach* is drawn in by attraction to replace *Metheg* at a place where *Metheg* could lawfully stand.

[3]Wickes, II, 80-83; for the distinction between *Light Metheg* and *Ga'ya* see Aharon Dotan, "The Minor *Ga'ya*," *Textus* (1964) 4:55-

use of *Munach-Metheg*.

TABLE 35
Numerical Summary of *Munach*
Serving in the Rank II Position

Serving:	Gen	Ex	Lev	Num	Deut	Total
Athnach	1	3	0	1	0	5
Segolta	4	4	2	1	7	18
Little Zaqeph	14	16	5	10	8	53
Pashta	26	26	19	21	37	129
Tebir	14	11	17	13	9	64
Zarqa	0	2	3	2	2	9
Pazer	3	1	5	8	6	23
Great Telisha	0	2	4	3	11	20
Total	62	65	55	59	80	321

Mahpak

The name *Mahpak* means "inverted." The accent mark
consists of two diagonal strokes joined at the left
(<). It is placed below the first letter of the
stressed syllable of the word and immediately to the
left of any vowel there. *Mahpak* looks like *Yethib* and
may be confused for it at times. *Yethib* is
prepositive, always preceding the first letter of a
word, whereas *Mahpak* usually follows a vowel, and is
always immediately followed by *Pashta*.

75; and Mordecai Breuer, "Toward the Clarification of Problems
in Biblical Accents and Vocalization: The *Ga'ya* for Improvement
of Reading," *Leshonenu* (1979) 44(1):3-11.

TABLE 36
Numerical Summary of *Munach*
Serving in the Rank III Position

Serving:	Gen	Ex	Lev	Num	Deut	Total
Pashta	1	1	1	1	2	6
Tebir	2	0	0	2	2	6
Zarqa	0	1	0	0	1	2
Rebia	0	0	0	1	0	1
Geresh	11	13	16	12	2	54
Pazer	1	0	0	1	1	3
Great Telisha	0	0	1	2	3	6
Total	15	15	18	19	11	78

TABLE 37
Numerical Summary of the Use of
Munach-Metheg

	Gen	Ex	Lev	Num	Deut	Total
Before Zaqeph	70	84	38	80	87	359
Exceptions	2	2	0	0	1	5
Total	72	86	38	80	88	364

Mahpak is the conjunctive accent of ordered rank I serving only *Pashta*. *Mereka* serves as its musical alternate.[4] Wickes recorded four instances where *Mahpak* replaces *Metheg* before *Pashta*.[5] Table 38

----

[4]According to Wickes (II, 107), *Mereka* is used when no syllable (and no *Paseq*) intervenes, and *Mahpak* when the interval is one or more syllables.

provides a numerical summary of the use of *Mahpak*.

TABLE 38
Numerical Summary of the Use of
Mahpak

	Gen	Ex	Lev	Num	Deut	Total
Before Pashta	798	654	452	567	569	3040
Exceptions	0	1	0	1	0	2⁶
Total	798	655	452	568	569	3042

Mereka

The name *Mereka* means "prolonged." The accent
mark consists of a diagonal stroke with its top
inclined to the right like an English slash (/);   in
some printed editions it has a slight downward
curvature.   It is placed below the first consonant of
the stressed syllable of the word and immediately to
the left of any vowel there.

Mereka is the sole conjunctive for two
disjunctives as follows:

> *Disjunctive*   *Number Permitted*
> *Silluq*.................0-1
> *Legarmeh*...............0-1

It is interesting to note that the accents that *Mereka*
serves all govern the domain of near subordinate
segments.   It has *Double Mereka* as a musical alternate
on rare occasions.

- - - - - - - - - - - - - - - - - -

⁵Song 1:7, 12; cf. 3:4; Eccl 1:7; 7:10.

⁶In Ex 10:13, BHS and BHK have *Mahpak* and *Mereka* serving
Pashta, whereas B and MG have *Maqqeph* instead of *Mereka*.   In Num
17:23, BHS and BHK have a double accent (*Mahpak* and *Mereka*) on the
same word before *Pashta*.

In addition, *Mereka* serves as the conjunctive of ordered rank I for *Tiphcha*; and it serves as the alternate conjunctive of ordered rank I for *Tebir*, *Zarqa* and *Pashta*--that is, in a few instances *Mereka* replaces *Darga* as the conjunctive of ordered rank I for *Tebir*, it replaces *Munach* as the conjunctive of ordered rank I for *Zarqa*, and it replaces *Mahpak* as the conjunctive of ordered rank I for *Pashta*. According to Wickes this substitution occurs for musical reasons. *Mereka* stands in place of *Mahpak* before *Pashta* when no syllables intervene (not even a *Paseq*); it stands in place of *Darga* before *Tebir* when no more that one syllable intervenes; and it stands in place of *Munach* before *Zarqa* for unexplained reasons.[7] *Mereka* is used

TABLE 39
Numerical Summary of the use of *Mereka*

Serving:	Gen	Ex	Lev	Num	Deut	Total
Silluq	643	461	372	514	381	2371
Tiphcha	1580	1237	865	1153	1055	5890
Zarqa	4	6	3	12	9	34
Pashta	25	28	26	36	37	152
Tebir	162	145	101	142	110	660
Legarmeh	1	1	4	0	3	9
Exceptions	0	1	0	0	0	1[8]
Total	2415	1879	1371	1857	1595	9117

----

[7] Wickes, II, 107-9.

only in the rank I position with any disjunctive it may
serve.   Table 39   provides a numerical summary of   the
use of *Mereka*.

Finally,   on rare occasions *Mereka* replaces *Metheg*
to mark a secondary stress.   Wickes noted eight places
where   *Mereka*   replaces   *Metheg* in the same   word   with
Tiphcha[9] and four places in the same word with *Tebir*.[10]
I found a few more in the Pentateuch in BHS.[11]

Double Mereka

The   name *Double Mereka* means "doubly   prolonged."
The accent mark is,   as its name implies,   two   *Merekas*
close together and placed in the same manner as *Mereka*.
It   functions   as a substitute for   *Mereka*   when   *Darga*
would   precede   it.   See   the   discussion   under   the
conjunctives   serving   *Tiphcha* which   is   the   only
environment where this conjunctive may occur.

Double   Mereka is   one   of   the   rare   accents,
occurring only five times in the Pentateuch.[12]   Wickes

----

[9] In Ex 38:12 BHS and BHK have *Mereka* serving *Zaqeph*, whereas
B and MG have *Munach*.

[9] Lev 23:21; 2 Kings 15:16; Jer 8:18; Ezek 36:25; 44:6 (BHS
has *Metheg*); Song 6:5 (BHS has *Metheg*); Dan 5:17; 1 Chr 15:31.

[10] Deut 13:10, 16; Ezr 6:2; 2 Chr 1:10.

[11] In Gen 9:24 it appears in the same word with *Tiphcha*; and
in Deut 5:7 it appears in the same word with *Tebir*.   In Ex 12:45
and Num 2:12 such a *Mereka-Metheg* appears before *Silluq*, but in Ex
12:45 BHK, B, and MG have *Metheg*.   In Num 17:23 BHS and BHK have a
Mereka marking secondary stress on the ultima of the word
נצׄ׳צׄ1, whereas B and MG have *Metheg*.

[12] Gen 27:25; Ex 5:15; Lev 10:1; Num 14:3; 32:42.   It occurs

regarded this accent as a weakened *Tebir* as the preceding *Darga* suggests.[13] This is possible because in every case *Tebir* could have been used. Weisberg pointed out that *Double Mereka* always occurs (except once) "on the fourth from the last word in the sentence and always on a monosyllabic word."[14] He also suggested that this rare accent was used by the Masoretes to signify the homiletical element of "an *aggadic* tale or lesson."[15]

Darga

The name *Darga* means "stopping." The accent mark consists of a serpentine stroke in the shape of a small English "s." It is placed below the first letter of the stressed syllable of the word and immediately to the left of any vowel there.

Darga serves as the conjunctive of ordered rank I for *Tebir*. It also serves as the conjunctive of ordered rank II for *Rebia* and *Tiphcha*. Table 40 provides a numerical summary of the use of *Darga*.

Azla

The name *Azla* means "proceeding." The accent mark consists of a diagonal stroke with its top inclined to the left like an English back-slash (\); in some

----

only nine other times in the rest of the Old Testament: 1 Kings 10:3; 20:29; Ezek 14:4; Hab 1:3; Zech 3:2; Ezra 7:25; Neh 3:38; 2 Chr 9:2; 20:30 (Wickes, II, 91-92).

[13]Wickes, II, 92.

[14]Weisberg, *JQR* 56(4):334.

[15]Weisberg, *JQR* 56(4):334.

TABLE 40
Numerical Summary of the Use of *Darga*

Serving:	Gen	Ex	Lev	Num	Deut	Total
Tebir	234	212	167	226	186	1025
Tiphcha	1	1	1	2	0	5[16]
Rebia	18	8	3	9	22	60
Exceptions	0	0	0	0	1	1[17]
Total	253	221	171	237	209	1091

printed editions it has a slight upward curvature.   It
is   placed   above the first consonant of   the   stressed
syllable of a word.   It appears much like *Pashta* except
that *Pashta* is postpositive.

   Azla functions as the conjunctive of ordered   rank
I for *Geresh*, and of ordered rank II for *Zarqa, Pashta,*
and *Tebir*.   *Munach* serves as an alternate whenever *Azla*
would   fall   on the first syllable of the   word   except
when   *Little   Telisha* precedes.   Table 41   provides   a
numerical summary of the use of *Azla*.

   Finally, *Azla* occasionally replaces *Metheg* to mark
secondary   stress.[18]   Most often it appears   before   a

----

   [16]This   occurs   only   before *Double Mereka* serving   *Tiphcha*.
Wickes   (II,   92) presented this as evidence that   *Double   Mereka*
should be regarded as a weakened *Tebir*.   See the discussion under
Double Mereka and *Tiphcha*.

   [17]In   Deut 13:15,   BHS and BHK have *Darga* serving *Tiphcha*   in
the   rank   I as well as the rank II position, whereas B   and   MG
correctly have *Tebir* instead of the rank I *Darga*.

   [18]Grammarians   call   this   use of *Azla* by   the   name   *Methiga*
(מְתִיגָא); see Wickes' discussion in II, 80‑83.

TABLE 41
Numerical Summary of the Use of *Azla*

Serving:	Gen	Ex	Lev	Num	Deut	Total
Geresh	213	195	160	192	209	969
Zarqa	12	14	10	17	16	69
Pashta	132	100	74	107	114	527
Tebir	69	64	63	77	73	346
Exceptions	1	0	0	0	1	2[19]
Total	427	373	307	393	413	1913

Little Zaqeph governing an empty segment, and less often before a *Geresh* governing an empty segment. On rare occasions it appears in ordered rank II position before *Pashta*[20] and *Zarqa*.[21] *Azla* naturally serves *Geresh* in ordered rank I, and *Pashta* in ordered rank II; thus it is likely drawn by attraction at times to replace *Metheg* in those positions. By analogy, one may expect to find an *Azla-Metheg* in ordered rank II position before *Tebir* on rare occasions somewhere else in the Hebrew Bible.[22] Table 42 provides a numerical

----

[19]In Gen 18:18, BHS and BHK have *Azla* before *Zaqeph*; it marks secondary stress on a word that lacks a required *Maqqeph*; B and MG correctly have the *Maqqeph*. In Deut 12:30, BHS and BHK have *Azla* serving *Geresh* in the rank II as well as the rank I position; whereas B and MG correctly have *Rebia* instead of the rank II *Azla*.

[20]See Ex 20:4; Lev 25:46; Num 20:1; and Deut 8:16; in the last case, the word involved has three accents. Yeivin (*Tiberian Masorah*, 197) recorded additional places: Lam 4:9; Ezek 43:11; Dan 3:2; Ezra 7:24; 2 Chr 35:25. He also noted one place where *Azla* and *Mahpak* appear on the same letter (Ezek 20:31).

[21]See Lev 10:12.

summary of the use of *Azla-Metheg.*

TABLE 42
Numerical Summary of the Use of
Azla-Metheg

	Gen	Ex	Lev	Num	Deut	Total
Before Zaqeph	27	22	21	30	11	111
Before Geresh	3	8	4	11	12	38
Before Pashta	0	1	1	1	1	4
Before Zarqa	0	0	1	0	0	1
Total	30	31	27	42	24	154

Little Telisha

The name *Little Telisha* means "a small drawing out." The accent mark consists of a diagonal stroke with its top inclined to the left and with a small circle on its top. The accent is postpositive, being placed above the last letter of a word regardless of which syllable is stressed.

Little Telisha serves only as the conjunctive of ordered rank II for *Geresh* and *Virtual Geresh,* and for musical reasons it must be followed by *Azla.* Table 43 provides a numerical summary of the use of *Little Telisha.*

Galgal

The name *Galgal* means "wheel." The accent mark consists of two diagonal strokes joined at the bottom

----

[11]Yeivin (*Tiberian Masorah,* 204) listed eight cases: Isa 30:16; 32:15; Job 1:15, 16, 17, 19; Neh 11:7; 2 Chr 17:8.

TABLE 43
Numerical Summary of the Use of
Little Telisha

Serving:	Gen	Ex	Lev	Num	Deut	Total
Geresh	64	70	61	59	83	337

Virtual Geresh in:

	Gen	Ex	Lev	Num	Deut	Total
ZAR	1	1	0	3	3	8
PASH	13	14	5	16	19	67
TEB	14	2	5	10	8	39
Total	92	87	71	88	113	451

to form a small angle like an English "v." It is placed below the first letter of the stressed syllable of the word and immediately to the left of any vowel there.

Galgal serves only as the conjunctive of ordered rank I for *Great Pazer*. Both accents are rare, occurring in the Pentateuch only in Gen 35:5.

Mayela

Mayela is not really a conjunctive accent. Instead it is a *Tiphcha-Metheg* (see under *Metheg* and under *Tiphcha*). Wickes provided convincing proof of this view.[23]

----

[23]Wickes, II, 73.

CHAPTER 9

Interpreting the Prose Accents

Although most accents are easy to interpret,
the tension between the rules that govern the
placement of the accents and the syntax of the language
itself causes the interpretation of the accents to be
difficult at times. The interpretation of the
conjunctive accents and disjunctive accents is
discussed separately.

Interpreting the Conjunctive Accents

Conjunctive accents join words that are closely
related syntactically. The follow are examples of
syntactic relationships that usually involve
conjunctive accents:[1]

(1) Two nouns in apposition;

(2) Two nouns joined by a conjunction and forming
a compound part of speech;

(3) A substantive with its modifier, such as:

(a) a substantive with an adjectival modifier;

(b) a substantive with a relative pronoun;

(c) a substantive with an adverbial modifier;

(4) A construct noun with its following absolute

----

[1] Wickes, II, 52-58.

noun;

(5) Two   verbs   in   the   same   grammatical
construction.

Conjunctive accents are usually used to join
constructions   like   the   above,   but   when   the
constructions are too long for the allowable number of
conjunctives,   then the syntax of the accents   demands
that   a   disjunctive be used in spite of the syntax   of
the language.

The   kind   of conjunctive accent used in   a   given
context is determined by the kind of disjunctive accent
that   the   conjunctive   accent   serves.   A   given
disjunctive   accent   may   be   served   only   by   those
conjunctives   admitted   by the rules of the   syntax   of
accents.   Some   disjunctive accents may be served   by
only one kind of conjunctive, whereas others permit the
service   of   more than one   kind.   Those   disjunctive
accents   that   may be served by more than one   kind   of
conjunctive require them to serve in a   specific
sequence by ordered rank.   Musical   considerations
determine   substitutions   when   such   are   lawful.
Otherwise,   there is no hierarchy among the conjunctive
accents.   The   kind   of   conjunctive   accent   has   no
significant   bearing on   the linguistic interpretation.
All conjunctive accents have equal conjoining force.

The Disjunctive Accents

The   disjunctive accents usually mark places   in   a
verse   where division occurs with respect to the syntax
of the Hebrew language itself.   This is nearly always
true   in the case of the remote subordinate disjunctive
accents, but less often in the case of near subordinate
disjunctives.   Disjunctive accents of high   hierarchic

rank mark the most prominent syntactic divisions and
govern the most prominent syntactic segments of a
verse. Those of low hierarchic rank mark less
prominent divisions and govern less prominent segments.
There is an approximate correspondence between the
hierarchy of the accents and the syntactic hierarchy of
the language, but the correspondence is relative within
the domain of a verse.

Accents in Hierarchy I and II

The accents in hierarchy I and II mark the
strongest syntactic divisions. Every verse in the
prose books is closed by *Soph Pasuq* which marks the end
and governs the domain of the whole verse. *Silluq* and
Athnach govern the two main segments of a verse. The
division is usually determined by logical or
syntactical relations. Thus, for example, the two
segments may consist of:[2]

Athnach Segment	Silluq Segment
Clause............	Clause
Subject...........	Predicate
Subject + Verb.....	Object
Object............	Verb + Subject
Adverbial Phrase...	Clause
Vocative..........	Clause
Phrase............	Phrase

----

[2]Wickes, II, 30-58.

(#1)   SOP

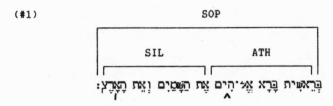

In the beginning God created / the heavens and the earth.
(Gen 1:1)

In (#1) the *Athnach* segment consists of the subject plus the verb phrase, and the *Silluq* segment consists of a compound object.

(#2)   SOP

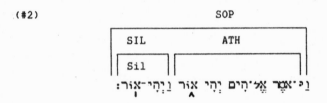

Then God said, "Let there be light"; / and there was light.
(Gen 1:3)

In (#2) the *Athnach* segment consists of an action clause, and the *Silluq* segment consists of a result clause. The segments are of equal syntactic rank, but not of equal length.

Accents in Hierarchy III

Zaqeph, *Segolta*, and *Tiphcha* divide the major segments into secondary segments. *Segolta*, when used, governs the first secondary segment in the domain of *Athnach*, otherwise *Zaqeph* governs it. There may be more than one *Zaqeph* segment. *Tiphcha* always governs

the last secondary segment, but from the next-to-last
word-unit. A *Tiphcha* segment may stand alone. These
secondary segments should be interpreted as being on an
equal par syntactically, logically, or rhetorically.[3]

(#1)

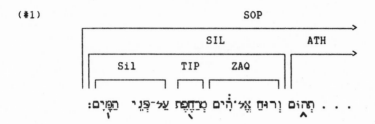

And the Spirit of God /
   was hovering over the   face of the waters.
                             (Gen 1:2)

In (#1) the *Silluq* segment consists of a clause.
The subject is contained in a *Zaqeph* segment,   and
the predicate is contained in the *Tiphcha* segment.[4]

----

[3] Wickes (II, 31) disagreed, regarding each successive
occurrence of *Zaqeph* as marking a less prominent division.   This
is unnatural in most instances.   It is better to grant equal
syntactic value to the repetition of an accent and to ponder over
the reason why the accentuators seem to have done unusual things
in some cases.   See the discussion of such unnatural binary
restraints in the section on continuous dichotomy.   A *Segolta*
segment often exhibits some semantic difference from a following
Zaqeph segment, but syntactically they may be regarded as of about
the same rank.

[4] As stated above, *Tiphcha* governs its segment from the next-
to-last word unit--that is,   its segment includes the word unit
bearing the *Silluq*, but a near disjunctive accent cannot stand
on the same word unit as the superior accent that governs its
domain.   Therefore it must govern its own domain from the
position adjacent to its own superior.   This is true of all
near disjunctive accents, as explained and illustrated in a later
section.

(#2)   SOP

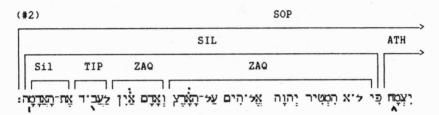

For the LORD God had not caused it to rain on the earth, /
and there was no man / to till the ground.   (Gen 2:5)

        In (#2)   the *Silluq* segment consists of three
clauses: two   independent clauses,   the second with a
dependent infinitive clause of purpose.   The first two
are contained in *Zaqeph* segments, and the last in the
Tiphcha segment.   The first is longer than the others,
but evidently on about the same par rhetorically.

(#3)   SOP

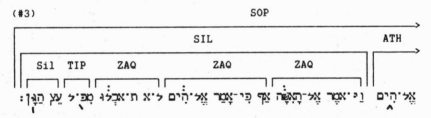

And he said to the woman, / "Has God indeed said, /
'You shall not eat / of every tree of the garden'?"
(Gen 3:1)

        In (#3) the *Silluq* segment contains four secondary
segments: three   clauses   plus   a dependent adverbial
phrase of source.   The   first three are contained in
Zaqeph segments, and the last in the *Tiphcha* segment.

(#4)   SOP

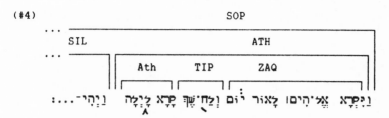

And God called the light Day, /
and the darkness He called Night.
(Gen 1:5)

In (#4) the *Athnach* segment consists of two
independent clauses. The first is contained in a
Zaqeph segment, and the last is in the *Tiphcha*
segment.[5]

Accents in Hierarchy IV

Tebir, *Pashta*, *Zarqa*, and *Rebia* divide the
secondary segments into tertiary segments. In the
domain of *Segolta*, *Zaqeph*, or *Tiphcha*, *Rebia* governs
the remote segments; and a *Tebir*, *Pashta*, or *Zarqa*
governs the near segment, depending on the governing
accent. A *Tebir*, *Pashta*, or *Zarqa* segment may stand
alone. These segments should be regarded as on about
equal par syntactically, logically, or rhetorically.

In (#1) the first *Zaqeph* segment consists of two
clauses. The first is contained in a *Rebia* segment,
and the second in a *Pashta* segment.[6]

----

[5] The *Tiphcha* segments includes the word unit bearing the
Athnach for the same reason that it included the word unit bearing
Silluq. See footnote 4.

[6] *Pashta*, being a near disjunctive, its segment includes the
word-unit bearing the *Zaqeph*.

(#1)

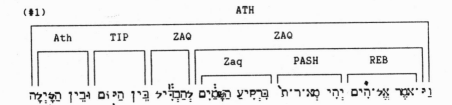

Then God said,   "Let there be lights
in the firmament of the heavens /
to divide / the day from the night..."   (Gen 1:14)

(#2)

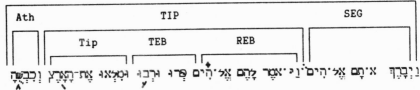

Then God blessed them, /
and God said to them, /
"Be fruitful, and multiply, and fill the earth /
and subdue it; . . ."   (Gen 1:28)

In   (#2)   a   *Tiphcha* segment contains two clauses:
the   first   introduces   the   second   which   has   a   compound
verb phrase.   The first clause is contained in a *Rebia*
segment, and the second in a *Tebir* segment.[7]

Accents in Hierarchy V
     Geresh, Pazer, and *Great Telisha* divide the domain
of the hierarchy IV accents into subordinate segments.
Pazer or its substitute   *Great   Telisha* govern the
remote segments.   More than one *Pazer* segment may
- - - - - - - - - - - - - - - - - -

     [7] *Tebir,* being a near disjunctive, its segment includes the
word-unit bearing *Tiphcha.* See further discussion of p. 152-53.

occur. The near segment is governed by *Geresh*. These
segments should be regarded as on about equal par
syntactically, logically, or rhetorically.

Influences of Poetic Structure
        On the other hand, the accentual division of a
verse may be determined by poetic meter rather than by
purely syntactical considerations.   Often   poetic
structure is dominant (even in so-called prose),   so
that the primary disjunctives (*Silluq* and *Athnach*)   and
even the secondary disjunctives (*Zaqeph*, *Segolta*, and
Tiphcha) may mark the end of poetic lines.   This   may
occur even when the logical or syntactical points of
division do not coincide with the ends of the poetic
lines.

(#1)   וַיְהִי־לִי לִישׁוּעָה   עָזִּי וְזִמְרָת יָהּ (15:2)

                  אֲרֹמְמֶנְהוּ: אֱלֹהֵי אָבִי וַאֲנְוֵהוּ   זֶה אֵלִי (15:2)

                  יְהוָה שְׁמֹו: יְהוָה אִישׁ מִלְחָמָה (15:3)

                  יָרָה בַיָּם   מַרְכְּבֹת פַּרְעֹה וְחֵילֹו (15:4)

                  בְיַם־סוּף: טֻבְּעוּ שָׁלִשָׁיו וּמִבְחַר (15:4)

    (2) The LORD is my strength and song, /
          And He has become my salvation; //
        He is my God, and I will praise Him; /
          My father's God, and I will exalt Him. //
    (3) The LORD is a man of war; //
          the LORD is His name. //
    (4) Pharaoh's chariots and his army
          He has cast into the sea; //
        His chosen captains also
          are drowned in the Red Sea. // (Ex 15:2-4)

      In (#1) above, verse two contains two poetic lines
each hemistich of which consists of one or two short

clauses;   the ends of the poetic lines are marked   by
Athnach   and *Silluq* and the end of the first   hemistich
of each line is is marked by a *Zaqeph*.   Verse three
contains   only   one   poetic line, so the ends   of   the
hemistichs   are marked by *Athnach* and *Silluq*.   Verse
four contains two poetic lines, each consisting of a
single clause;   so the ends of the lines are marked by
the same.   In this example the poetic lines and accents
are in harmony with the syntax of the language.
However, the poetic lines, all of about equal syntactic
rank,   are marked by different accents because the
verses do not contain an equal number of poetic lines.

(#2)   (34:6) וַיַּעֲבֹ֨ר יְהוָ֥ה ׀ עַל־פָּנָיו֮ וַיִּקְרָא֒

יְהוָ֣ה ׀ יְהֹוָ֔ה אֵ֥ל רַח֖וּם וְחַנּ֑וּן

אֶ֥רֶךְ אַפַּ֖יִם וְרַב־חֶ֥סֶד וֶאֱמֶֽת׃

(34:7) נֹצֵ֥ר חֶ֙סֶד֙ לָאֲלָפִ֔ים נֹשֵׂ֥א עָוֺ֛ן וָפֶ֖שַׁע וְחַטָּאָ֑ה

וְנַקֵּה֙ לֹ֣א יְנַקֶּ֔ה

פֹּקֵ֣ד ׀ עֲוֺ֣ן אָב֗וֹת עַל־בָּנִים֙ וְעַל־בְּנֵ֣י בָנִ֔ים

עַל־שִׁלֵּשִׁ֖ים וְעַל־רִבֵּעִֽים׃

(6) And the LORD passed before him / and proclaimed, //
    "The LORD, the LORD, / the merciful and gracious God, //
    Longsuffering, / and abounding in kindness and truth, //
(7) Keeping mercy for thousands, /
        forgiving iniquity and transgression and sin, //
    By no means clearing (the guilty), /
    Visiting the iniquity of the fathers
        upon the children and the children's children /
    To the third and the fourth generation." // (Ex 34:6-7)

The verses of (#2) above, although contained in a
so-called prose passage, exhibit poetic structure.

Verse six contains three poetic lines. The first line consists of a *Segolta* segment which introduces the declaration of the divine name; the second line consists of an *Athnach* segment; and the third consists of the *Silluq* segment. Each line has two hemistichs. In the second line, the first hemistich (a *Zaqeph* segment) contains a double declaration of the name יהוה separated by *Paseq* (in BHK but not BHS); and the second (a *Tiphcha* segment) contains an appositive with a compound adjectival modifier. The third line contains two additional compound adjectival modifiers, one in each hemistich. Apart from the influence of the poetic structure (which requires an *Athnach* to set off the poetic line), the *Athnach* should be a *Zaqeph* (on purely syntactic grounds), because it is unnatural to have such a strong disjunctive between adjectival phrases in the same syntactic structure.

Verse seven is a quatrain, the first and third lines containing two hemistichs, and the second and fourth containing only one. The first four hemistichs are participle clauses, parallel in thought and grammatical form; and the last two are adverbial phrases, parallel in thought and form, modifying the fourth participle clause. The *Athnach* segment contains the first two hemistichs (which make positive statements), and the *Silluq* segment contains the last two (which make negative statements) along with the two adverbial phrases. Apart from the influence of the poetic structure the *Silluq* segment surely would be divided differently. This example illustrates how poetic structure may determine the placement of the accents rather than purely syntactic relations of the language.

Interpreting Near Disjunctives

The remote disjunctives (*Athnach, Zaqeph, Segolta, Rebia, Great Telisha,* and *Pazer*) rest on the last word of the domain they govern. Thus they unambiguously mark a place of division in the verse. The same is not true for the near disjunctives (*Silluq, Tiphcha, Tebir, Pashta, Zarqa,* and *Geresh*). Except for *Silluq,* these accents cannot rest on the last word of the domain they govern, because their immediate superior is already there governing the domain of a larger segment that also ends with that word. Therefore, they must of necessity stand one word-unit short of the end of their domain, and then govern their own subordinate segments from that position. From an analytical and syntactical point of view, these disjunctives pose several problems.

Replacing a Conjunctive. One problem is that a near disjunctive accent may occur where a conjunctive accent is expected syntactically. For example, *Silluq* and *Tiphcha* may be served, at the most, by only one conjunctive (*Mereka*); and *Athnach, Zaqeph,* and *Segolta* may be served, at the most, by only one conjunctive (*Munach*).[a] Thus when a segment ends with a compound phrase requiring more conjunctive accents than is permitted by the syntax of the accents, the near subordinate disjunctive must occur of necessity where the syntax of the Hebrew language (or logic) expects a conjunctive.

----

[a]Two *Munachs* may occur on rare occasions in places where two short words could (and probably should) have been joined by *Maqqeph.*

(#1)

וַיֹּאמֶר יַעֲקֹב אֶל־פַּרְעֹה

יְמֵי שְׁנֵי מְגוּרַי שְׁלֹשִׁים וּמְאַת שָׁנָה

מְעַט וְרָעִים הָיוּ יְמֵי שְׁנֵי חַיַּי

וְלֹא הִשִּׂיגוּ אֶת־יְמֵי שְׁנֵי חַיֵּי אֲבֹתַי בִּימֵי מְגוּרֵיהֶם:

And Jacob said th Pharaoh, /
"The days of the years of my pilgrimage
    are one hundred and thirty years; //
few and evil have been
    the days of the years of my life, /
and they have not attained
    to the days of the years of my fathers /
    in the days of their pilgrimage." (Gen 47:9)

In (#1) the phrase שְׁלֹשִׁים וּמְאַת שָׁנָה (thirty and a hundred of years) is the near subordinate *Tiphcha* segment of the *Athnach* segment. Syntactically the phrase should be one unit, and particularly the construct מְאַת should be joined with שָׁנָה; but *Tiphcha* divides them. This is because, in the rules of the accents, *Tiphcha* must stand on the first or second word before *Athnach* regardless of linguistic syntax or logic. In interpreting this accentuation, the *Tiphcha* should be understood to close its segment on the same word with *Athnach* (which closes its larger segment with the same word), and to stand in place of a conjunctive accent.

Also in this verse, the phrases יְמֵי שְׁנֵי מְגוּרַי (the days of the years of my pilgrimage) and יְמֵי שְׁנֵי חַיַּי (the days of the years of my life) are the *Pashta* segments of *Zaqeph* segments. Syntactically the phrases each should be one unit, particularly because the words constitute a string of construct forms which should not be divided, according to the syntax of the language.

But *Pashta* divides the first from the last two.   This
is because, in the rules of the accents,   *Pashta* must
stand on the first or second word before *Zaqeph*
regardless of linguistic syntax or logic.   In
interpreting this accentuation, the *Pashta* should be
understood to close its segment on the same word with
Zaqeph, and to stand in place of a conjunctive accent.[9]

(#2)   :וְאֶת־פַּתְרֻסִים וְאֶת־כַּסְלֻחִים אֲשֶׁר יָצְאוּ מִשָּׁם פְּלִשְׁתִּים וְאֶת־כַּפְתֹּרִים:

The Pathrusites and Casluhites (from whom come the Philistines
and the Caphtorites). (Gen 10:14)

The verse in (#2) has no verb, but consists of a
compound phrase.   The entire verse lies in the domain
of both *Silluq* and *Tiphcha*, but *Tiphcha* of necessity
must rest on the next to last word.   Yet syntactically
the word should have a conjunctive accent.   Otherwise,
if a genuine major division were intended here,   it
should have been marked unambiguously with *Athnach*.
Consequently,   instead of the *Tiphcha* separating the
Chaphtorites from the Philistines, making only the
Philistines descendants of the Casluhites (as some
interpreters suppose),[10] the *Tiphcha* stands in place of

----

[9] On the word היוּ the *Pashta* governs a *Pashta-B* segment,
standing in place of a *Rebia* segment (see discussion on pp.   93-
95).   On the word יֹמִי in the phrase יֹמִי שְׁנֵי חַיֵּי אֲבִיתִי the *Pashta*
is anomalous.   It cannot be a *Pashta-B* (in place of *Rebia*) because
Rebia would never stand on a construct form.   The phrase should
have a conjunctive with שְׁנֵי or יֹמִי, or a *Maqqeph*.

[10] Of course, it is possible that *Tiphcha* stands in place of
its own subordinate *Rebia* or its own remote companion *Zaqeph* as
explained later.   These possibilities would support the alternate
view.   However, the author could have avoided the ambiguity by
alternate word order.   So when a conjunctive is possible, that is
the better choice.

a conjunctive accent and joins the two as common
descendants. A corresponding interpretation should be
given to any of the near disjunctive accents when they
occur where a conjunctive accent is expected
syntactically.

   Replacing Its Own Subordinate. A second problem
is that a near disjunctive accent may occur at a place
where its own subordinate is expected syntactically.
For example, in a *Tiphcha* segment (which is a near
subordinate segment in the domain of *Silluq* or
Athnach), if its own near subordinate segment (*Tebir*)
is only one word-unit long, then *Tiphcha* must stand
where its own remote subordinate disjunctive accent
(*Rebia*) is expected syntactically.[11]

(#1)   SOP

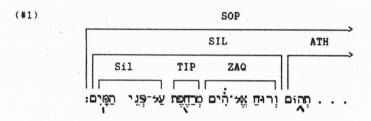

And the Spirit of God /
was hovering over the face of the waters.
                                    (Gen 1:2)

   In (#1) *Tiphcha* stands where its own remote
subordinate *Rebia* is expected. The entire *Tiphcha*
segment (הַמָּֽיִם עַל־פְּנֵי מְרַחֶפֶת) stands in parallel with
its companion Zaqeph segment (אֱלֹהִים וְרוּחַ), and the
accents should be interpreted in this way

----

[11] *Tiphcha* cannot stand on the same word unit bearing *Silluq*
or *Athnach*, so, because its domain consists of only one word unit,
it is impossible for *Tiphcha* to stand within the domain which it
should govern syntactically.

syntactically.

In (#2) also, *Tiphcha* stands where its own remote subordinate *Rebia* is expected.   The entire *Tiphcha* segment (ולחׁ'שֶׁ קְרָא לַיְלָה) stands in parallel with its companion Zaqeph segment (וַיִּקְרָא אֱלֹ׳הִים׀ לָאוֹר יוֹם), and the accents should be interpreted in this way syntactically.

(#2)

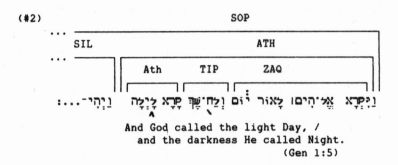

And God called the light Day, /
and the darkness He called Night.
(Gen 1:5)

In (#3) *Tiphcha* stands where one of its own subordinates is due to close the third of four parallel segments in the domain of the *Tiphcha*.   Thus God's command consists of four imperatives of equal rank syntactically.   The *Tiphcha* is there because of demands of the rules of accents, not to grant special emphasis to the last imperative.   A corresponding interpretation should be given to any of the near disjunctive accents when they occur where one   of its   own subordinate accents is expected syntactically.

(#3)   ATH

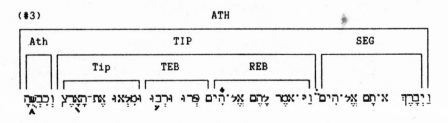

Then God blessed them, /
and God said to them, /
"Be fruitful, and multiply, and fill the earth /
and subdue it; ..." (Gen 1:28)

Replacing Its Own Remote Companion. A third
problem is that a near disjunctive may occur where its
own remote companion is expected syntactically. For
example, if a *Tiphcha* segment is short, consisting of
only one word-unit, then the *Tiphcha* must of necessity
stand outside its own domain on the word where its
remote companion *Zaqeph* is expected.

(#1)

מַרְכְּבֹ֤ת פַּרְעֹ֥ה וְחֵיל֖וֹ   יָרָ֣ה בַיָּ֑ם

וּמִבְחַ֥ר שָׁלִשָׁ֖יו   טֻבְּע֖וּ בְיַם־סֽוּף׃

(4) Pharaoh's chariots and his army /
He has cast into the sea; //
His chosen captains also /
are drowned in the Red Sea. //
(Ex 15:4)

The verse in (#1) consists of two poetic lines,
each with two hemistichs. In both lines, *Tiphcha* marks
the end of the first hemistich, but it stands in place
of its remote companion *Zaqeph.* In each case the
second hemistich belongs to *Tiphcha*, but it is so short
that *Tiphcha* must of necessity stand outside its own
domain. The accents should be interpreted such that
the segment actually closed by *Tiphcha* and the segment
following *Tiphcha* are on equal par syntactically.
Whenever a near disjunctive accent stands in place of
its own remote companion, it governs its own
subordinates (if any) from that place. A corresponding

interpretation should be given to any of the near
disjunctive accents when it occurs where one of its own
remote companion accents is expected syntactically.

The Problem of Altered Accentuation

The laws of substitution provide for one accent to
substitute for another for musical or rhythmic reasons.
In these cases, no syntactic significance should be
implied. However, a few exceptions to the common rules
of the accents are probably not due to musical
considerations. It is likely that the early form of
the syntax of the accents was simple and consistent,
and that in later times the accentuators deliberately
violated the rules for exegetical purposes. It is
likely, for example, as previously discussed, that
Shalsheleth and *Great Pazer* were new substitutes
introduced later for exegetical purposes.

(#1)

וַתּוֹצֵא הָאָרֶץ דֶּשֶׁא עֵשֶׂב מַזְרִיעַ זֶרַע לְמִינֵהוּ

וְעֵץ עֹשֶׂה פְּרִי אֲשֶׁר זַרְעוֹ־בוֹ לְמִינֵהוּ

וַיַּרְא אֱלֹהִים כִּי־טוֹב׃

> And the earth brought forth grass,
>   the herb that yields seed according to its kind,
> and the tree that yields fruit according to its kind.
> And God saw that it was good.   (Gen 1:12)

It is also likely that the occasional trans-
position of *Geresh* and *Great Telisha* may have been a
later exegetical innovation. For example (#1), in Gen
1:12, the word הָאָרֶץ should be accented with *Geresh*.
However, this would produce an ambiguity, because
Geresh, being a near subordinate accent, could be
interpreted either disjunctively or conjunctively.

Furthermore, the word רֵאשׁ is ambiguous, being either an
absolute or construct form. So the word could be
understood to be the head of a construct chain
governing עֵשֶׂב מַזְרִיעַ זֶרַע, thus indicating that God
commanded only two kinds of vegetation rather than
three (v. 11). On the other hand, *Geresh* could be
functioning disjunctively, in which case רֵאשׁ would be
an absolute form, standing in parallel with עֵשֶׂב מַזְרִיעַ
זֶרַע, and indicating that God commanded three kinds of
vegetation, in agreement with verse 11. Perhaps, in
order to resolve the ambiguity, later accentuators
transposed *Geresh* and *Great Telisha*.[12] In those places
where such unusual accentuation occurs, is it possible
that the accentuators altered the accents for
exegetical purposes? Only further study will resolve
this question.

The Problem of Double Accentuation

Besides the problems that have been mentioned,
additional problems exist because the Masoretes
provided double accentuation in a few places. Double
accentuation occurs on single words, on single verses,
and on groups of verses. In all these places I
selected only one set of accents for computer analysis.

On a Single Word

In Gen 5:29 the Masoretes recorded both *Geresh* and
Great Telisha on the word זֶה, possibly for special

----

[12]The verse bears evidence of further tampering because
the *Tebir* has an anomalous sequence of conjunctives serving
it in BHS and BHK. The word עָשָׂה before *Tebir* has *Mereka* instead
of *Maqqeph* (as in B and M), thus forcing the *Darga* into the
anomalous rank II position.

emphasis. Either accent would be lawful in that place, or both if there were two words. The normal order of the accents on separate words would be *Great Telisha* followed by *Geresh*. But a Masoretic note recorded in B states

הקורא יטעים הגרש קודם התלשא

> The reader should cantillate the *Geresh*
> before the *Telisha*.

So BHS and BHK record the accents in that order even though it violates the prepositive position of *Telisha*. However, B and MG record them with *Telisha* first, in its normal position. Yeivin recorded four additional places where this same set of accents occurs.[13]

On a Single Verse

In Gen 35:22 the Masoretes recorded two sets of accents: one set is the normal set of accents for a single verse; the other divides the verse into two accentuation units at the word *Israel* for obvious reasons. A dividing פ occurs between the two parts. Both sets conform to the syntax rules. Translators usually have followed the tradition that divides the verse, but they retain only one verse number.

On the Decalog

In the two places where the Decalog is recorded

----

[13]Yeivin, "A Unique Combination...," 209; see also 2 Kings 17:13; Ezek 48:10; Zeph 2:15; and Lev 10:4. BHS does not record the *Great Telisha* in Lev 10:4, but it is present in BHK, MG, and B (with the same note as above).

(Ex 20:2-17 and Deut 5:6-21) the Masoretes recorded two sets of accents: one for public reading and one for private study.

One set of accents views each traditional verse as a single unit of cantillation. That is the set of accents I used in this analysis. Its accents conform to the syntax rules.

The other set of accents clusters several verses together into larger logical units as follows:

    (1) Ex 20:2-6   (= Deut 5:6-10): Commandments 1 and 2
    (2) Ex 20:7   (= Deut 5:11):   Commandment 3
    (3) Ex 20:8-11   (= Deut 5:12-15): Commandment 4
    (4) Ex 20:12   (= Deut 5:16):   Commandment 5
    (5) Ex 20:13-16 (= Deut 5:17-20): Commandments 6-9
    (6) Ex 20:17   (= Deut 5:21):   Commandment 10

These sections are separated by the closed paragraph marker *Samek*; and, in addition, Commandments 6-9 are thus separated. The alternate set of accents seems to conform to the syntax rules except for the following anomalies:

(1) Verses 2 and 5 both end with *Athnach*. If verses 2 through 6 form one complete unit of accentuation, then only one *Athnach* segment is lawful. However, verses 2-3 comprise the traditional First Commandment. Assuming that the Masoretes intended a division between Commandments 1 and 2, then verse 3 should end with *Silluq*; but the MSS and editions record a *Rebia* there. The problem is further complicated because the passage in Deuteronomy (5:6) that is parallel with 20:2, although closed by *Athnach* in BHS and BHK, is closed by *Rebia* in B and MG.

(2) In Deut 5:17, BHS lacks the *Tiphcha* found in BHK, B, and, MG; thus setting off Commandment 6 by

itself,   apart from 7 through 9.   This is contrary to
the   parallel in Exodus,   and is a possible   defect   in
BHS.

Interpreting Problem Texts

The   accents   are   a helpful   guide   to   resolving
problem   texts,   at least for determining the   rabbinic
interpretation   of such problem texts.   The   following
exposition of the difficult text in Eccl 8:10   uses the
accents in this manner.

וּבְכֵן רָאִיתִי רְשָׁעִים קְבֻרִים וָבָאוּ
וּמִמְּקוֹם קָדוֹשׁ יְהַלֵּכוּ
וְיִשְׁתַּכְּחוּ בָעִיר   אֲשֶׁר כֵּן־עָשׂוּ
גַּם־זֶה הָבֶל:

Then I saw wicked men
  being buried and departing,[14]
And they used to go and come[15]
  from the Holy Place;
And it was forgotten[16] in the city
  where[17] they had done so:
This too is vanity.

----

[14]The   passive participle קְבֻרִים expressive   durative   action.
The   preacher   continually   saw   wicked men being honorably   buried.
The perfect וָבָאוּ with *Waw* consecutive   perpetuates   the durative
aspect of the previous verb.

[15]The   verb   הלך in the *piel* stem suggests traversing in and
out,   and the imperfect aspect suggests habitual behavior.   Note
that   *Zaqeph* produces a pausal form here,   contrary to   the   usual
practice.

[16]Literally "they were forgotten."

[17]The antecedent of אֲשֶׁר is the preceding noun עִיר.

The verse consists of four poetic lines. *Athnach*
divides the verse logically at the end of the third
line. The first three lines describe the disgusting
circumstances that the fourth labels as vanity.
Zaqeph logically divides the three line description at
the end of the second line, so the first two lines
relate the frustrating practices that the third laments
as forgotten. *Rebia* logically divides the first two
lines into two parallel conditions that result in the
lamentation: (1) wicked men were continually being
buried and departing this life with dignity and honor;
(2) during their life time these wicked men had regular
access in and out of the Temple (the Holy Place).
These conditions should have resulted in public outrage
but instead were forgotten by a lethargic populance.
The preacher regarded such public indifference as a
vain frustration.

Most translators and expositors ignore the *Rebia*
and divide the first two lines with the *Geresh* at
קברים. However, the rabbinic interpretation requires
that the division take place at the unambiguous *Rebia*.
Here ambivalent *Geresh* stands in place of a conjunctive
that binds the two verbs together as a compound verb
phrase. By following the divisions defined by the
accents and by following the regular rules of Hebrew
syntax, one is able to derive a meaning from this
difficult text that makes good sense (the ultimate test
of exposition). Hopefully the reader will be able to
successfully interpret other difficult texts with the
aid of these laws of the accents and good Hebrew
grammar.

PART II

THE SYNTAX OF THE MASORETIC ACCENTS USED IN THE THREE BOOKS OF POETRY

CHAPTER 10
The Poetic Accents Marks

The masoretic accentuators provided a separate
system of accents for the three so-called books of
poetry (Psalms, Job, and Proverbs), also referred to as
the Books of Truth, based on the acronym אֱמֶת (truth)
constructed from the first letters of their Hebrew
names אִיּוֹב (Job), מִשְׁלֵי (Proverbs), and תְּהִלִּים (Psalms).[1]
Several of the accent marks used in the books of poetry
are the same as those used in the prose books, but
their syntactic function is usually different, and for
some their names are different. In addition, several
of the accent marks used in the prose books are not
used in the books of poetry, and instead different
marks are employed.

----

[1]Yeivin noted that the accents in the prose sections of Job
(1:1-3:2 and 42:7-17) belong to the set used in the prose books,
not the books of poetry (*Tiberian Masorah*, 157-8). However, the
section of prose in 32:1-6a has the accents of the books of
poetry; these verses exhibit minor deviations from the rules of
accentuation due to their non-poetic structure. Yeivin devoted
comparatively little space (only eleven pages) to the discussion
of the accents in the books of poetry. BHS and BHK have the books
in the order Psalms, Job, Proverbs; whereas B and MG have the
order Psalms, Proverbs, Job. BHS, following L, counts only 149
psalms with the Hebrew numbering system, regarding Psalms 114 and
115 as a single psalm (along with the LXX, the Syriac, Theodotian,
Jerome, and many Hebrew mss); but, BHS follows the tradition of B
and MG, counting 150 psalms when numbering with Arabic numerals.

Part II provides a description of each of the accents used in the books of poetry together with a discussion of their laws of accentuation. A commentary on each accent defines its rules of syntactic governance. The rules have been exhaustively tested and tabulated by means of a computer; they have proven to be relatively simple and consistent.

List of Poetic Accents

The following is a list of the accents used in the three so-called books of poetry. They are listed and numbered according to the list provided as a companion to BHK.[2]

Disjunctive Accents

	Name[3]	Example
(1)	Silluq (סִלּוּק)	דָּבָ֖ר
(2)	Ole-WeYored (עוֹלֶה וְיוֹרֵד)	דָּבָ֫ר
(3)	Athnach (אַתְנָח)	דָּבָ֑ר
(4)	Great Rebia (רְבִיעַ גָּדוֹל)	דָּבָ֗ר
(5)	Rebia Mugrash (רְבִיעַ מֻגְרָשׁ)	דָּבָ֝ר
(6)	Great Shalsheleth (שַׁלְשֶׁלֶת גָּדוֹלָה)	דָּבָ֓ר׀
(7)	Sinnor (צִנּוֹר) (Postpositive)	דָּבָ֮ר
(8)	Little Rebia (רְבִיעַ קָטוֹן)	דָּבָ֔ר
(9)	Dechi (דְּחִי) (prepositive)	דָּבָ֙ר

---

[1] *Erläuterung der Accente zu Kittels Biblia Hebraica*, Privileg. Bibelanstalt, Stuttgart. Some authorities have used different names for some of the accents. These are not regarded as important for this work. Consult Wickes for more detail.

[2] Unlike the prose books, in the poetic books *Soph Pasuq* has no part in the syntax of the accents. In the poetic books, *Silluq* governs the domain of the entire verse.

(10) Pazer (פָּזֵר) .... הָדָבָ֡ר

(11) Mahpak Legarmeh (מַהְפָּךְ לְגַרְמֵהּ) .... הָדָבָ֤ר׀

(12) Azla Legarmeh ((אַזְלָא לְגַרְמֵהּ) .... הָדָבָ֨ר׀

Conjunctive Accents
  Name   *Example*

(13) Munach (מוּנַח) .... הָדָבָ֣ר

(14) Mereka (מֵרְכָא) .... הָדָבָ֥ר

(15) Illuy (עִלּוּי) .... הָדָבָ֬ר

(16) Tarcha (טַרְחָא) .... הָדָבָ֖ר

(17) Galgal (גַּלְגַּל) .... הָדָבָ֪ר

(18) Mahpak (מַהְפָּךְ) .... הָדָבָ֤ר

(19) Azla (אַזְלָא) .... הָדָבָ֨ר׀

(20) Little Shalsheleth (שַׁלְשֶׁלֶת קְטַנָּה) .... הָדָבָ֓ר

(21) Sinnorit Mereka (צִנּוֹרִית מֵרְכָא) .... הָדָבָ֥֘ר

(22) Sinnorit Mahpak (צִנּוֹרִית מַהְפָּךְ) .... הָדָבָ֤֘ר

(23) Paseq (פָּסֵק) .... יְהָדָבָר׀

The following tables list the frequency of
occurrence of each of the accents used in the books of
poetry. The tables include the secondary accents and
the substitutes used for *Metheg*.[5]

----

[4]*Paseq* is not on the standard list of accents, but it must be
included in any discussion of them. It is not a conjunctive
accent as its position in the list implies; nor does it mark a
stressed syllable as do most of the other accents. But it does
call for a slight pause in imitation of a weak disjunctive accent.
It appears last on the list in order to keep the index numbers in
correspondence with the list in the companion to BHK and BHS.

[5]See the discussion of secondary accents in the Introduction.

TABLE 44
Numerical Summary of the Use of the Accents
in the Books of Poetry

Accent	Psa	Job	Prov	Total
Silluq	2527	1023	915	4465
Ole-WeYored	352	40	29	412
Athnach	2335	977	904	4216
Great Rebia	408	96	76	580
Rebia Mugrash	1828	703	654	3185
Great Shalsheleth	23	6	2	31
Sinnor	219	18	14	251
Little Rebia	153	23	18	194
Dechi	1412	615	657	2684
Pazer	72	8	11	91
Mahpak Legarmeh	197	36	26	259
Azla Legarmeh	252	45	27	324
Munach	3661	1649	1601	6911
Mereka	2297	749	717	3767
Illuy	146	20	14	180
Tarcha	582	288	242	1112
Galgal	195	15	9	219
Mahpak	293	98	60	451
Azla	40	1	6	47
Little Shalsheleth	6	0	2	8
Sinnorit Mereka	17	1	0	18
Sinnorit Mahpak	138	23	16	177
Paseq	51	6	5	62

TABLE 45
Numerical Summary of the Use of the Secondary Accents
in the Books of Poetry

Secondary Accent	Psa	Job	Prov	Total
Metheg-Left	1415	497	361	2273
Metheg-Right	72	26	11	109
Metheg-Ultima	28	13	21	62
Total	1515	536	393	2444

TABLE 46
Numerical Summary of the Use of the Metheg Substitutes
in the Books of Poetry

Metheg Substitute	Psa	Job	Prov	Total
Munach	6	4	4	14
Mereka	5	5	1	11
Illuy	5	0	0	5
Tarcha	13	8	5	26
Dechi	2	2	0	4
Galgal	13	2	3	18
Mahpak	25	2	4	31
Total	69	23	17	109

CHAPTER 11
The Laws of Poetic Accentuation

The use of the accents in the Hebrew Bible is
governed by strict well-behaved rules. They have
their own laws of grammar and syntax, which are in
turn in approximate harmony with the grammar and syntax
of Biblical Hebrew.

The Laws of Hierarchic Governance

The early authorities recognized a hierarchic
order among the disjunctive accents, referring to the
various ranks in terms of European nobility. Wickes
noted a hierarchic order among the accents, but he
avoided specific categories and terms of nobility.
Evident differences in the classification of the
accents demonstrate the lack of agreement among the
authorities. My own research supports the existence of
hierarchic order among the accents in the poetical
books, but with the following hierarchic ranks:

Hierarchy	Disjunctive Accents
I	*Silluq*[1]
II	*Rebia Mugrash, Athnach, Ole-WeYored*
III	*Dechi, Sinnor, Great Rebia*
IV	*Pazer, Legarmeh*

----

[1] Unlike the accents of the prose books, *Soph Pasuq* does not
govern its own segments. In the poetical books *Silluq* governs the

The disjunctive accents used in the poetical books observe rules of governance similar to those used in the prose books with minor differences. These differences are noted in the commentary on the individual accents. The following lists the governance of each disjunctive accent.

		Defined Subordinate	
Hierarchy	Disjunctive	Near	Remote
I	Silluq	Rebia Mugrash	Athnach/Ole-WeYored[2]
II	Rebia Mugrash	Dechi	Great Rebia
	Athnach	Dechi	Great Rebia
	Ole-WeYored	Sinnor	Great Rebia
III	Dechi	Legarmeh	Pazer
	Sinnor	Legarmeh	Pazer
	Great Rebia	Legarmeh	Pazer
IV	Pazer	Legarmeh	Empty
	Legarmeh	Legarmeh	Empty

The distinguishing characteristic of each hierarchic rank is that it embraces the segments of the next lower rank in its domain. Thus in hierarchy II, both *Rebia Mugrash* and *Athnach* have *Dechi* as the near subordinate segment in their domain, and both they and *Ole-WeYored* have *Great Rebia* as the principal remote segment. In hierarchy III, *Dechi, Sinnor,* and *Great Rebia* all have *Legarmeh* in their domain as the near subordinate segment, and each has *Pazer* as the remote

----

entire verse.

[2] In the domain of *Silluq,* only one *Athnach/Ole-WeYored* segment may occur. If two are required, the first is an *Ole-WeYored* segment and the second is an *Athnach* segment. In this case Wickes (I, 31-32) would regard *Ole-WeYored* to mark the principle division and *Athnach* to mark a minor division. However, the division of the verse is more complex than this. According to the governance of the accents, *Ole-WeYored, Athnach* and *Rebia Mugrash* have equal rank. This disagreement with Wickes is discussed in a later section.

subordinate segment from hierarchy IV.[3]   I propose that
this governance determines how the division of a verse
is decided, contrary to Wickes.

The Law of Substitution

Some of the disjunctive accents do not appear in
the laws of hierarchic governance, but serve the role
of designated substitutes for some of the accents in
those laws.   In most cases substitution takes place
when the regular segment is empty and the associated
disjunctive accent has no preceding conjunctives. More
specific conditions for substitution are given in the
commentaries on the individual accents. The following
is a list of the substitute segments and the segments
which they replace:

Regular Segment   Substitute Segment

Rebia Mugrash..........*Great Shalsheleth*
Sinnor................*Little Rebia*

The Law of Conjunctives

A sequence of words closely related grammatically
and syntactically is joined together by conjunctive
accents; that is, the first and any intermediate words
in the sequence have conjunctive accents, and the last
word has a disjunctive accent.   As far as the
governance of the disjunctive accents is concerned,
such a conjoined sequence of words functions as a
single word (or word-unit);   that is,   the presence of
conjunctive accents has little or no effect on the

----

[3] Note that the hierarchy breaks down in hierarchy IV in that
Pazer and *Legarmeh* may govern a near subordinate *Legarmeh*.

syntax of the disjunctive accents.[4]

On the other hand, a given disjunctive accent determines the number and kind of conjunctive accents that may appear on the words conjoined preceding it. The following is a list of the number and kind of conjunctive accents that may precede each of the disjunctives:[5]

Disjunctive Accent	Number and Kind of Permitted Conjunctive Accents
Silluq...................	0-1 *Munach/Mereka/Illuy*
Rebia Mugrash.............	0-1 *Mereka*
Great Shalsheleth.........	0-1 *Mereka*
Athnach...................	0-1 *Munach/Mereka*
Ole-WeYored...............	0-1 *GalGal/Mahpak*
Dechi.....................	0-1 *Munach*
Sinnor....................	0-1 *Munach/Mereka*
Little Rebia..............	0-1 *Mereka*
Great Rebia...............	0-1 *Illuy/Mahpak/Sinnorit-Mahpak*
Pazer.....................	0-1 *Galgal*
Azla Legarmeh.............	0-1 *Illuy/Mahpak/Sinnorit-Mahpak*
Mahpak-Legarmeh...........	None

The law of conjunctives allows only one conjunctive to serve a given disjunctive. If more that two words occur in a close syntactical relationship, then *Maqqeph* is employed to limit the sequence to two phonetic-units. In some cases this required *Maqqeph* is lacking (usually after a monosyllabic particle); in such instances *Mereka* or *Mahpak* is used in lieu of the expected *Maqqeph*. This may result in two conjunctives

----

[4] Conjunctive accents have influence on the operation of some of the rules of substitution.

[5] Minor deviations from these general rules are discussed in the later commentary on the individual accents. Where alternatives are given, the choice is determined by musical (rhythmic) laws. In some cases, when a disjunctive becomes virtual it governs a different conjunctive.

before a given disjunctive in apparent violation of
this law. But the law regards this use of *Mereka* and
Mahpak as the equivalent of the *Maqqeph* for which they
stand.

Under appropriate musical conditions, the law of
transformation converts certain disjunctives into their
virtual form, in which case a conjunctive stands in
place of the virtual disjunctive. Such transformations
may produce sequences of two or more conjunctives
before a given disjunctive in apparent violation of the
law of conjunctives. However, any conjunctive accent
that stands in place of a virtual disjunctive is
regarded by this law as the equivalent of the
disjunctive for which it stands.

The Law of Transformation

Wickes documented the musical restraints that
govern the proximity of certain accents.[6] In the prose
books, for musical reasons, *Geresh* cannot stand very
close to the disjunctive that governs it without being
transformed into a *Virtual Geresh* which has a
conjunctive standing in its place. In such cases the
transformed *Geresh* functions musically as a
conjunctive, while continuing to function syntactically
as a disjunctive. A similar musical restraint causes
Rebia to transform into *Pashta* under certain
conditions.

In the books of poetry, three of the near
subordinate disjunctives (*Rebia Mugrash, Dechi,* and
Legarmeh) are subject to a similar transformation.
Wickes recorded the first two and alluded to the

----

[6]Wickes, II, 117.

third.[7] The transformation of all three has been
confirmed to be simple and quite consistent, even when
they occur in sequence.   He also noted a similar
musical restraint that causes *Great Rebia* to transform
into *Sinnor*.[8] Although few instances exist, this too
has been confirmed.

The Law of Continuous Dichotomy

The law of continuous dichotomy is discussed in
the section on the accentuation of the prose books.
What is said there also applies for the books of
poetry.   However,   one serious difficulty must be
addressed. According to Wickes,[9] when both *Ole-WeYored*
and *Athnach* occur in a verse, the *Ole-WeYored* marks the
primary division,   and *Athnach* marks the secondary
division between the *Ole-WeYored* and *Silluq*.   This is
commonly accepted by scholars. Gesenius stated:

> In   shorter   verses 'Athnâh suffices as principal
> distinctive;   in longer verses '*Olè weyôrêd* serves as
> such,   and is then mostly followed by 'Athnâh as the
> principal disjunctive of the second half of the
> verse.[10]

Yeivin echoed the same rule:

> If the verse is long, and the main division is distant
> from *silluq*, it is marked by '*oleh we-yored*. . . . If
> the verse is short,   and the main division is
> relatively close to *silluq*,   it is marked by *atnah*.

----

[7] Wickes, I, 60, 62, 74, 83.

[8] Wickes, I, 56.

[9] Wickes, I, 30-35.

[10] E Kautzsch, ed, *Gesenius' Hebrew Grammar*, 2nd ed. Revised
by A. E. Cowley (London: Oxford Press, 1910), 15h.

> . . . *Atnah* in the Three Books has the same form as
> in the twenty-one books [sic], and a similar use, but
> its pausal value is less than that of *'oleh we-yored*
> and similar to that of *zaqef* in the Twenty-One
> Books.[11]

However, there are several reasons why *Ole-WeYored*
and *Athnach* should be regarded as having equal
disjunctive rank:

(1) Both govern hierarchy III disjunctives in
their domain; and both evoke pausal forms, even in the
same verse (Psa 1:1), although the pausal form fails
with *Athnach* at times.

(2) When the verse is short, either may mark the
principal division: *Athnach* marks it when it falls
near the end of the verse, *Ole-WeYored* when remote from
the end; this must be a musical not a grammatical
restraint. In the mid-range (neither near nor far),
either one may occur, evidently on the basis of
arbitrary choice.

(3) An *Ole-WeYored* segment (the alleged first half
of the verse) is not divided by *Athnach* (as supposed
for the second half), but by *Great Rebia*, the same
disjunctive that marks the major division of the
Athnach and *Rebia Mugrash* segments; thus *Athnach* does
not parallel the use of *Zaqeph* in the prose books, as
Yeivin suggested.

(4) Frequently *Ole-WeYored* and *Athnach* mark the
divisions between triplets of equal syntactic and
poetic value as in the following examples:

----

[11]Yeivin, *Tiberian Masorah*, 265-67; capitalization (and lack
of it) his.

(#1)

תּוֹדִיעֵנִי אֹ֛רַח חַיִּ֑ים

שׂ֣בַע שְׂמָחוֹת אֶת־פָּנֶ֗יךָ

נְעִמ֖וֹת בִּימִינְךָ֣ נֶֽצַח׃

You will show me the path of life;
In Your presence is fullness of joy;
At Your right hand are pleasures forevermore.
(Psa 16:11)

(#2)

הָאֵ֖ל תָּמִ֣ים דַּרְכּ֑וֹ

אִמְרַת־יְהוָ֣ה צְרוּפָ֑ה

מָגֵ֣ן ה֭וּא לְכֹ֥ל ׀ הַחֹסִ֣ים בּֽוֹ׃

As for God, His way is perfect;
The word of the LORD is proven;
He is a shield to all who trust in Him.
(Psa 18:31)

(#3)

הַמְקָרֶ֣ה בַמַּ֗יִם עֲלִיּ֫וֹתָ֥יו

הַשָּׂם־עָבִ֥ים רְכוּב֑וֹ

הַֽמְהַלֵּ֗ךְ עַל־כַּנְפֵי־רֽוּחַ׃

Who lays the beams of His upper chambers
in the waters,
Who makes the clouds His chariot,
Who walks on the wings of the wind.
(Psa 104:3)

(#4)

זֶ֤ה ׀ הַיָּ֥ם גָּד֗וֹל וּרְחַ֪ב יָ֫דָ֥יִם

שָֽׁם־רֶ֭מֶשׂ וְאֵ֣ין מִסְפָּ֑ר

חַיּ֥וֹת קְטַנּ֗וֹת עִם־גְּדֹלֽוֹת׃

This great and wide sea,
In which are innumerable teeming things,
Living things both small and great.
(Psa 104:25)

Examples of such triplets abound when one is free to view the two accents as of equal rank.[12] At times the triplets consist of three pairs of parallel lines (a hexastich) as in the following examples:

(#1)

רַבּוּ מִשַּׂעֲרוֹת רֹאשִׁי / שֹׂנְאַי חִנָּם
עָצְמוּ מַצְמִיתַי / אֹיְבַי שֶׁקֶר
אֲשֶׁר לֹא־גָזַלְתִּי / אָז אָשִׁיב:

> Those who hate me without a cause
> Are more than the hairs of my head;
> They are mighty who would destroy me,
> Being my enemies wrongfully;
> Though I have stolen nothing,
> I still must restore it.
> (Psa 69:5)

(#2)

יְהוָה מָלָךְ / גֵּאוּת לָבֵשׁ
לָבֵשׁ יְהוָה / עֹז הִתְאַזָּר
אַף־תִּכּוֹן תֵּבֵל / בַּל־תִּמּוֹט:

> The LORD reigns,
> He is clothed with majesty;
> The LORD is clothed,

----

[12]The determination of syntactic and poetic equality is somewhat subjective, but the following verses seem to exhibit three parallel clauses in three poetic lines: Psa 2:7; 9:7; 14:4 (= 53:5); 16:4, 11; 18:31, 36, 44, 49; 21:10; 22:17; 24:4; 27:14; 29:3; 30:12; 35:8, 21; 36:5; 46:10; 50:3; 52:7; 56:9; 60:8; 63:12; 66:12; 68:17, 35; 69:21; 72:15, 16; 74:9; 77:3, 7; 78:7, 50; 80:15; 81:8; 84:12; 86:16; 88:9, 10; 90:17; 97:10; 99:8; 102:27; 104:3, 29; 115:12; 135:7; 138:8; 139:14; 144:14; Job 3:4, 6, 9; 7:11; 10:1; 11:20; 20:26; 24:13; 30:12, 13, 15; 31:7; 34:20; Prov 1:11; 3:3; 23:7; 30:15, 20. In addition, the following verses have three clauses in three poetic lines, except that one clause has an elided element: Psa 35:17; 68:14; 140:11; 142:6; Job 36:11; Prov 7:22.

He has girded Himself with strength.
Surely the world is established,
So that it cannot be moved.

(Psa 93:1)

(5) In addition, there are many poetic triplets in which the lines are not syntactically equal, but are comparable according to the criteria provided for division in the prose books, that is, besides clauses paralleling clauses, dependent clauses may parallel independent clauses,[13] phrases (subject, predicate, verb, object, adverb, or vocative) may parallel a clause,[14] and phrase may parallel phrase.[15] In the case

----

[13] All the following verses have three poetic lines the first of which is closed by *Ole-WeYored* and the second by *Athnach*. The following have one or two dependent clauses: Psa 14:7 (= 53:7); 31:8, 24; 67:5; 73:28; 79:8; 106:43; 130:7; 138:7; 139:15; Job 14:7, 14; 21:33; 32:12; 38:41; Prov 1:22, 23; 23:5; 24:14; 25:8; 30:20. In the following verses the first poetic line contains two short clauses, and the next two lines each contain a clause that expounds on one of the first two: Psa 6:3; 68:3; Job 14:12; Prov 23:31. It is true that *Ole-WeYored* often sets off the independent clause; but since dependent and independent clauses may stand in parallel in a doublet (e.g., Psa 45:8, 12), then they may stand in parallel in a triplet.

[14] All the following verses have three poetic lines the first of which is closed by *Ole-WeYored*, the second by *Athnach*. The following contain two clauses followed by a parallel phrase: Psa 7:9; 25:7; 27:11; 32:9; 35:20; 37:7, 25; 42:7; 45:6; 59:14; 84:11; 86:2; 100:3; 109:18; 118:27; 125:2; 128:5; Job 29:25; 42:3; Prov 8:30; 25:7. The following verses contain a clause followed by a phrase followed by another clause: Psa 24:10; 79:11; 87:4; 110:3. The following verses contain one clause followed by two parallel phrases: Psa 4:9; 11:5; 12:7; 32:8, 10; 10:18; 18:3; 24:8; 45:15; 50:23; 51:19; 68:29; 71:13; 78:19, 71; 107:3; 116:8; 130:2; 135:6; 140:12; 144:11; Job 30:3; Prov 8:34. The following verses have a phrase (*casus pendens*) followed by two clauses to which the phrase applies: Job 18:4 (vocative); Prov 24:24 (accusative). It is true that *Ole-WeYored* usually separates an independent clause from a dependent clause, and the phrase usually modifies the dependent clause; but in some verses both clauses are independent (Psa 100:3), and the phrase may modify both (Psa 128:2). Again, since

of triplets, it appears that the accents are setting
off parallel poetic lines without strict regard for
their relative syntactic rank, but with greater regard
for poetic and musical meter as in the following
examples:

(#1)

אִם־תִּשְׁכְּבוּן בֵּין שְׁפַתָּיִם

כַּנְפֵי יוֹנָה נֶחְפָּה בַכֶּסֶף

וְאֶבְרוֹתֶיהָ בִּירַקְרַק חָרוּץ:

> Though you lie down among the sheepfolds,
> Yet you will be like the wings of a dove
>   covered with silver,
> And her feathers with yellow gold.
>   (Psa 68:14)

(#2)

וַאֲנִי ׀ קִרֲבַת אֱלֹהִים לִי־טוֹב

שַׁתִּי ׀ בַּאדֹנָי יְהוִה מַחְסִי

לְסַפֵּר כָּל־מַלְאֲכוֹתֶיךָ:

> But it is good for me to draw near to God;
> I have put my trust in the Lord GOD,
> That I may declare all Your works.
>   (Psa 73:28)

(6) In at least one place, *Ole-WeYored* and *Athnach*
mark equal segments, and the last segment of the verse
consists of a musical notation, as in the following
example:

----

a clause and a phrase may stand in parallel in a doublet (e. g.,
Psa 31:19), they may stand in parallel in a triplet.

[15]All the following verses have three poetic lines, each
containing only phrases: Psa 71:20; 103:20; 104:25; 123:4; 137:8;
Prov 30:16.

(#1)   נוֹדַע| יְהוָה מִשְׁפָּט עָשָׂה
                  בְּפֹ'עַל כַּפָּיו| נוֹקֵשׁ רָשָׁע
                                    הִגָּיוֹן סֶלָה:

The LORD is known by the judgment He executes;
The wicked is snared in the work of his own hands.
                    Meditation.   Selah
                                        (Psa 9:17)

(7) In addition to the poetic triplets, most of
which support the thesis that *Ole-WeYored* and *Athnach*
have equal disjunctive rank, numerous verses with four
poetic lines have three parallel clauses, one
consisting of two lines, and the other two consisting
of one line each. Usually the first two lines
constitute a long clause closed by *Ole-WeYored*,[16] but
one verse has the long clause in the last two lines.[17]
These also suggest that *Ole-WeYored* and *Athnach* are of
equal rank, as in the following examples:

(#1)   אַל-תַּסְתֵּר פָּנֶיךָ| מִמֶּנִּי[1]
                      בְּיוֹם צַר לִי,
                      הַטֵּה-אֵלַי אָזְנֶךָ
                  בְּיוֹם אֶקְרָא מַהֵר עֲנֵנִי:

Do not hide Your face from me
   in the day of my trouble;
Incline Your ear to me;
In the day that I call, answer me speedily.
                                   (Psa 102:3)

(3-3/2/4) Three clauses,
   one is two lines with *Ole-WeYored*.

----

[16] Psa 1:1;   27:5;   28:4;   30:10; 40:4; 42:3; 52:9;   55:20;
78:8;   101:3;   102:3;   127:5.

[17] Psa 99:4.

(#2)

וַיֹּאמֶר לְהַשְׁמִידָם

לוּלֵי מֹשֶׁה בְחִירוֹ

עָמַד בַּפֶּרֶץ לְפָנָיו

לְהָשִׁיב חֲמָתוֹ מֵהַשְׁחִית׃

> Therefore He said that He would destroy them,
> Had not Moses His chosen one
>   stood before Him in the breach,
> To turn away His wrath, lest He destroy them.
> (Psa 106:23)

>   (2/3-3/3) Four clauses,
>   the one with *Athnach* is two lines,
>   two short clauses in the last line.

(8) In addition to the poetic triplets, there are numerous places where *Ole-WeYored* sets off an auxiliary element of the verse, obviously not the principal division. In these cases *Athnach* marks the principle syntactic division. These consist of (a) setting off a short title,[18] (b) setting off an introduction to a quotation,[19] and setting off an initial refrain.[20] Also there are several places where

----

[18] The title usually consists of only two words: *lamenatseach ledawid* (Psa 11:1; 14:1); *mizmor ledawid* (15:1; 29:1; 50:1; 141:1; 143:1); *ledawid mizmor* (24:1; 101:1; 110:1); *mizmor le'asaph* (79:1; 82:1); *maskil le'asaph* (74:1; 78:1); *tephillah ledawid* (17:1; 86:1); *tehillah ledawid* (145:1); *mishley shelomoh* (Prov 10:1); the Songs of Ascents *shir hamma'aloth* (Psa 120:1; 121:1; 123:1; 125:1; 126:1; 128:1; 129:1; 132:1; 133:1; 134:1); a few consist of three words: *shir hamma'aloth ledawid* (122:1; 124:1; 131:1; 133:1); *shir hamma'aloth lishlomoh* (127:1); one consists of four words (Prov 30:1).

[19] Job 32:6; such introductions are not usually set off by a major disjunctive.

[20] Psa 104:1.

Ole-WeYored with *Athnach* appears in prose sections of
the poetic books.[21]   None of these instances prove the
superiority of *Ole-WeYored* over *Athnach*.   Instead they
suggest an equality of rank similar to that of *Zaqeph*
and *Segolta* in the prose books.

   (9)   Finally,   there   are several   places   where
syntactically *Athnach* seems   to   mark   the   principal
division   of   the   verse,   and *Ole-WeYored* to   mark   the
division of the first half of the verse.[22]   Contrary to
Wickes'   proposed dichotomy,   these   instances   suggest
that *Athnach* is   of   superior   rank   to *Ole-WeYored*.   It
seems better, however, to understand that   these verses
have been divided on   the   basis   of poetic parallelism
rather than strict syntactic function, and that the two
accents   are   of   equal   rank,   as   in   the   following
examples:

(#1)

מִנִּ֫יגַהּ נֶגְדּ֑וֹ

עָבָ֑יו עָבְר֑וּ

בָּרָ֖ד וְגַחֲלֵי־אֵֽשׁ׃

From the brightness before Him
His thick cloud passed by,
With hailstones and coals of fire.
                                                (Psa 18:13)

(#2)

מֵאֹ֫פֶךְ תֵּהָמְתִ֑י בְּסֵ֖תֶר רָ֑ב

נִדְרַ֖י אֲשַׁלֵּ֑ם נֶ֖גֶד יְרֵאָֽיו׃

----

   [21]They   appear in five prose titles of the Psalms (Psa   18:1;
52:2;   59:1;   60:2; 88:1),   and in two prose verses of Job (32:2,
3).

   [22]See Psa 5:13;   18:13;   22:26; 37:40; 48:3; 56:5;   59:13:
64:8;   71:19;   85:9; 86:17; 115:1; 116:16; 139:12;   143:12;   Job
36:7; Prov 5:19; 9:15; 12:6.

> My praise shall be of You
> in the great assembly;
> I will pay my vows
> before those who fear Him.
> (Psa 22:26)

In all, about 238 examples are cited above which suggest that the two accents are of equal rank. This constitutes approximately 65% of all the occurrences of *Ole-WeYored* and *Athnach* together. It remains to consider those places where *Ole-WeYored* seems to mark the principal division.

When the number of poetic lines is three or a multiple of three, *Ole-WeYored* and *Athnach* nearly always divide the verse into thirds: for three poetic lines the meter would be something like 3/3/3, 4/3/3, etc.; for six lines it would be something like 2-2/2-2/2-2, or 2-3/3-2/2-2, etc. But when the verse has four or five poetic lines, there is no way of indicating this kind of quadruple or pentuple parallelism, because *Ole-WeYored* and *Athnach* cannot be repeated, and they are the accents of highest rank.[23] Therefore, one or the other (or both) must govern more than one poetic line, and *Great Rebia* must be used to mark the end of the lines not marked by *Athnach* or *Ole-WeYored*.

Usually when there are four poetic lines containing four parallel clauses, *Ole-WeYored* governs two, *Athnach* one, and *Rebia Mugrash* one.[24] But

----

[23]This is one of the deficiencies of the simple accent grammar that make it inadequate for reflecting the more complex poetic structure of long verses.

[24]The following verses have four poetic lines and four parallel clauses of approximately equal syntactic rank, and are accented in this manner: Psa 5:10; 10:14; 11:4; 18:7; 22:15;

occasionally   the   situation   reverses,[25]   as   (#1)
demonstrates.   These forty-one instances add   to   the
previous 238 that suggest that the two accents are   of
equal rank, raising the percentage to 76%.[26]

(#1)

גַּם אָנֹכִי כָּכֶם אֲדַבֵּרָה

לוּ־יֵשׁ נַפְשְׁכֶם תַּחַת נַפְשִׁי

אַחְבִּירָה עֲלֵיכֶם בְּמִלִּים

וְאָנִיעָה עֲלֵיכֶם בְּמוֹ רֹאשִׁי׃

> I also could speak as you do.
> If your soul were in my soul's place,
> I could heap up words against you,
> And shake my head at you.
>   (Job 16:4)

(4/4-3/4) Four clauses, two with *Athnach*

The   remaining instances of four-line   verses   may
more   easily   be interpreted to support   Wickes'   law.
They consist of intermixtures of clauses and phrases in
various   combinations   that   often lead   to   a   logical
division   of   the verse at the end of the   second   line

31:11;   40:18;   57:7;   62:5; 70:6; 72:17;   78:38;   139:16;   142:5.
The following have four lines and four clauses some of which are
dependent but poetically parallel: Psa 5:11; 13:6; 14:3 (= 53:4);
19:10; 27:3;   28:1, 7; 31:14; 39:2; 53:13; 57:2; 62:10, 11;   69:4;
142:7, 8; 143:7, 8, 10; Job 7:20, 21; Prov 23:35; 30:9.   Since
independent and dependent clauses may stand parallel in doublets
and triplets, then they may do so in quatrains.

[25] The following verses have four poetic lines and four
parallel clauses of approximately equal syntactic rank, and have
Athnach setting off the middle two: Psa 35:15; Job 16:4;   Prov
24:12.

[26] This,   of course, is fully consistent with the fact that
both accents govern *Dechi* (or *Sinnor*) and *Great Rebia* as their
immediate subordinates.

(usually marked with *Ole-WeYored*).   These combinations
include clause-clause/clause/phrase,[27]   clause-clause/
phrase/clause,[28] clause-phrase/clause/phrase,[29] clause-
phrase/phrase/clause,[30] clause-clause/phrase/ phrase,[31]
phrase-clause/phrase/clause,[32]   clause-phrase/phrase/
phrase,[33] and phrase-phrase/phrase/ phrase.[34] But   in
view of the previous evidence that the use of the   two
accents may be governed   by musical considerations
related to setting off parallel poetic lines, and that
clauses and phrases appear in poetic parallelism, it is
possible to explain the accents in these verses on that
basis.   Such an explanation is just as reasonable as
Wickes' attempt to impose a dogmatic dichotomy on 76%
of the cases.   The same reasoning may apply to those
few verses containing five lines[35] and six lines.[36]

    A few doublets remain for discussion.   The use of
----

[27]Psa 20:7; 57:19; 65:5; 69:9; 71:18; 96:13; 137:6.

[28]Psa 29:9; 142:4.

[29]Psa 14:2 (= 53:3); 69:7; 71:22; 98:9; 126:6; 128:3; 133:3;
144:12.

[30]Psa 101:6.

[31]Psa 15:5;   18:16;   32:7; 35:10; 37:14; 56:14; 57:5;   62:4;
78:5; 79:10; 106:47; 131:2; 132:11; 144:7 (*Athnach* sets off two
lines in this last one).

[32]Psa 8:3; 101:5.

[33]Psa 28:3;   31:20; 79:6; 98:3; 106:23 (*Athnach* sets off
two lines); 132:12; Prov 30:14.

[34]Psa 27:2; 32:4; 35:4, 26; 40:15, 17; 68:21, 22, 24; 70:3,
5; 79:13; 84:3; 101:7; 137:7; 144:2; Job 30:1; Prov 6:26; 30:17.

[35]Psa 1:3;   17:4;   27:9; 32:6; 35:27; 39:13; 42:12;   43:5;
53:6; 75:9; 78:20; 84:4; 88:6; 126:2.

[36]Psa 27:4; 31:12; 40:6; 69:5; 93:1; 123:2.

both *Ole-WeYored* and *Athnach* in a two-line verse is rare and unexpected in view of what has been seen of their use. However, even some doublets support the equal rank of the accents. In four instances the accents set off three clauses.[37] In three instances *Athnach* closes the first line, with *Ole-WeYored* dividing it, at least according to the editors of BHS.[38] In only three instances do the verses have two clauses in which *Athnach* divides the second into phrases.[39] These can be regarded as within the flexibility of the above considerations.

The results of this statistical study support the thesis that *Ole-WeYored* and *Athnach* are of equal disjunctive rank. This is in harmony with the manner in which they govern similar subordinate segments. The evidence suggests that, particularly in the books of poetry, the use of the major accents is determined as much by the musical and rhythmic elements of poetry as it is by the linguistic syntax of the verses themselves.

In the vast majority of cases, *Athnach* and *Ole-WeYored* occur at the end of poetic lines, even when a major syntactic division fails to coincide with the end of a poetic line. Wickes himself noted this fact:

> In the more *musical* accentuation of the three books, there is an apparent reluctance to place the main dividing accent after the *first*, or before the *last* word of the verse. In cases where, according to the logical (or syntactical) division, it would come there, it is generally moved forwards or backwards to

----

[37] Psa 3:6; 9:21; Job 27:5; 33:9.

[38] Psa 5:13; 18:13; 22:26.

[39] Psa 12:3; 76:12; 140:4.

where a convenient resting-place is found for it.[40]

All his examples show the major accent conveniently resting at the end of a poetic line. In fact, almost all the problems of dichotomy that Wickes noted in the books of poetry can be explained in this way. This is as common sense would dictate: when reading poetry, major pauses occur at the end of poetic lines; and when major syntactic divisions fail to coincide with the end of poetic lines, they necessarily require secondary pause. Short verses having neither *Athnach* or *Ole-WeYored* should be regarded as containing only one poetic line.

This is in agreement with the conclusion of Revell who argued that the end of poetic lines are marked by pausal forms.[41] Wilfred G. E. Watson, a contemporary authority on Hebrew poetry, observed that "a guide to marking off lines in Hebrew [poetry] is the occurrence of pausal forms."[42] Thus it is necessary to differ with Wickes' Law of Continuous Dichotomy. It may seem presumptuous to dispute such a widely accepted principle formulated by such a highly competent authority, but it has been done only after careful thought and with deep respect. Most of Wickes' other laws have been rigorously confirmed.

----

[40]Wickes, I, 29; emphasis his.

[41]E. J. Revell, "Pausal Forms."

[42]W. G. E. Watson, *Classical Hebrew Poetry*, Journal for the Study of the Old Testament, Supplement Series 26 (Sheffield, England: JSOT Press, 1984), 14.

This chapter has described the general laws that govern the use of the accents in the books of poetry. It has defended a law of hierarchic governance that differs somewhat from Wickes' law of continuous dichotomy. The chapters that follow define the governance of the individual accents according to their hierarchic rank.

CHAPTER 12
The Poetic Accent In Hierarchy I

This chapter and those that follow discuss each of the accents used in the books of poetry, giving an exhaustive account of their conformity to the laws of hierarchic governance, substitution, conjunctives, and transformation. Any deviations from these laws are noted, examples are given, problems are discussed, and a count is given of the number of times each alternative is used. The accents are discussed in the order of their hierarchic rank rather than the order in which they are presented on the BHK list. This facilitates clarity.

Hierarchy I contains only one accent, *Silluq*. Unlike the use of *Silluq* in the prose books where it governs only the second half of the verse, in the books of poetry *Silluq* governs the entire verse. This is equivalent to the function of *Soph Pasuq* in the prose books. In the books of poetry, however, *Soph Pasuq* has no independent function in the syntax of the accents, but rather is wholly redundant with *Silluq*.

Silluq

The name *Silluq* means "separation." Like the *Silluq* used in the prose books, the accent mark

consists of a small vertical bar placed below the first
letter of the stressed syllable in the last word of the
verse and to the left of the vowel there. It is the
unfailing companion of *Soph Pasuq*.[1]   It has no
substitute segment.

Silluq evokes the pausal forms of the words upon
which it appears. The domain of *Silluq* is

(Rule 1a)   SIL = $\begin{cases} \text{Sil + RMUG} \\ \text{Sil + [LEG] + RMUG + ATH/OLE} \\ \text{Sil + [LEG] + RMUG + ATH + OLE} \end{cases}$

where "SIL" represents the domain of *Silluq*, "Sil"
represents the word-unit bearing the accent *Silluq*,
"RMUG" represents the domain of a *Rebia Mugrash* near
subordinate segment or its substitute *Great
Shalsheleth*, and "ATH" represents the domain of an
Athnach remote subordinate segment,[2] "OLE" represents
the domain of an *Ole-WeYored* alternate remote
subordinate segment, and "LEG" represents the domain
of an optional *Legarmeh* (#3, #6) segment which may be
merely virtual.[3]   SIL is never empty, but must have at

----

[1] In Psa 59:5, 78:41, and Prov 8:28, BHS lacks a *Silluq*;
whereas BHK, B, and MG have it (BHS has a note in Prov 8:28
acknowledging that L is defective there). I regard *Silluq* to be
correct in these places.

[2] In Job 22:21, on the word ‏יֹמַע‎ BHS has Athnach, leaving the
word ‏וְשָׁלֵם‎ without a vowel and accent, with a note indicating that
L is defective here. On the word ‏וְשָׁלֵם‎ BHK, B, and MG have *Athnach*
and on the word ‏יֹמַע‎, *Munach*. I accept this latter reading as
correct here.

[3] See the discussion under *Virtual Legarmeh*.   LEG has an

least a RMUG segment (#1);[4]   or it may be full, having
Sil + RMUG + ATH (#2, #3) or OLE (#4) or both (#5, #6).
The segments of the verse may not repeat.[5]   If the
verse requires three divisions, the first segment must
be OLE and the second ATH (#5, #6).

According to Wickes,

> Probably the musical relation between Athnach and
> R'bhîa mugrash was such that a break, or pause, in the
> melody between them would have produced an unmusical
> effect.   For this or some other reason connected with
> the melody, *the dichotomy always fails in R'bhîa
> mugrash's clause, when Athnach precedes.*[6]

That is, when *Athnach* precedes, RMUG is always empty.
This is true musically except for two cases.[7] However,
syntactically RMUG is not always empty following
Athnach.   A V-RMUG segment may be fractional following
Athnach, having a virtual *Dechi* near subordinate
segment,[8]   or a real *Dechi* near subordinate segment.[9]

----

auxiliary function here and is not regarded as being in Hierarchy
II.

[4] RMUG is obligatory, but may be only Virtual-RMUG.   See the
discussion under *Virtual Rebia Mugrash*.

[5] In Psa 53:2, on הִשְׁחִיתוּ BHS and BHK have *Rebia Mugrash*,
whereas B has *Tarcha* and MG has *Mereka*.   This results in a
repeated *Rebia Mugrash* in BHS and BHK contrary to the rule.

[6] Wickes, I, 74; emphasis his.

[7] In Psa 14:1 *Great Rebia* intervenes between *Athnach* and *Rebia
Mugrash*; however, the *Rebia Mugrash* is defective in BHK and BHS
(but not in B and MG), lacking the *Geresh*.   In Psa 53:2 BHK and
BHS have a *Rebia Mugrash* intervening between *Athnach* and *Rebia
Mugrash*, but compare B and MG.

[8] Psa 3:5; 4:8; etc.

[9] Psa 104:1; 112:2; 115:3, 8; 119:16; 135:18.

Also a RMUG segment may be fractional following
Athnach, having a virtual *Dechi* near subordinate
segment.[10]   Usually a long RMUG segment stands alone,
or is preceded by *Ole-WeYored*.[11]

    If the main syntactic division of the verse is
strong then SIL usually has both RMUG and ATH/OLE
subordinate segments. If on rare occasions the main
division fails to coincide with the ends of a poetic
line, then *Athnach* and *Ole-WeYored* are usually moved to
the end of the poetic lines; and from these positions
they govern their subordinate segments. If the verse
contains more that three poetic lines, then *Athnach* or
Ole-WeYored (or both) must govern more than one poetic
line, and *Great Rebia* must mark the end of the
intermediate lines in the domain of *Athnach* or *Ole-
WeYored*. If the main division is weak, then the near
subordinate segment RMUG may define the structure. If
either major segment of SIL has at least one
subordinate segment with minor divisions that extend to
a depth involving accents in Hierarchy IV, then the
domain of SIL must include an ATH or OLE segment--all
the lower ranks are employed, thus demanding the
governance of Hierarchy II accents. If this major
division would be on the first word-unit before Sil,

----

[10]Psa 8:2; 18:1; 19:8; etc.

[11]According to Wickes (I, 30-31), if the main division of the
verse occurs on the sixth word-unit from the end of the verse or
earlier, the division must be marked by *Ole-WeYored*; but on the
fourth or fifth word-unit from the end, it may be marked by either
Athnach or *Ole-WeYored*. I found no instances of *Ole-WeYored* on
the third word-unit from the end. It occurs seventeen times on
the fourth word, twenty times on the fifth word, ten times on the
sixth word, four times on the seventh word, never on the eighth
word, and twice on the ninth word.

and the restraints of poetic structure do not overrule, then RMUG (or V-RMUG) must replace ATH,[12] because the syntax of the accents demand that Rmug (or at least V-Rmug) must precede Sil.   Table 47 provides a numerical summary of the structures of the *Silluq* segment.

(#1)

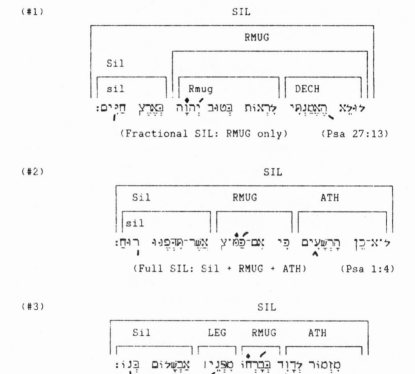

(Fractional SIL: RMUG only)   (Psa 27:13)

(#2)

(Full SIL: Sil + RMUG + ATH)   (Psa 1:4)

(#3)

(Full SIL: Sil + LEG + RMUG + ATH)   (Psa 3:1)

----

[12]This seldom happens, but in such cases *Rebia Mugrash* evokes a pausal form whenever the *Athnach* it replaces would do so (Wickes, I, 74). See Psa 37:23; 52:6.

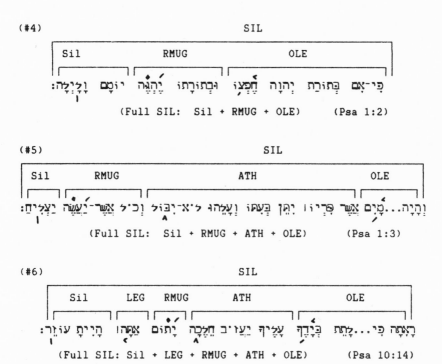

(#4)

(Full SIL: Sil + RMUG + OLE)   (Psa 1:2)

(#5)

(Full SIL: Sil + RMUG + ATH + OLE)   (Psa 1:3)

(#6)

(Full SIL: Sil + LEG + RMUG + ATH + OLE)   (Psa 10:14)

The conjunctives that serve *Silluq* are determined by the sequences of conjunctives that occur between *Silluq* and the various disjunctives that lawfully precede it: *Rebia Mugrash* (or its substitute *Great Shalsheleth*), or *Mahpak-Legarmeh*.[21] Table 48 lists the sequences of conjunctives that occur between *Silluq* and *Rebia Mugrash* or its substitute *Great Shalsheleth*.

----

[21]Other disjunctives are found before *Silluq*, but these always involve the presence of *Virtual Rebia Mugrash*, and may also involve the presence of *Virtual Dechi* and even *Virtual Legarmeh*.

TABLE 47
Numerical Summary of the Structures
of the *Silluq* Segment

	Psalms	Job	Prov	Total
Empty	0	0	0	0[13]
Sil + RMUG	132	42	9	183[14]
Sil + V-RMUG	13	0	0	13[15]
Sil + RMUG + ATH	1990	930	872	3792
Sil + LEG + RMUG + ATH	16	5	3	24[16]
Sil + V-LEG + RMUG + ATH	3	0	0	3[17]
Sil + V-LEG + GSHAL + ATH	21	5	2	28
Sil + RMUG + OLE	47	4	2	53[18]
Sil + RMUG + ATH + OLE	298	36	27	361
Sil +LEG +RMUG +ATH+OLE	5	0	0	5[19]
Sil+V-LEG+GSHAL+ATH+OLE	2	1	0	3[20]
Total	2527	1023	915	4465

----

[13] In eleven titles of the Psalms, *Silluq* is the only disjunctive of the verse (36:1; 38:1; 44:1; 47:1; 49:1; 61:1; 69:1; 81:1; 83:1; 85:1; and 108:1). Such short titles are not representative of the accentuation of the regular verses of the poetical books, having unusual sequences of conjunctives. It is assumed in this study that these verses have virtual segments in accordance with the regular rules.

[14] Nearly always with defective Rmug. Exceptions are in Psa 25:1; 40:1; 70:1; 89:1, 53; 137:9; 146:1; Prov 1:10. These monocolons include numerous short titles of psalms and short introductions to speeches in Job.

[15] Psa 18:2; 30:1; 36:1; 38:1; 44:1; 47:1; 49:1; 61:1; 69:1; 81:1; 83:1; 85:1; 108:1.

TABLE 48
Summary of the Conjunctives
Serving *Silluq*

	Psalms	Job	Prov	Total
Sil + mun + Rmug	349	187	183	719
Sil + mer + Rmug	768	271	283	1322
Sil + ill + Leg-M + Rmug	21	5	3	29
Sil + mun + tar + Rmug	3	0	0	3[11]
Sil + mun + tar + Gshal	22	6	2	30[13]
Sil + sin-mer + Rmug	6	1	0	7[14]

----

[16] Psa 3:1;   20:2;   45:2;   47:9;   56:8; 68:19;   73:20;   74:2; 88:11;   98:6;   102:20;   104:8; 105:3; 119:69, 104;   148:4;   Prov 19:10; 21:29; 25:1;   Job 3:13; 15:24; 21:28; 36:28; 37:14.

[17] Psa 46:8, 12; 66:3.

[18] Psa 1:2;   3:3;   4:5, 7; 5:7; 7:10;   11:6;   18:51;   30:6,   8; 31:3, 6, 16, 19, 21, 23;   32:1;   40:3; 42:5, 6, 10; 43:2, 4; 44:4; 45:8; 47:10;   49:15;   51:6; 55:22, 23;   58:3; 64:10; 68:5, 20, 35; 72:19; 73:1, 26; 90:1; 92:12;   109:16, 28;   124:7;   125:3; 144:10, 13; 145:21; Job 11:6; 20:25;   24:16;   34:10;   Prov 1:21; 8:13.   In BHS and BHK, in most instances defective *Rebia Mugrash* follows *Ole-WeYored*;   the following have *Virtual Rebia Mugrash* instead: Psa 3:3;   4:7; 109:16; 125:3; and Prov 8:13.   Only twice does a normal *Rebia Mugrash* follow *Ole-WeYored*: Psa 58:3; and Job 11:6.

[19] Psa 10:14; 18:7, 31; 99:4; 127:1.

[20] Psa 67:5; 131:1; Job 32:6.

[21] Psa 46:8, 12; 66:3.

[23] In Psa 146:3, BHS and BHK have *Mahpak* with *Metheg-Ultima* on the word שִׁבּוֹ;   whereas B and MG have   *Mahpak-Metheg* with   the expected *Tarcha*. I accept the latter reading as correct here.

[24] Psa 18:20;   22:9;   118:25; Job 20:27. Psa 41:14;   72:19; 89:53;   note that these last three occur on the double Amen at the end of sections of the Psalter.

The   evidence indicates that *Silluq* may be   served
by one conjunctive:[25] It may be *Munach*[26] or *Mereka*[27]
after *Rebia Mugrash*, and *Illuy*[28] after *Mahpak-Legarmeh*.
In Hebrew order the rule is

(Rule 1b)   Sil = $\left[\begin{array}{l} \text{sil} \\ \text{sil + mun/mer/ill} \end{array} \right]$

Regarding the conjunctives serving *Silluq*, Wickes
declared:

----

[25]In Prov 25:28   (in BHS and BHK), *Silluq* has three
conjunctives between it and *Rebia Mugrash* (*Mahpak*, *Tarcha*, and
Munach), the Rank III conjunctive being *Mahpak*; however, B and MG
have *Mahpak-Legarmeh* there.   This is a strange case. If B and MG
are accepted, this would be the only instance of *Mahpak-Legarmeh*
before *Silluq* with *Tarcha* and *Munach* intervening;   all other cases
have only *Illuy* intervening.   This suggests the possibility of V-
Leg following Leg-M. This does occur in other places. Otherwise,
the *Mahpak* must be understood to replace *Maqqeph* here.

[26]According to Wickes (I, 69-70), *Munach* is used when the
stress is on the first syllable of the word. I have not verified
this statement.   It is also used after *Tarcha* almost always,
that is, when it represents V-Leg.

[27]According to Wickes (I, 69-70), *Mereka* is used when the
stress is not on the first syllable of the word, or when the word
is followed by *Paseq*. I have not verified the first part of this
statement, but the last part is not true in Psa 58:7; 61:9; and
66:18.   In a few places *Sinnorit-Mereka* replaces *Mereka* (Psa 5:7;
10:3;   18:20; 22:9; 41:14; 70:4; 72:19; 89:53;   118:25;   Job
20:27);   in all but the last two cases, *Paseq* intervenes or the
word has a *Metheg* on the ultima.   In BHS and BHK in Job 12:15;
19:14;   34:21; and Prov 17:14 *Tarcha* replaces *Mereka*, but B and
MG have *Mereka*.

[28]In Psa 3:3 and in eight short titles (Psa 36:1; 44:1; 47:1;
49:1; 61:1; 69:1; 81:1; 85:1) it is *Illuy* after *Illuy*;   in Psa
4:7; 109:16; 125:3; and Prov 8:13, it is *Illuy* after *Azla*; in
Psa 68:20, it is *Illuy* after *Sinnorit-Mahpak*.

Indeed, in *all* cases, in which Silluq has two or
more servi, the servus adjoining Silluq stands, by
transformation, for R'bhia mugrash. . . . Without
the law of transformation, Silluq would--as in the
prose system--*never have more that one servus.*[29]

But unless he meant that *Virtual Rebia Mugrash* may
stand after regular *Rebia Mugrash* or after *Great
Shalsheleth*, this statement must be modified. Indeed,
two conjunctives occasionally stand between *Silluq* and
Rebia Mugrash, and always between *Silluq* and *Great
Shalsheleth*. Wickes regarded these cases to be
instances of *Virtual Legarmeh.*[40] In light of this
evidence, Wickes' law should be revised to state:

Following *Rebia Mugrash* or *Great Shalsheleth*, if
more than one conjunctive intervenes between *Silluq*
and *Rebia Mugrash* or *Great Shalsheleth*, the
conjunctive immediately preceding *Silluq* (usually
Munach) stands in place of *Virtual Legarmeh*; and the
other conjunctive (usually *Tarcha*) serves the *Virtual
Legarmeh*.
In the absence of *Rebia Mugrash* or *Great

----

[40]Wickes, 1, 70; emphasis his.

[30]Wickes, 1, 67. For musical reasons *Legarmeh* may not stand
on the first word before *Silluq*. When it is called for in that
place, it becomes virtual, being replaced by *Munach*, but retaining
the *Tarcha* that serves it. *Virtual Legarmeh* served by *Tarcha*
occurs after *Great Shalsheleth* in the following verses: Psa 7:6;
10:2; 12:8; 13:2, 3; 20:8; 29:11; 33:12; 41:8; 44:9; 49:14;
50:6; 52:5; 66:7; 67:5; 77:4; 89:2, 3; 94:17; 131:1; 143:6, 11;
Job 5:19; 15:23; 16:9; 32:6; 37:12; 40:23; Prov 6:10; 24:33.
It occurs after *Rebia Mugrash* in the following verses: Psa 46:8,
12; 66:3; Prov 14:13. It occurs in short titles in the following
verses: Psa 38:1; 83:1; 108:1. In Psa 146:3, in BHS and BHK,
the word ‏שׁער‎ has *Mahpak* following *Great Shalsheleth*, and its
ultima has *Metheg*; whereas in B and MG the word has *Tarcha* and
Mahpak-Metheg according to expectation; B19a is probably
defective here, having confused *Tarcha* for *Metheg*. However, if B
and MG are correct, this would be a rare instance where *Munach*
failed to follow *Tarcha*.

> Shalsheleth, the conjunctive adjoining Silluq is a
> Virtual Rebia Mugrash, having been transformed from a
> Rebia Mugrash that would stand too close to Silluq.
> The conjunctive bearing Virtual Rebia Mugrash is
> nearly always Munach or Mereka.[11]

This must further be modified to state:

> When the context expects it, Virtual Dechi is borne by
> the conjunctive adjoining Virtual Rebia Mugrash,[12] and
> Virtual Legarmeh is borne by the conjunctive adjoining
> Virtual Dechi.[13]

Table 49 provides a numerical summary of the
conjunctives serving Silluq.

----

[11] It is Munach after Dechi or Tarcha, and it is Mereka after
Athnach with no intervening conjunctive. Illuy bears Virtual
Rebia Mugrash in Psa 3:5; 4:7; 68:20; 109:16; 125:3; Prov 8:13.

[12] See discussion under Virtual Dechi. For examples see Psa
18:2; 30:1; 68:1.

[13] See Wickes (I, 85), also the discussion under Virtual
Legarmeh. For an example see Psa 42:2.

TABLE 49
Numerical Summary of the Conjunctives
Serving *Silluq*

	Psalms	Job	Prov	Total
Munach	899	467	424	1790
Mereka	900	310	303	1513
Sinnorit-Mereka	9	1	0	10[34]
Illuy	34	5	4	43
Tarcha	0	3	1	4[35]
None	685	237	183	1105
Total	2527	1023	915	4465

----

[34] Psa 18:20; 22:9; 118:25; Job 20:27.

[35] Job 12:15; 19:14;   34:21;   Prov 17:14;   but B and MG have *Mereka* or *Maqqeph* in these cases.

CHAPTER 13
Poetic Accents In Hierarchy II

The accents in Hierarchy II consist of *Rebia Mugrash* (and its substitute *Great Shalsheleth*), *Athnach*, and *Ole-WeYored*. The segments governed by these accents function in the domain of *Silluq*. The *Rebia Mugrash* segment functions as the near subordinate segment of *Silluq*, and the *Athnach* and *Ole-WeYored* segments function as its remote subordinate segments.

The accents of Hierarchy II govern segments in Hierarchy III. All three (*Rebia Mugrash*, *Athnach*, and *Ole-WeYored*) govern a *Great Rebia* remote subordinate segment; *Rebia Mugrash* and *Athnach* govern a *Dechi* near subordinate segment; and *Ole-WeYored* governs a *Sinnor* near subordinate segment.

Rebia Mugrash

The accent mark consists of a prominent diamond-shaped dot placed above the first consonant of the stressed syllable of the word (like the *Rebia* used in the prose books), together with a stroke resembling a *Geresh* placed above the first letter of the word. The name *Rebia* means "quarter" or "resting" and the word *Mugrash* means "bearing *Geresh*." Wickes regarded this name to be

> quite inappropriate, for Geresh is altogether unknown
> in the accentuation of the three books. Rabinical
> writers term our accent מִפְעָה, because it occupies the
> same position before Silluq, as Tiphcha does in the
> prose accentuation. Nay more, the stroke over the
> first letter is, no doubt, *the Tiphcha-sign itself*,
> transferred from below.[1]

But *Tiphcha* likewise is unknown in the accentuation of
the books of poetry, and *Rebia Mugrash* has no
comparable position before *Athnach* as *Tiphcha* does in
the prose books. So the resemblance of the stroke with
Geresh is just as appropriate as with *Tiphcha*,
especially since *Geresh* appears above the word, and
Tiphcha would have to reverse its inclination on being
moved from bottom to top.

   Rebia Mugrash governs the near subordinate segment
of *Silluq,* and its segment is required in every verse,
whether real or virtual. Its companion remote
subordinate segment is *Athnach* or *Ole WeYored.* The
domain of *Rebia Mugrash* is

$$
\text{(Rule 2a)} \qquad \text{RMUG} = \left\{ \begin{array}{l} \text{RMug/GShal} \\ \text{RMug + LEG} \\ \text{RMug + DECH} \\ \text{RMug + DECH + (GREB)} \end{array} \right.
$$

where "RMUG" represents the domain of the *Rebia Mugrash*
segment; "RMug" represents the word-unit bearing the
accent *Rebia Mugrash*; "GShal" represents the word-unit

----

[1]Wickes, I, 15-16; emphasis his.

bearing the accent *Great Shalsheleth*, the substitute for RMug; "LEG" represents an auxiliary *Legarmeh* segment that may occur before RMug at times;[2] "DECH" represents the domain of the near subordinate *Dechi* segment; and "GREB" represents the domain of the remote subordinate *Great Rebia* segment. The parentheses indicate that GREB may repeat.

RMug (or its substitute GShal) is mandatory, but RMug may be merely virtual.[3] When RMug is virtual, I refer to the segment as a *Virtual Rebia Mugrash* segment (V-RMUG). RMUG is often empty, having only one word-unit (RMug or GShal); it may be fractional, having only RMug + DECH (#1); or it may be full, having RMug + DECH + GREB (#2). On rare occasions GREB may repeat (#3). If RMUG is not empty, then DECH is mandatory, but it too may be only a *Virtual Dechi* segment.[4]

If the main syntactic division of RMUG is strong, then it usually has both DECH and GREB subordinate

----

[2] In two instances, LEG occurs before RMug in an otherwise empty segment. In both instances rmug is defective (see later discussion of defective rmug). This rare phenomenon may not warrant being included in the rule, but note a similar rare auxiliary use of LEG in the domain of *Athnach*.

[3] See the discussion of *Virtual Rebia Mugrash* that follows.

[4] See the discussion under *Virtual Dechi*. Wickes seems to deny that DECH is mandatory (I, 58), but I found no instance where it is lacking, at least as V-DECH. It is better to understand that *Dechi* (or at least *Virtual Dechi*) must follow its remote companion segment (GREB), just as all other near subordinate accents must follow their remote companion segments. *Rebia Mugrash* occurs on the first word of the title of fourteen psalms: Psa 13:1; 19:1; 20:1; 21:1; 31:1; 40:1; 41:1; 42:1; 51:1; 52:1; 64:1; 70:1; 89:1; 140:1. It also occurs on the first word of Job 9:1.

segments. If the main division is weak, then the near
subordinate segment DECH may define the structure.   If
either major segment of RMUG has at least one
subordinate segment with minor divisions that extend to
a depth involving accents in Hierarchy IV, then the
domain of RMUG must include a GREB;   otherwise the
division may be defined by DECH only.   If this major
division occurs on the first word-unit before RMug,
then DECH replaces GREB;   because the syntax of the
accents demands that *Dechi* must precede *Rebia Mugrash*
unless RMUG is empty.   Table 50   privides a   numerical
summary of the structures of RMUG.

(#1#)

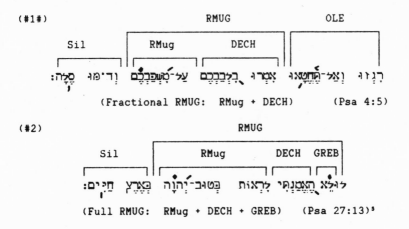

(Fractional RMUG: RMug + DECH)   (Psa 4:5)

(#2)

(Full RMUG: RMug + DECH + GREB)   (Psa 27:13)[5]

(#3)

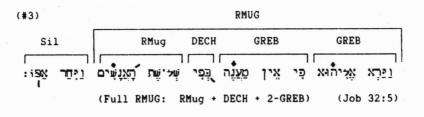

(Full RMUG: RMug + DECH + 2-GREB)   (Job 32:5)

- - - - - - - - - - - - - - - - - - - -

[5] Note that ליּלֹא is marked with *Niqqudim*. BHS has *Great Rebia*
with ליּלֹא, whereas B and MG have *Munach*, and BHK has *Zaqeph*(!).

TABLE 50
Numerical Summary of the Structures
of the *Rebia Mugrash* Segment

	Psalms	Job	Prov	Total
RMug alone	1680	666	636	2982
RMug + LEG	2	0	0	2[6]
RMug + DECH	58	19	5	82
RMug + V-DECH	63	13	12	88
RMug + DECH + GREB	15	1	0	16[7]
RMug + V-DECH + GREB	12	1	1	14[8]
RMug + DECH + 2-GREB	0	3	0	3[9]
Total	1830	703	654	3187

According to Wickes, under certain circumstances *Rebia Mugrash* functions as a substitute for *Athnach* and governs the ATH segment as though *Athnach* were present. He declared:

> If Athnach be *not* present it is because R'bhia mugrash has, by the law of transformation, taken its place in the first or second word before Silluq.

----

[6] Psa 71:21; 109:28 (both defective rmug, see later discussion).

[7] Psa 27:13; 31:23; 41:14; 49:15; 55:7; 57:9; 68:4, 36; 90:1; 99:5; 104:35; 119:48; 146:10; 148:14; 149:9; and Job 10:22 (all defective rmug).

[8] Psa 14:1; 18:51; 76:8; 79:3; 106:48; 113:9; 115:18; 116:19; 117:2; 121:6; 135:21; 147:20; Job 24:19; and Prov 7:7 (all defective rmug).

[9] Job 32:5; 33:24, 27 (all defective rmug); note that no words intervene between the two GREB's.

> Athnach's clause has in consequence become transferred
> to R'bhîa mugrash. This transfer, however, does not
> in any way affect the *division* of the same. Great
> R'bhîa and D'chî appear, just as if Athnach were
> present. . . . In short, R'bhîa mugrash is the
> complete representative of the Athnach it has
> displaced. *The rules for the dichotomy of its clause
> are, in consequence, . . . strictly carried out.*[10]

This is true under very special conditions. For
musical reasons *Rebia Mugrash* must occur before *Silluq*
without fail, so whenever a major division of a verse
occurs on the first or second word-unit before *Silluq*,
then *Rebia Mugrash* must replace the *Athnach* that would
otherwise be expected there. This is the case where
the near subordinate RMUG segment is both empty and too
short to contain the accent that governs it. But this
special circumstance must not be construed to indicate
that *Rebia Mugrash* does not govern its own segment.
Although the syntax of the RMUG segment and the ATH
segment are the same, several facts confirm that *Rebia
Mugrash* governs its own segment:

(1) A full or fractional RMUG segment may follow
an ATH segment (Psa 14:1;   104:1;   112:2;   115:3,8;
119:16;   135:18);   an empty RMUG frequently stands
after ATH;   and RMUG (or at least V-RMUG)   is never
lacking in a verse.

(2) The *Rebia Mugrash* accent has its own
substitute, *Great Shalsheleth.*

(3) *Rebia Mugrash* governs different conjunctives
than *Athnach* and governs them under different

----

[10]Wickes, I, 74-75; emphasis his.

circumstances. This is true whether RMug is an alleged "transformed" Ath or not.

(4) *Rebia Mugrash* undergoes transformation to V-RMug, whereas *Athnach* does not become virtual. It is begging the question to assert that Ath transforms to V-RMug on the first word before *Silluq*. It could just as easily be explained that OLE is used instead of ATH when RMUG is long.

(5) *Athnach* never occurs without a following RMUG (or V-RMUG) segment.

Rebia Mugrash may be served by only one conjunctive, and that is nearly always *Mereka*. In Hebrew order the rule is:

(Rule 2b)   RMug = rmug + [mer]

When rmug has more than one conjunctive, it is due to the presence of *Virtual Dechi* with its residual conjunctive. In these cases, *Virtual Dechi* is borne by the *Mereka* serving rmug, and any conjunctives preceding the *Mereka* must be regarded as serving V-Dech.[11] Table 51 provides a numerical summary of the conjunctives that serve *Rebia Mugrash*.

Defective Rebia Mugrash

Frequently *Rebia Mugrash* is written defectively in BHK and BHS, appearing as *Rebia* without the

- - - - - - - - - - - - - - - - - - - -

[11] *Dechi* is normally served by *Munach*, but *Virtual Dechi* before RMug is served by *Mereka* or *Tarcha*, or on rare occasions by *Sinnorit-Mereka* (Psa 18:1). See the discussion under *Virtual Dechi*.

TABLE 51
Numerical Summary of the Conjunctives
Serving *Rebia Mugrash*

	Psalms	Job	Prov	Total
None	1144	458	399	2001
Mereka	675	245	252	1172
Other	9	0	3	12[12]
Total	1828	703	654	3185

accompanying *Geresh*.   I   interpret every *Rebia* on   the
first   or   second word-unit before *Silluq* as   *Rebia*
Mugrash.   Defective *Rebia Mugrash* is used in BHS   and
BHK almost always (less often in B and MG)   when SIL is
fractional,   that is,   when RMUG is its only segment.[13]

----

[12] *Rebia Mugrash* is never served by *Munach* (as Ath may be),
but on rare occasions it is served by a substitute: *Sinnorit-
Mereka* (Psa 31:22;   66:20), but B and MG have *Mereka*;   *Mahpak*
(Prov 27:1,   19), but these replace *Maqqeph*; or *Sinnorit-Mahpak*
(Psa 31:16;   34:8;   68:15; 79:3; 116:19; 135:21;   Prov 7:7).   On
one occasion it is served by *Illuy* with *Little Shalsheleth* (Psa
137:9);   see discussion under *Little Shalsheleth*.

[13] It occcurs thus in BHS,   BHK,   B,   and MG in the   following
titles: Psa 4:1;   5:1;   8:1;   9:1; 13:1; 19:1; 20:1; 21:1;   31:1;
42:1; 51:1; 52:1;   53:1;   54:1; 55:1; 58:1; 64:1; 65:1; 92:1;   and
140:1;   also before a final *Hallelujah* in Psa 113:9;   117:2;
135:21:   and 150:6;   also in the following introductions   to a
speech: Job 3:2 (= 3:1 in MG); 6:1; 9:1; 11:1; 12:1; 15:1; 16:1;
18:1;   19:1;   20:1;   21:1; 22:1; 23:1; 25:1;   26:1;   27:1;   29:1;
34:1;   35:1; 36:1; 38:1; 40:1, 3, 6; and 42:1.   It also occurs in
the following additional places: Psa 48:4;   50:2;   57:9;   59:7,
15; 68:15; 69:32; 71:21; 76:5; 79:3; 83:18; 92:9;   102:24;   106:6,
37; 119: 4, 5, 12, 14, 17, 24, 26, 33, 36, 44, 47, 48, 54, 64, 68,
103, 112, 124, 140, 144; 121:6; 126:5; 128:4; 129:7; 137:5; 143:9;
Job 3:26   (= 3:25 in MG); 10:22; 14:4; 24:19; 32:5; 33:24,   27;
34:26, 30, 31;   Prov 7:7;   8:33; 24:10; 26:18.
     It occurs in BHS,   BHK,   and MG (where B has   normal *Rebia*
Mugrash)   in the following titles: Psa 41:1;   and 68:1;   and

Likewise it is used almost always when an RMUG segment
follows an OLE segment with no intervening ATH.[14]
Defective *Rebia Mugrash* occurs only five other times
(following *Athnach*).[15]

----

before a final *Hallelujah* in Psa 149:9; and also in the following
additional places: Psa 34:8; 73:4; 86:7, 8; 99:3.   It occurs in
BHS, BHK, and MG (where B has *Athnach*) in Job 9:21;   and Prov
2:11.
     It occurs in BHS, BHK, and B (where MG has normal *Rebia
Mugrash*) in the following titles: 39:1 (MG lacks an accent here);
62:1;   and 67:1; also before a final *Hallelujah* in Psa 104:35;
115:18;   116:19;   and 148:14.   It occurs in these three in the
following additional places: Psa 29:7; 68:4; 76:8; 108:3; 119:57,
130   (MG lacks an accent here);   120:3;   Job 9:9;   and Prov 8:23.
Also it occurs in BHS, BHK, and B (where MG has *Athnach*) in the
following places: Psa 49:9; 52:8; 83:7; and 119:34.
     It occurs in BHS and BHK (where B and MG have normal *Rebia
Mugrash*) in the following titles: Psa 6:1; 12:1;   22:1;   and
77:1;   also before a final *Hallelujah* in Psa 105:45;   106:48;
146:10;   and 147:20;   and also in an introduction to a speech:
Job 4:1;   and 8:1.   It occurs also in the following additional
places: Psa 27:7, 13; 35:24; 37:23; 45:13; 47:8; 52:6;   65:8;
84:2; 99:5 (MG has *Geresh* without *Rebia*);   109:4; 119:46, 52, 145;
Job 17:1;   Prov 3:28; and 6:7.
     It occurs in BHS and BHK (where B and MG have *Athnach*) in the
following places: Psa 5:2;   26:11; 35:12; 37:27; 41:14; 55:7, 21;
63:4;   91:3;   119:2; 126:3; Job 30:27.
     Nine exceptions occur. In the following places, normal *Rebia
Mugrash* is used instead of the expected defective one: Psa 25:1;
40:1; 48:1 [*Geresh* without *Rebia*]; 70:1; 89:1, 53; 137:9; 146:1;
and Prov 1:10.

     [14] It occcurs in BHS, BHK, B, and MG following an *Ole-WeYored*
in Psa 30:6; 31:6; 47:10; 55:22, 23; 64:10; 144:10.   It occurs in
BHS, BHK, and MG (where B has normal *Rebia Mugrash*) following an
Ole-WeYored in Psa 7:10; 109:28; and Job 20:25. It occurs in BHS,
BHK, and B (where MG has normal *Rebia Mugrash*) following an *Ole-
WeYored* in Psa 4:5; 31:21; 42:10; 49:15. It occurs in BHS and BHK
(where B and MG have normal *Rebia Mugrash*)   following an *Ole-
WeYored* in Psa 1:2;   5:7; 11:6; 18:51; 30:8; 31:3, 10, 19, 23;
32:1; 40:3; 42:5; 43:2, 4; 44:4; 45:8; 51:6; 68:5, 36; 72:19;
73:1, 26; 90:1; 92:12; 124:7; 144:13; 145:21; Job 34:10; Prov
1:21.   It occurs in BHS and BHK (where B and MG have *Athnach*)
following an *Ole-WeYored* in Psa 42:6; and Job 24:16.
     Only two exceptions occur where normal *Rebia Mugrash* is used
instead of the expected defective one: Psa 58:3 and Job 11:6.

Wickes   did not regard this use of defective *Rebia*
Mugrash   to   have   originated   with   the   original
accentuators,   but   to have been   a   later   innovation
introduced   to   mark   places   where   *Rebia   Mugrash*
supposedly replaces *Athnach*.   He argued that

> We .must   not,   however,   assign it to   the   original
> accentuators,   for it is impossible to suppose   that,
> when they were selecting the accentual symbols,   they
> should   have   designedly   represented--in   the   short
> verses   of the three Books--*three different accents by
> one and the same sign.*[16]

He   noted   that,   although   the   defective   *Rebia*
Mugrash   is   found in the oldest manuscripts,   and   is
sanctioned   by   the   Masorah,   yet   many   writers   and
accentuators regarded it as awkward,   and preferred the
use   of the normal sign.   He seems to have agreed with
this preference by concluding:

> No   doubt   we have a   *different kind* of R'bhîa   mugrash
> . . . (just as we have two different kinds of   *Rh'bhîa*
> *simplex*);   but the essential (musical)   character of
> the accent may well have been retained in the   changes
> it   underwent.   As foretone to Silluq,   it cannot   be
> dispensed with.[17]

It   is   doubtful   that there are really   two   different
kinds of *Rebia Mugrash*.   The analogy with *Little Rebia*
and   *Great   Rebia*   does   not   apply,   because   (as   is
demonstrated later)   *Little Rebia* and *Great Rebia* occupy
two   different syntactic positions and govern different

----

[15]Psa 14:1; 44:19; 61:9; 88:4; Job 9:10.

[16]Wickes, I, 75;   emphasis his.

[17]Wickes, I, 76;   emphasis his.

sets of conjunctives, thus demonstrating their essential difference; but, no such differences exist between the supposed two kinds of *Rebia Mugrash*. As the data cited above indicates, much confusion exists among the editions over the use of the defective sign, and BHS itself exhibits some inconsistency. Therefore, perspicuity would be served, were all the defective signs to be restored to their normal form.

There is another way in which *Rebia Mugrash* frequently is defective in BHS. It appears as *Geresh* without *Rebia* (nearly always with a note indicating that BHS is defective).[18] The irregularity is much less

----

[18]This irregular *Rebia Mugrash* occurs forty-eight times in Psalms, thirteen times in Job, and fourteen times in Proverbs. It occurs in the following places each with a note that L is defective: Psa 2:2; 8:7; 14:2; 18:15, 38; 21:6, 9; 24:3, 9; 28:6; 30:11; 31:5; 35:9, 20, 28; 46:8, 12; 47:3; 48:1; 49:17; 63:5; 66:1; 68:34; 73:20; 78:35, 38; 94:16; 97:7; 105:15, 24; 107:9; 109:9; 113:1; 118:15, 16, 19; 119:21, 42, 155; 129:1, 2; 132:1; 134:2; 135:1, 7; 139:17; 143:8; 147:1; Job 5:10, 24; 8:2; 12:9; 22:10; 24:18; 26:4; 28:12; 29:3; 31:20 [note missing in the bottom apparatus]; Prov 7:25; 10:14; 15:13; 16:24; 17:4; 19:22; 22:24, 29 [note it is defective]; 26:27; 27:4; 28:22; 31:2, 5, 6. It occurs in the following places without a note: Job 17:2; 29:8; and 39:25.
    In Prov 14:13, BHS has a *Tarcha* with *Geresh*, whereas BHK, B, and MG have *Rebia Mugrash*; L must be defective here. In Psa 124:1, BHS has the *Rebia* before the *Geresh*, whereas BHK, B, and MG have the correct order; L is probably defective here. In Job 31:15, BHS has a superfluous *Geresh* on the first word, whereas BHK, B, and MG do not have it; I regard L to be defective here.
    In Job 5:1, BHS and BHK have double accents on the word מַעֲשֵׂי־יָדָיו, *Rebia* with *Munach*; whereas B and MG have only *Munach*. Either one would be correct, but not both--*Rebia* for defective *Rebia Mugrash*, or *Munach* for *Virtual Rebia Mugrash*. The preceding *Tarcha* favors the *Munach*, which I accept as correct here. L must have been recording two traditions.
    In Psa 53:2 (cf. 14:1), BHS and BHK have two *Rebia Mugrashim* contrary to law; whereas B has *Tarcha* for the first, MG has *Mereka*, and 14:1 has *Great Rebia*. Either *Tarcha* or *Great Rebia* would be acceptable; I regard *Tarcha* as correct here.

frequent in BHK, B, and MG. I found no apparent reason
for   the irregularity,   and assume that L is   seriously
defective in this instance.   I   also interpret these as
Rebia Mugrash.

Virtual Rebia Mugrash

According to Wickes,[19] for musical reasons *Rebia
Mugrash* cannot stand on the first word before *Silluq* if
the word bearing *Silluq* is short.[20]   *Rebia Mugrash* may
stand   if   at least two syllables precede   the   *Silluq*;
and if only two, the first must have a full vowel.   If
the   word is short, *Rebia Mugrash* must transform   into
the appropriate conjunctive that serves *Silluq*.[21]   The
transformed   accent   functions   musically   as   a
conjunctive,   but syntactically as a disjunctive--that

----

[19]Wickes, I, 69.

[20]Rmug stands on the first word before *Silluq* 685 times   in
Psalms, 237 times in Job, and 181 times in Proverbs. I have not
checked every instance, but I suspect that the transformation
occurs at times even when the word is long (see Psa 18:14;   27:10;
119:175; Job 6:4;   30:18; Prov 29:4).   In fact, it is right to
assume that *Dechi* has transformed whenever it fails to follow
Great Rebia (its remote companion), *Legarmeh* or *Pazer* (its own
subordinate segments), or whenever *Rebia Mugrash* has more than one
conjunctive,   regardless of whether logic or syntax call for a
division,   or whether the word bearing *Rebia Mugrash* is long or
short.   It is the law of the accent grammar that a near
subordinate   accent must be present if the domain of the
disjunctive that governs it is not empty.

[21]*Rebia Mugrash* is transformed into *Mereka* immediately after
Athnach (the only exceptions being in Job 12:19 and Prov 18:10).
It is transformed into *Munach* when V-RMug has its own conjunctive
or is immediately preceded by *Dechi* (real or virtual): Psa 104:1;
112:2; 115:3, 8; 119:16; 135:18.   It is transformed into *Illuy*
when RMug has a conjunctive after *Dechi* (Psa 4:7; 109:6;   Prov
8:13),   or after *Virtual Dechi* with a preceding *Great Rebia* (Psa
68:20), or after the beginning of the verse in short titles (eight
times), and in two other cases (Psa 3:3 and 125:3).

is,   the   transformed accent continues to   govern   its
segment   as though it were still *Rebia   Mugrash*.   The
conjunctive accents that serve it remain in place,   and
any   subordinate   segments function as though   it   were
still   there.   I   refer to this transformed   RMug   as
"*Virtual   Rebia   Mugrash*"   (V-RMug),   and   the   segment
governed   by V-RMug as a *Virtual Rebia Mugrash*   segment
(V-RMUG).   A   V-RMUG segment usually is empty,   but
occasionally has a near subordinate *Dechi* segment,   and
on   one   occasion has a remote subordinate *Great   Rebia*
segment   (Psa 68:20).   Table 52   provides a   numerical
summary   of   the   conjunctives to which   *Rebia   Mugrash*
transforms.

TABLE 52
Numerical Summary of the Conjunctives
to which *Rebia Mugrash* Transforms

	Psalms	Job	Prov	Total
Mereka	137	38	20	195
Munach	525	276	238	1039
Illuy	14	0	1	15
Total	676	314	259	1249

The   syntactic structure of V-RMUG is the same   as
RMUG   except   that GShal does not substitute,   LEG does
not occur in   the structure,   and the conjunctives that
serve V-RMug differ.   V-RMUG is often empty, consisting
of V-RMug only;   it may be fractional, consisting of V-
RMug   +   DECH   (#1)   or V-DECH (#2);   or it may be   full,
consisting   of V-RMug + V-DECH + GREB (#3).   Table   53
provides   a numerical summary of the structures   of   V-
RMUG.   In Hebrew order, the rule is

$$\text{(Rule 2c)} \qquad \text{V-RMUG} = \begin{cases} \text{V-RMug} \\ \text{V-RMug + DECH} \\ \text{V-RMug + DECH + GREB} \end{cases}$$

(#1)

(Fractional V-RMUG: V-RMug + DECH)   (Psa 4:7)

(#2)

(Fractional V-RMUG: V-RMug + V-DECH)   (Psa 3:5)

(#3)

(Full V-RMUG: V-RMug + V-DECH + GREB)   (Psa 68:20)

TABLE 53
Numerical Summary of the Structures of the
Virtual Rebia Mugrash Segment

	Psalms	Job	Prov	Total
V-RMug alone	608	300	255	1163
V-RMug + DECH	8	0	1	9[22]
V-RMug + V-DECH	57	14	3	74[23]
V-RMug + V-DECH + GREB	1	0	0	1[24]
Total	674	314	259	1247

Virtual Rebia Mugrash may be served by one conjunctive, but the conjunctives that serve it differ from those that serve real RMug. Usually V-RMug is served by *Tarcha*, but by *Azla* after real *Dechi*, by *Sinnorit-Mahpak* after *Great Rebia*, and by *Illuy* after the beginning of the verse. The rule is

(Rule 2d)   V-RMug = v-rmug + [tar/azl/sin-mah/ill]

TABLE 54
Numerical Summary of the Conjunctives
Serving *Virtual Rebia Mugrash*

	Psalms	Job	Prov	Total
None	163	46	26	235
Tarcha	498	268	232	998
Illuy	9	0	0	9[23]
Azla	3	0	1	4[26]
Sinnorit-Mahpak	1	0	0	1[27]
Total	674	314	259	1247

----

[23]Psa 4:7; 104:1; 109:16; 112:2; 115:3, 8; 119:16; 135:18; Prov 8:13.

[23]Psa 3:5;   4:8; 9:11; 18:2; 24:6, 10; 25:8, 15; 28:8; 30:1; 32:5; 33:21; 39:12; 41:12; 42:2; 45:3; 47:5; 48:9; 51:21; 52:7; 54:5, 8; 55:10; 56:1, 3; 59:6; 61:5; 62:13; 65:9; 66:15; 67:2; 68:11, 25, 30; 69:2; 71:15; 73:15; 74:10; 75:4; 76:4; 78:25; 79:12; 81:8; 83:9; 84:9; 89:5, 46, 49; 94:13; 106:34; 119:84; 125:3; 127:2; 143:2 145:15, 18; 148:5; Job 8:9;   11:7;   12:6; 14:3, 13; 20:4; 21:9; 22:12; 27:8; 32:1, 4; 36:2; 38:5, 36; Prov 3:27; 26:1, 25.

[24]Psa 68:20;   note that the accents of this verse have several peculiarities.

where v-rmug is one of the conjunctives that   normally
serve *Silluq*. Table 54 privides a numerical summary of
the conjunctives serving *Virtual Rebia Mugrash*.

Great Shalsheleth

The name *Shalsheleth* means "triplet"   or   "chain."
Like its counterpart in the prose books,   the accent
mark consists of a vertical,   three-stepped zigzag line
placed above the first consonant of the stressed
syllable, together with a vertical stroke like a *Paseq*
immediately following the word.   In the poetic books,
Great Shalsheleth is a musical substitute for *Rebia
Mugrash*.   Substitution takes place under the following
conditions:

(1) The RMUG segment is empty, or at the most with
a *Virtual Dechi* (#1).[25]

(2) *Silluq* has a *Virtual Legarmeh* intervening with
Tarcha serving it.[26]

(3)   *Athnach* immediately precedes GShal and the
conjunctives serving it.

----

[25]Psa 3:3 (after *Little Shalsheleth*); 36:1; 44:1; 47:1; 49:1;
61:1;   69:1;   81:1; 85:1; all but the first instance are short
titles, where v-rmug = *Illuy*.

[26]Psa 4:7; 109:16: 125:3 (before *Dechi*); Prov 8:13.

[27]Psa 68:20.

[28]See Job 32:6; 37:12.

[29]Wickes (I, 67) stated that for musical reasons *Rebia
Mugrash* cannot precede *Tarcha*, thus substitution must occur.
There are a few exceptions: Psa 46:8, 12; 66:3 (note that BHS and
BHK have defective Rmug in 46:8, 12, consisting of *Geresh* only).
In Prov 14:13, BHS alone has a defective accent, consisting of
Geresh with *Tarcha* instead of *Rebia*; this gives the appearance of
Rmug before *Tarcha*.

Table 55 provides a numerical summary of the structures of the *Great Shalsheleth* segment.

(#1)

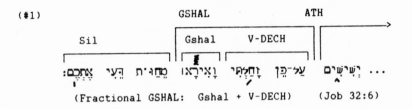

(Fractional GSHAL: Gshal + V-DECH)   (Job 32:6)

TABLE 55
Numerical Summary of the Structures
of the *Great Shalsheleth* Segment

	Psalms	Job	Prov	Total
Gshal alone	23	4	2	29[10]
Gshal + V-Dech	0	2	0	2[11]
Total	23	6	2	31

Although seldom used, *Great Shalsheleth* has the same conjunctive serving it (*Mereka*) as serves *Rebia Mugrash* for which it substitutes. The evidence is found in Psa 89:2; Job 32:6; 37:12. Table 56 provides a numerical summary of the conjunctives used with GShal. In Hebrew order, the rule is:

(Rule 3)   Gshal = gshal + [mer]

----

[10] Psa 7:6;   10:2;   12:8; 13:2, 3; 20:8; 29:11;   33:12;   41:8; 44:9; 49:14; 50:6; 52:5; 66:7; 67:5; 77:4;   89:2, 3; 94:17; 131:1; 143:6, 11; 146:3; Job 5:19; 15:23; 16:9; 40:23; Prov 6:10; 24:33.

[11] Job 32:6; 37:12;   V-DECH is empty in both.

TABLE 56
Numerical Summary of the Conjunctives
Serving *Great Shalsheleth*

	Psalms	Job	Prov	Total
None	22	4	2	28
Mereka	1	2	0	3
Total	23	6	2	31

Athnach

The name *Athnach* means "rest." The accent mark,
like the *Athnach* used in the prose books, consists of
two strokes joined at the top to form an inverted "V"
($_\wedge$). It is placed below the first letter of the
stressed syllable and to the left of any vowel there.
Athnach, like *Silluq* and *Ole-WeYored*, evokes the pausal
form of a word.[32] It usually governs the first
principal segment of a verse, the remote subordinate
segment in the domain of *Silluq*. An *Athnach* segment is
never repeated, never occurs without its companion RMUG
segment, is seldom omitted (see under *Silluq*), and has
no substitute segment. The domain of *Athnach* is like
that of *Rebia Mugrash*, except that it does not become
virtual.

$$(Rule\ 4a) \qquad ATH = \left\{ \begin{array}{l} Ath + [LEG] \\ Ath + [LEG] + DECH \\ Ath \qquad\quad + DECH + (GREB) \end{array} \right\}$$

----

[32]Cf. Psa 1:1; some instances of *Athnach* do not have the
expected pausal form (Psa 9:7).

where "ATH" represents the domain of the *Athnach* segment, "Ath" represents the word-unit bearing the accent *Athnach*, "DECH" represents the domain of a *Dechi* near subordinate segment, "GREB" represents the domain of a *Great Rebia* remote subordinate segment,[33] "LEG" represents an optional *Legarmeh* segment, and the parentheses indicate repetition. ATH is often empty, having only one word-unit, Ath (#1 disregarding LEG); it may be fractional, having Ath + DECH only (#2, #3); or it may be full, having Ath + DECH + GREB (#4). A DECH segment must intervene between Ath and GREB (if any). GREB may repeat (#5), and an optional LEG may precede Ath on rare occasions (#1 ,#2). If ATH is not empty (neglecting a rare LEG before Ath), then DECH is mandatory, but it may be only a *Virtual Dechi* segment.[34] According to Wickes, *Athnach* may not appear on the first word of a verse; however, this rare phenomenon does occur in Psa 102:28.[35] Table 57 provides a numerical summary of the structures of the *Athnach* segment.

---

[33] In Psa 40:11 on the word לְבִּי, BHS lacks *Great Rebia*, whereas BHK, B, and MG correctly have *Great Rebia*; L is probably defective here. I regard *Great Rebia* to be there for the sake of statistics.

[34] See the discussion in the section on *Virtual Dechi*. Wickes denied that DECH is mandatory (I, 58), but I found no instance where the rule failed, at least as V-DECH. The problem is that he did not admit division with only two words in a clause (I, 38) and his musical context for transforming to *Virtual Dechi* was too restrictive. See the discussion under *Rebia Mugrash*.

[35] This is true in BHS, BHK, and B; but to Wickes' credit, MG does not have *Athnach*.

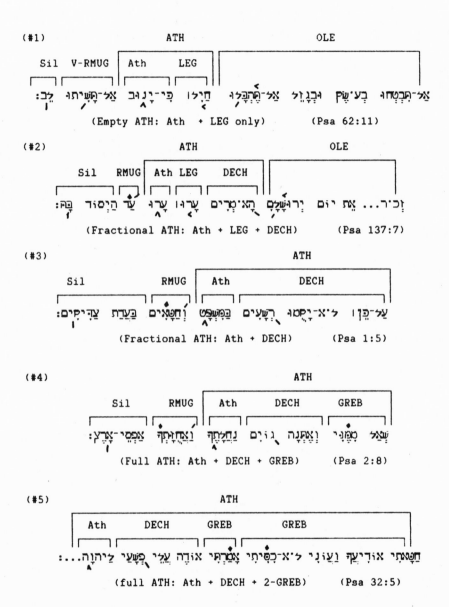

(#1)

(Empty ATH: Ath + LEG only)   (Psa 62:11)

(#2)

(Fractional ATH: Ath + LEG + DECH)   (Psa 137:7)

(#3)

(Fractional ATH: Ath + DECH)   (Psa 1:5)

(#4)

(Full ATH: Ath + DECH + GREB)   (Psa 2:8)

(#5)

(full ATH: Ath + DECH + 2-GREB)   (Psa 32:5)

Athnach may have only one conjunctive serving it:
either *Munach* or *Mereka*.   The conjunctive is   nearly

TABLE 57
Numerical Summary of the Structures
of the *Athnach* Segment

	Psalms	Job	Prov	Total
Ath alone	381	128	99	608
Ath + LEG	1	0	1	2[36]
Ath + LEG + DECH	1	0	2	3[37]
Ath + DECH	1165	544	604	2313
Ath + V-DECH	465	220	126	811
Ath + DECH + GREB	159	46	44	249
Ath + V-DECH + GREB	148	36	26	210
Ath + DECH + 2-GREB	6	1	1	8[38]
Ath + V-DECH + 2-GREB	9	2	1	12[39]
Total	2335	977	904	4216

always *Munach* immediately after *Dechi*, or *Virtual Dechi*,[40] and nearly always *Mereka* after any other

----

[36] Psa 62:11; Prov 16:10. Wickes would correct the text to remove *Legarmeh* in these cases (I, 60).

[37] Psa 137:7; Prov 8:30, 34; these may be *Mahpak* with *Paseq*, where the *Paseq* marks the redundant text, but *Mahpak* does not serve *Athnach*.

[38] Psa 32:5; 78:4; 89:20; 97:5; 102:25; 140:6; Job 7:4; Prov 27:10.

[39] Psa 17:1; 41:7; 46:5; 50:21; 59:6; 71:3; 95:10; 105:11; 133:2; Job 24:24; 33:23; Prov 4:4. Wickes (I, 59) regarded the second *Rebia* to be a substitute for *Dechi*. But *Virtual Dechi* is present in every case, and *Rebia* never substitutes for *Dechi* anywhere else.

[40] So about 1947 times after *Dechi*, and 651 times after *Virtual Dechi* in BHS. According to Wickes (I, 61) *Munach* becomes *Mereka* in this context when *Paseq* follows; this is true in Psa

preceding disjunctive or the beginning of the verse.[41]
Table 58 provides a numerical summary of the
conjunctivs that serve *Athnach*. In Hebrew order the
rule is:

(Rule 4b)   Ath = ath + [mun/mer]

- - - - - - - - - - - - - - - - - -

77:8, 116:1, Job 27:9, 35:13, and Prov 15:25; but it fails in Psa
35:1 and 74:18. In the following places BHS has *Mereka*
immediately after *Dechi*:   Psa 1:1; 3:7; 7:5; 10:11; 15:2; 73:15;
74:16; 84:6; 89:12; 90:17; 106:32; Job 5:12; 15:16; 33:33; Prov
2:14; 11:24; 25:11; 28:16--in every case MG has *Munach* and B
mostly so. In Psa 118:25, *Sinnorit-Mereka* replaces *Munach* in this
context. Wickes also noted that whenever *Paseq* follows V-Dech,
the accent bearing V-Dech is *Mereka* and the conjunctive serving V-
Dech is *Tarcha*; this is true in every instance but one: Psa
10:13; 18:50; 44:24; 57:10; 59:2; 66:8; 67:4, 6; 78:65; 89:9,
50, 52; 94:3; 108:4; 113:4; 119:156; 139:19, 21; Job 27:13; 40:9;
Prov 6:9; 8:21; the exception is Job 33:31 (but cf. B and MG).

   [41]So about 718 times in BHS. In BHS and BHK, *Munach*
intervenes between Ath and a preceding disjunctive (other than
Dechi) in Psa 14:5; 18:16; 93:4; 104:7; and Prov 31:6. In all
cases but the last, either MG or B, or both have *Mereka*. In Prov
31:6, B and MG have *Dechi* rather than *Munach*. In Job 22:21, BHS
and BHK have *Munach* intervening between Ath and the beginning of
the verse; however, L is defective here, having no accent on
שלום; cf. B and MG.
   In Prov 3:12, *Athnach* has five conjunctives serving it--more
than can be explained on the basis of Ath + V-Dech + V-Leg +
Conjunction. B and MG have only four by using *Maqqeph* with one
word; the first *Mahpak* may be understood to replace *Maqqeph* on a
monosyllabic particle.
   In Psa 5:5, 65:2, and 72:3, *Sinnorit-Mereka* replaces *Mereka*
in this context. In Prov 6:3, *Sinnorit-Mahpak* replaces *Mereka* in
this context. In Prov 3:4, BHS and BHK have *Tarcha* serving Ath
after the beginning of the verse; whereas MG has *Mereka* as
expected, and B is accentuated according to the presence of
Virtual Dechi.
   In Psa 14:3 (= 53:4) BHS and BHK have *Mahpak* serving *Athnach*
whereas B and MG have the expected *Mereka*; note the strange
double accent in MG (14:3 only) where *Dechi* and *Rebia Mugrash*
occur on the same word. In Prov 24:29 BHS and BHK have *Mahpak*
serving *Athnach*, whereas B and MG have the expected *Munach*.

TABLE 58
Numerical Summary of the Conjunctives
Serving *Athnach*

	Psalms	Job	Prov	Total
None	349	135	131	615
Munach	1476	685	646	2807
Mereka	506	157	123	786
Other	4	0	4	8[42]
Total	2335	977	904	4216

If more than one conjunctive precedes *Athnach*, a *Virtual Dechi* is present. The conjunctive adjacent to Ath bears the V-Dech and the remaining conjunctives serve the V-Dech. See the discussion of V-Dech in a subsequent section. The conjunctive bearing V-Dech before Ath is *Munach* when V-Dech has a *Munach* serving it; and it is *Mereka* under all other conditions--that is, when V-Dech has no conjunctive after another disjunctive or the beginning of the verse, or when V-Dech is served by *Tarcha* or *Mereka*.

Ole-WeYored

The name *Ole-WeYored* means "ascending and descending." The accent consists of two separate marks: a sign like *Mahpak* (<) above the word and before the stressed syllable (which sign I refer to as

----

[42]*Sinnorit-Mereka* in Psa 5:5; 65:2; 72:3; and 118:25; *Illuy* after *Little Shalshelleth* in Prov 1:9 and 6:27; *Tarcha* in Prov 3:4; and *Sinnorit-Mahpak* in Prov 6:3.

"*Ole*"),   and a sign like *Mereka* (/)   below the first
letter   of the stressed syllable and to the left of any
vowel   there (which sign I refer to as "*Yored*").   In
BHS and BHK,   if   the word   bearing this accent has the
primary   stress on its first syllable,   then the   *Ole*
(<)   appears   on the preceding word.[43]   Usually   the
preceding   word has a construct form without   *Maqqeph*[44]
and any accent of its own.   Occasionally the preceding
word   has   a conjunctive accent   of its own   marking
secondary   stress   in   place   of   *Metheg*,   usually
Galgal,[45]   but   once   *Mahpak*.[46]   Occasionally   *Ole-
WeYored*   is   written defectively in BHS,   having   the
Yored   (/),   but   lacking   the   *Ole* (<);[47]   in all
these cases   (except   Psa   86:2)   the condition is as
described   above,   but the *Ole* failed to be placed on

----

[43]Psa 1:3;   6:3;   8:3; 14:4; 18:44; 28:3; 30:8; 31:19,   21;
37:7;   40:18;   44:4;   45:8; 53:3, 5, 6; 56:9; 62:10;   88:1,   10;
97:10;   102:3;   115:1;   142:7; 144:2;   Job 3:4,   6;   7:11;   21:33;
32:2; 33:9; 34:10; 37:6;   42:3;   Prov 1:22; 6:26; 8:13, 34; 24:12;
25:7; 30:16, 19.   In Psa 53:3 (cf. 14:2) and 142:7   the phenomenon
occurs even when the stress is not on the first syllable.

[44]Wickes (I,   54)   suggested that *Maqqeph* is not necessary in
this case, that is, the *Ole* replaces *Maqqeph*.

[45]Psa 8:3;   14:4; 18:44; 28:3; 37:7; 44:4; 53:6; 56:9; 142:7;
Job 3:6;   32:2; Prov 8:34; 24:12; 30:16.   In Prov 8:34,   BHS has a
superfluous *Metheg* on the same word with *Yored* and *Galgal*.

[46]Psa 53:5;   but B and MG have *Galgal* as expected (cf. 14:4).

[47]Psa 30:12;   42:3;   55:20;   68:20;   78:21;   86:2;   118:27;
125:2;   Job 8:6;   29:25;   34:20;   Prov 24:24;   30:15.   Yeivin
(*Tiberian   Masorah*,   266)   explained that this   occurs   when   the
preceding   word   is   stressed on the ultima or   is   marked with
Rebia.   This   is   true for all the above instances except   Psa
118:27.   In   nearly all these instances,   B   and MG have the
expected   *Ole*.   In Psa 130:7   and Prov 30:14,   BHS has an *Ole*
without *Yored*;   whereas BHK,   B,   and MG have both (MG has *Yored*
without *Ole* in Psa 130:7).

the preceding word;   yet the accent   must be   *Ole-*
WeYored and   not   *Mereka* because   of   a   preceding
Sinnor which always anticipates an *Ole-WeYored.*

Ole-WeYored, like *Silluq* and *Athnach,* evokes the
pausal form of the word bearing it.   It governs the
first principal segment of a verse (the   remote
subordinate segment in the domain of *Silluq*)   if   the
division is distant from the end of the verse,   or   if
the verse has more than one principal division.   An
Ole-WeYored segment is never repeated, never occurs
without its companion *Rebia   Mugrash* segment,   and
has no substitute segment.   The   domain   of   *Ole-*
WeYored is like that of *Rebia Mugrash* and *Athnach*
except that it   has   a *Sinnor* segment or a *Little Rebia*
segment as its near subordinate segment.   In Hebrew
order, the rule is

$$\text{(Rule 5a)} \qquad \text{OLE} = \left\{ \begin{array}{l} \text{Ole + SIN/LREB} \\ \text{Ole + SIN/LREB + (GREB)} \end{array} \right\}$$

where   "OLE" represents the domain of the   *Ole-WeYored*
segment,   "Ole" represents the word-unit bearing the
accent *Ole-WeYoreb;*   "SIN" represents the domain of a
Sinnor near subordinate segment;   "LREB" represents the
domain of a *Little Rebia* segment, the substitute for
SIN;[**] and "GREB" represents a *Great Rebia* remote
subordinate segment.   OLE is never empty, but always
has at least Ole + SIN or LREB (#1, #2);   and it may be

[**]According to Wickes (I, 55)   LREB is used when Ole has no
conjunctive serving it, and SIN is used when it does.   This is
true except for five minor instances (see the actual evidence that
follows).

full, having Ole + SIN (or LREB)   +   GREB (#4, #5).   A
SIN (or LREB) segment must intervene between Ole and
GREB (if any).

       GREB may repeat, but not SIN or LREB.   According
to Wickes,[49] for musical reasons, in the poetic books a
Little Rebia may not follow *Great Rebia* without at
least two words intervening.   If this is not the case,
then *Sinnor* replaces the *Great Rebia* (#3). Likewise a
Great Rebia may not follow another *Great Rebia* without
at least two words intervening.   If this is not the
case, then *Sinnor* replaces the second *Great Rebia* (#6).
I   refer   to this   substitute as   GREB-B.   Such
substitution produces the apparent sequence of LREB +
SIN (= GREB-B) (#7),   or SIN + SIN (= GREB-B) (#6).
However, this restriction is true only in the domain
of *Ole-WeYored*,   and not in the domain of *Athnach* or
Rebia Mugrash.   Table 59 provides a numerical summary
of the structures of the *Ole-WeYored* segment.

(#1)   OLE

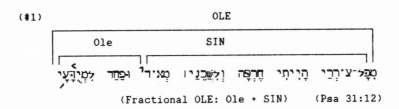

(Fractional OLE: Ole + SIN)   (Psa 31:12)

(#2)   OLE

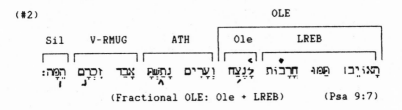

(Fractional OLE: Ole + LREB)   (Psa 9:7)

- - - - - - - - - - - - - - - - - - - -

[49]Wickes I, 56.

(#3)   OLE

| Ole | LREB | GREB-B (= SIN) |

בְּרִישׁ֫וּעָתֶ֗ךָ   בְּלִבִּ֗י   יָגֵ֫ל   בְטַחְתִּי֮   בְּחַסְדְּךָ   וַאֲנִי ׀

(Full OLE: Ole + LREB + GREB-B)   (Psa 13:6)

TABLE 59
Numerical Summary of the Structures
of the *Ole-WeYored* Segment

	Psa	Job	Prov	Total
Ole only	0	0	0	0
Ole + SIN	164	18	10	192
Ole + LREB	129	21	15	165
Ole + LREB + GREB-B	18	1	3	22[50]
Ole + SIN + GREB	35	0	1	36
Ole + LREB + GREB	4	0	0	4[51]
Ole+SIN+GREB-B+GREB	1	0	0	1[52]
Ole+LREB+GREB-B+GREB	1	0	0	1[53]
Total	352	40	29	421

----

[50]Psa 13:6;   15:1;   22:15; 27:9; 28:7; 32:4;   35:10;   39:13;
40:6, 15; 51:6; 55:20; 56:14; 59:17; 69:7; 79:13; 132:12; 144:13;
Job 30:1; Prov 23:35; 30:9, 19.   In all instances less than two
words intervene between *Sinnor* (= GREB-B) and *Little Rebia*
except Psa 28:7   where two short words   (three   syllables)
intervene.

[51]Psa 20:7;   52:9;   127:5; 139:14;   in all these instances
at least two words intervene between *Great Rebia* and *Little
Rebia*.   Psa 133:2   may be a violation of the rule if a
defective *Ole-WeYored* is understood in the verse, but this is
unlikely.

[52]Psa 17:14;   only one word intervenes between *Great Rebia*

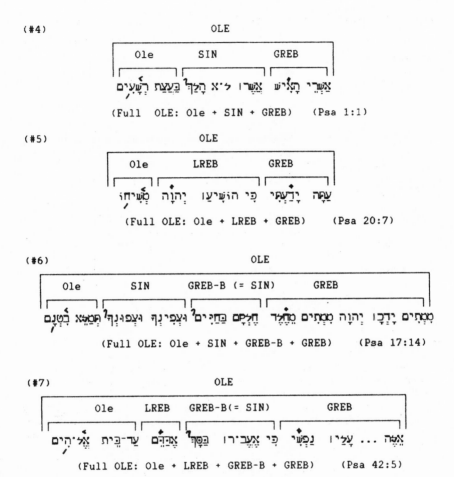

(#4)   OLE

Ole	SIN	GREB

אַשְׁרֵי הָאִישׁ אֲשֶׁר׀ לֹ־א הָלַךְ בַּעֲצַת רְשָׁעִים

(Full OLE: Ole + SIN + GREB)   (Psa 1:1)

(#5)   OLE

Ole	LREB	GREB

עַתָּה יָדַעְתִּי כִּי הוֹשִׁיעַ׀ יְהוָה מְשִׁיחוֹ

(Full OLE: Ole + LREB + GREB)   (Psa 20:7)

(#6)   OLE

Ole	SIN	GREB-B (= SIN)	GREB

מְמְתִים יָדְךָ׀ יְהוָה מְמְתִים מֵחֶלֶד חֶלְקָם בַּחַיִּים וּצְפִינְךָ תְּמַלֵּא בִטְנָם

(Full OLE: Ole + SIN + GREB-B + GREB)   (Psa 17:14)

(#7)   OLE

Ole	LREB	GREB-B (= SIN)	GREB

אֵלֶּה ... עָלַי׀ נַפְשִׁי כִּי אֶעֱבֹר׀ בַּסָּךְ אֶדַּדֵּם עַד־בֵּית אֱלֹהִים

(Full OLE: Ole + LREB + GREB-B + GREB)   (Psa 42:5)

The conjunctives that may serve *Ole-WeYored* are determined by the conjunctives that occur between it and *Sinnor* or *Little Rebia*, because it never occurs

- - - - - - - - - - - - - - - - - -

and *Sinnor* (= GREB-B).

''Psa 42:5; no words intervene between *Sinnor* (= GREB-B) and *Little Rebia*.

without   one   or   the other preceding   it.   Table   60
provides   a   numerical summary of   the   sequences   that
occur:

TABLE 60
Numerical Summary of the Conjunctives
Serving *Ole-WeYored*

	Psa	Job	Prov	Total
Ole + Sin	21	3	5	29[54]
Ole + gal + Sin	164	13	5	182
Ole + mah + Sin	14	1	1	16[55]
Ole + Lreb	149	23	17	189
Ole + mer + Lreb	4	0	1	5[56]
Total	352	40	29	421

----

[54]Psa 55:22;   80:15;   104:29; 106:47;   140:4;   Job 24:13.
The following verses have a word intervening between Ole and Sin
which has no accent of its own: Psa 31:21; 45:8; Prov 1:22;   and
8:13.   In the following verses, the word bearing   *Ole-WeYored*
also   has   *Galgal* marking secondary stress   in place of *Metheg*:
Psa 5:11   and 29:9.   In the following verses,   a   word
intervenes between Sin and Ole,   but the word bearing *Ole-WeYored*
is stressed on the first syllable, so the *Ole* marks the principal
stress of the intervening word which also has a *Galgal* marking its
secondary stress in place of *Metheg*:   Psa 8:3;   14:4   (=53:5
except that *Mahpak* marks the secondary stress); 18:44; 28:3; 37:7;
44:4;   53:6; 56:9; 142:7; Job 3:6; 32:2; Prov 8:34;   24:12.   In
the following verses,   BHS and BHK have an intervening negative
attached by *Maqqeph* with no accent of its own, but in B and MG
the negative is a separate intervening word with *Galgal*:   Psa 35:8
and 78:38.

[55]Psa 6:3;   12:3;   16:11;   24:8, 10;   31:10;   32:9;   49:15;
68:20,   21,   22; 78:5;   100:3; 137:7; Job 7:11; Prov 30:15;   in
each case the principal stress is on the first syllable of the
word.

[56]Psa 15:5;   35:10; 42:5; 74:9; Prov 30:9;   in each case the

The evidence indicates that *Ole-WeYored* may be
served by only one conjunctive, by either *Galgal* or
Mahpak[57] after *Sinnor*. Wickes[58] suggested that *Mahpak*
is used when *Paseq* intervenes, but I found no instances
of this in BHS. Instead, *Mahpak* is used when the
principal stress is on the first syllable, and Galgal
otherwise.[59] In Hebrew order, the rule is

(Rule 5b)   Ole = ole + [gal/mah]

----

word bearing *Mereka* is a monosyllabic particle that could (and
probably should) be joined by *Maqqeph* to the word bearing Ole.
BHS often uses *Mereka* to accent such words when *Maqqeph* is
lacking.   These are the only instances where a conjunctive
accent follows *Little Rebia*.

[57] In   Psa 68:20   *Ole-WeYored* appears to have a preceding
Mahpak-Legarmeh.   However,   this should be understood as a
regular *Mahpak*.   The *Paseq* that follows is not for marking
Legarmeh, but for calling attention to the redundancy of the
text.

[58] Wickes I, 57.

[59] The only exceptions are in Psa 51:19; 68:14;   and Prov
23:31.

CHAPTER 14
The Poetic Accents In Hierarchy III

The disjunctive accents in Hierarchy III govern
the immediately subordinate segments in the domain of
those in Hierarchy II. Thus they mark divisions of
secondary significance. They are *Dechi, Sinnor* (and
its alternate *Little Rebia*), and *Great Rebia*. They all
have essentially the same syntactic structure as far as
their subordinate segments are concerned.

Dechi

The first accent mark, *Dechi*, consists of a single
diagonal stroke with its top inclined to the left
similar to the English back-slash (\) and like the
Tiphcha used in the prose books; in some printed
editions it has a slight downward curvature. It is
prepositive, being placed below the line and to the
right of the first letter of the word bearing it. Thus
it does not mark the stressed syllable of the word, so
the stress must be determined by the conventional rules
of Hebrew phonology. Many manuscripts repeat the sign
on the stressed syllable if the stress is not on the
first syllable and the location of the stress may not
be certain.[1] If the word-unit bearing it consists of a

string of two or more words joined by *Maqqeph*, then
Dechi is placed before the first letter of the last
word in the string.

When the word is stressed on the first syllable
and the vowel of the stressed syllable is not below the
line, then *Dechi* may be confused as *Tarcha*, the
conjunctive accent of similar shape. Actually, *Dechi*
should precede the first letter, whereas *Tarcha* should
be under the first letter. But the printed editions do
not always make this distinction. In this case, the
identity must be determined by the syntax rules of the
accents.[2]

A *Dechi* segment, like a *Tiphcha* segment in the
prose books, serves as the near subordinate segment in
the domain of *Athnach*; and it also serves the same role
in the domain of *Rebia Mugrash*. Its companion remote
segment (if any) is *Great Rebia*. A *Dechi* segment never
is repeated. In Hebrew order the domain of *Dechi* is

----

[1]Something similar occurs several times in BHS and BHK; in
Psa 86:7, 118:5, and 139:7 the stressed syllable is marked with
Mereka; in Job 19:26 the stress is marked by *Metheg*. In Psa
7:10, 89:29, and Job 11:13, BHS has *Rebia* marking the stressed
syllable, whereas BHK, B, and MG have only *Dechi*.

[2]*Dechi* occurs where a syntactic division is required, and
Tarcha where a syntactic connection is required. The following
are places where *Dechi* may be confused as *Tarcha* (but should be
Dechi): Psa 5:4; 22:3; 24:2; 25:3; 29:11; 33:3; 41:10; 42:8;
44:27; 45:16; 46:7; 68:36; 77:18; 78:17; 94:9, 13; 97:10, 11;
105:2; 109:12, 19; 110:3; 112:4; Job 3:3; 8:16; 13:1; 18:6; 19:26;
20:23; 22:14; 23:6; 28:24; 30:18, 22, 30; 31:26, 28; 34:3, 19,
22; 37:20, 21; 39:11, 12; 40:19, 20, 29; Prov 7:13; 10:25; 11:4,
27; 13:11, 15; 18:10; 20:19; 22:21, 22; 24:2.

The following are places where *Tarcha* may be confused as
Dechi (but should be *Tarcha*): Psa 73:1; 148:5; Job 22:12. In Psa
73:15, on the word דּוֹר (a construct) BHS and BHK erroneously have
Dechi; whereas B and MG correctly have *Tarcha* here.

(Rule 6a)   DECH = $\left\{ \begin{array}{l} \text{Dech} \\ \text{Dech + (LEG)} \\ \text{Dech + (LEG) + PAZ} \end{array} \right\}$

where "Dech" represents the word-unit bearing the
accent *Dechi* or *Virtual Dechi*, "LEG" represents the
domain of the near subordinate *Legarmeh* segment, and
"PAZ" represents the domain of the remote subordinate
Pazer segment. DECH is very often empty, having only
one word-unit (Dech);[3] it is frequently fractional,
having only Dech + LEG (#1); and it is occasionally
full, having Dech + LEG + PAZ (#2). A LEG segment
should intervene between Dech and PAZ (if any), but it
fails in some instances (#4) and repeats rarely (#1);
and LEG may be only virtual (#3).[4] PAZ never repeats.
Dech may be only virtual (see next section). The
current discussion includes only those segments with
real *Dechi*. Table 61 provides a numerical summary of
the context in which *Dechi* is used, and Table 62
summarizes the structures of the *Dechi* segment.

- - - - - - - - - - - - - - - - - -

[3] *Dechi* appears as the first disjunctive in a verse 480 times
in Psalms, 311 times in Job, and 217 times in Proverbs.

[4] According to Wickes (I, 83), *Legarmeh* cannot stand on the
first word before *Dechi*. In such cases it is transformed into the
conjunctive accent that would normally serve *Dechi*. I refer to
such a transformed *Legarmeh* as *Virtual Legarmeh* (V-LEG).

TABLE 61
Numerical Summary of the Context
in Which *Dechi* Is Used

Segment:	Psa	Job	Prov	Total
RMUG	73	23	5	101
V-RMUG	8	0	1	9
ATH	1331	592	651	2574
Total	1412	615	657	2684

(#1)

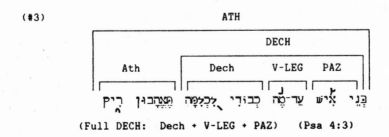

ATH

(Fractional DECH: Dech + 2-LEG)   (Psa 27:1)

(#2)

ATH

(Full DECH: Dech + LEG + PAZ)   (Psa 98:1)

(#3)

ATH

(Full DECH: Dech + V-LEG + PAZ)   (Psa 4:3)

(#4)   ATH

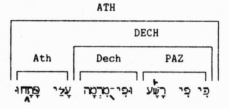

(Defective DECH: Dech + PAZ--Missing LEG) (Psa 109:2)

TABLE 62
Numerical Summary of the Structures
of the *Dechi* Segment

	Psa	Job	Prov	Total
Dech only	1304	586	629	2519
Dech + LEG	47	1	7	55
Dech + V-LEG	47	25	20	92
Dech + 2-LEG	1	0	0	1[5]
Dech + V-LEG + LEG	2	1	0	3[6]
Dech + LEG + PAZ	1	0	0	1[7]
Dech + V-LEG + PAZ	7	2	1	10[8]
Dech + PAZ	3	0	0	3[9]
Total	1412	615	657	2684

----

[5] Psa 27:1, a title.

[6] Psa 23:6; 56:1; Job 24:15; cf. Psa 56:10 in B and MG--BHS has two V-Legs.

[7] Psa 98:1.

[8] Psa 4:3; 5:12; 28:5; 44:3; 45:8; 68:5; 109:16; Job 3:5; 32:1; Prov 27:22.

[9] Psa 109:2; 122:4; 137:3.

Dechi is used to mark a secondary stress on rare occasions where Metheg would be expected.[10] The phenomenon occurs at times by attraction when a disjunctive accent governs an empty segment; the conjunctive accent that would naturally serve the given accent is drawn into the word-unit to replace Metheg. Here a disjunctive accent is drawn into the same function by analogy; Dechi is drawn into a word-unit governed by Virtual Rebia Mugrash to replace Metheg, because Dechi naturally precedes this accent.

Dechi may have only one conjunctive serving it, and that must be Munach.[11] Whenever Dechi has more than one conjunctive serving it, those preceding Munach are due to the presence of Virtual Legarmeh.[12] When Legarmeh becomes virtual before Dechi it transforms into Munach. Table 63 provides a numerical summary of the conjunctives that may serve Dechi. In Hebrew order

----

[10]Psa 25:4; 109:26; Job 10:6; 30:16. Actually the Dechi cannot replace Metheg, because Dechi is prepositive and does not mark the syllable receiving secondary stress. Nevertheless, in these verses Dechi stands on the same word bearing Virtual Rebia Mugrash.

[11]Dechi appears to be served by Mereka in Psa 78:21; 125:2; Job 8:6; and 29:25; but these are instances of defective Ole-WeYored where the Ole is lacking.

[12]This is verified by the fact that the conjunctives that precede Munach are either Illuy, Mahpak, or Sinnorit-Mahpak--the conjunctives that normally serve Legarmeh. Wickes (I, 86) suggested that LEG sometimes transforms into the second conjunctive before Dechi; but Dechi is served by only one conjunctive, therefore a Rank II conjunctive before Dechi must, of necessity, belong to Virtual Legarmeh. In Psa 31:2, Dechi is served by Tarcha and Munach in BHS and BHK; but Tarcha does not serve Legarmeh. However, B and MG have Maqqeph joining the two words with no Tarcha. At times BHS employs Mereka in places where Maqqeph is lacking.

the rule is

(Rule 6b)   Dech = dech + [mun]

TABLE 63
Numerical Summary of the Conjunctives
Serving *Dechi*

	Psa	Job	Prov	Total
None	679	358	261	1298
Munach	733	257	395	1385
Other	0	0	1	1[13]
Total	1412	615	657	2684

Virtual Dechi

According to Wickes[14]   *Dechi* may not stand on the
first word before *Rebia Mugrash* or *Athnach* when the
word bearing either of these accents is short.   *Dechi*
may stand when two or more syllables intervene, and, if
only two, the first syllable has a full vowel.   If the
word is short, then the *Dechi* is transformed into the
conjunctive accent that normally would serve the *Rebia
Mugrash* or *Athnach*.   However, the content of the DECH
segment governed by such a transformed *Dechi* remains
intact,   including the conjunctive that may have been
serving the *Dechi* before it was transformed.   I refer
to such a transformed *Dechi* as *Virtual Dechi* (v-dech)

----

[13] In Prov 10:10 the word קִרֵץ has two accents, the expected
Munach and an extra *Mereka*, placing *Mereka* before *Dechi* contrary
to expectation.   In Psa 86:7, 118:5, and 139:7 *Mereka* appears in
the same word with *Dechi*.

[14] Wickes, I, 60, 75.

and to the segment governed by v-dech as a *Virtual Dechi* segment (V-DECH). Musically v-dech functions as a conjunctive in cantillation, but syntactically it functions as a disjunctive governing a near subordinate segment. Usually V-DECH is empty, but occasionally it is found with a fractional or full domain. The syntax of the domain of *Virtual Dechi* is the same as that of real *Dechi* given above. Table 64 provides a numerical summary of the use of *Virtual Dechi*, and Table 65 summarizes the structures of *Virtual Dechi*.

TABLE 64
Numerical Summary of the Use of
Virtual Dechi

Segment:	Psa	Job	Prov	Total
RMUG	75	14	13	102
V-RMUG	58	14	3	75
GSHAL	0	2	0	2
ATH	622	257	153	1032
Total	755	287	169	1211

Before *Rebia Mugrash*, *Virtual Dechi* is transformed into *Mereka* nearly always.[15] Before *Virtual Rebia Mugrash* it is transformed into *Tarcha* nearly always;[16]

----

[15]About 153 times, but into *Illuy* (Psa 137:9) after *Little Shalsheleth* according to the rules of LShal; into *Sinnorit-Mereka* (Psa 31:22 and 66:20) probably for special meaning; and into *Sinnorit-Mahpak* (Psa 31:16; 34:8; 68:15; 79:3; 116:19; 135:21; and Prov 7:7).

[16]But also into *Illuy* (Psa 3:3; 68:20); into *Azla* (Psa 89:20; 125:3); and into *Sinnorit-Mahpak* (Psa 68:20).

TABLE 65
Numerical Summary of the Structures
of the *Virtual Dechi* Segment

	Psa	Job	Prov	Total
V-Dech only	652	246	141	1039
V-Dech + LEG	26	12	3	41
V-Dech + V-LEG	70	27	23	120
V-Dech + V-LEG + LEG	0	1	1	2[17]
V-Dech + V-LEG + PAZ	2	1	0	3[18]
V-Dech + PAZ	5	0	1	6[19]
Total	755	287	169	1211

and before *Athnach* it is transformed into *Munach* nearly
always.[10]

The conjunctives that may serve *Virtual Dechi* are
varied. In an ATH segment, the conjunctive is *Munach*
when v-dech is *Munach*; it is *Tarcha* when v-dech is
Mereka followed by *Paseq*; and it is *Mereka* or
Sinnorit-Mereka when v-dech is otherwise *Mereka*.[11] In
a RMUG segment, the conjunctive is *Mereka* after *Athnach*
or *Pazer*;[22] and it is *Tarcha* otherwise.[23] In a V-RMUG

- - - - - - - - - - - - - - - - - -

[17]Job 12:3; Prov 1:9. In Job 12:3 the *Azla* should be *Azla-Legarmeh*, producing a double *Legarmeh*; however, B and MG have
Great Rebia instead of *Azla*.

[18]Psa 19:15; 125:3; Job 11:6.

[19]Psa 18:2; 25:1; 30:1; 58:3; 146:1; Prov 1:10.

[20]But also into *Mereka* immediately after *Great Rebia*.

[21]It is *Mereka* in Psa 39:2; 109:8; Job 9:22; it is
Sinnorit-Mereka in Psa 2:7; otherwise it is *Mahpak* in Psa 5:5;
and it is *Little Shalsheleth* in Psa 65:2; 72:3; and Prov 1:9.

segment, the conjunctive is *Illuy* when the stress is on
the second syllable after an open syllable with a full
vowel (not vocal *Shewa*);[24]   it is *Mahpak* when the
stress is on the first syllable;[25]   it is *Sinnorit-
Mahpak* when the stress is on the third syllable
following an open syllable with a full vowel;[26] and it
is *Azla* otherwise (i.e., after a closed syllable or an
open syllable with vocal *Shewa*).[27]   This is
significantly different from real *Dechi* which admits
only *Munach*.   Table 66 provides a numerical summary of
the conjunctives that serve *Virtual Dechi*.   In Hebrew
order, the rule is

(Rule 6c)   Dech = v-dech + [mun/mer/ill/tar/mah/azl/sin-mah]

----

[24]Exceptions are found in Psa 23:5;   27:12;   42:11;   52:11;
53:2; and 74:3 where *Tarcha* appears after *Athnach*.

[25]Exceptions are found in Psa 18:1 (*Sinnorit-Mereka*);   Psa
34:8;   68:15; 137:9 (all *Little Shalsheleth*).

[26]Psa 4:8; 76:4; 78:25; 119:84.

[27]Job 8:9;   11:7;   14:13; 21:9; 27:8; 32:1, 4; 36:2; 38:5, 36;
Prov 26:1, 25. Note exceptions in Psa 12:6; 20:4; and 22:12.

[28]Psa 28:8; 48:9; 68:25; 74:10; 79:12; Job 14:3;   but note an
exception in Psa 32:5 where *Illuy* is expected.

[29]Psa 3:5;   24:6;   42:2; 47:5; 52:7; 54:5; 55:10; 56:1, 3;
59:6;   61:5; 62:13; 75:4; 81:8; 84:9; 89:46, 49; Prov 3:27; but
note an exception in Psa 89:5 where *Sinnorit-Mahpak* is expected.
Four times it is *Mereka* where strange or double accents occur (Psa
66:15; 67:2; 68:11; 83:9);   and once it is *Little Shalsheleth* (Psa
3:3).

TABLE 66
Numerical Summary of the Conjunctives
Serving *Virtual Dechi*

In ATH Segment:

	Psa	Job	Prov	Total
Munach	494	231	129	854
Tarcha	19	3	2	23
Mereka	2	1	0	3[28]
Other	4	0	1	5[29]

In RMUG Segment:

Mereka	22	6	6	34
Tarcha	36	7	3	46
Other	4	0	0	4[30]

In V-RMUG Segment:

Mereka	4	0	0	4[31]
Illuy	4	0	0	4[32]
Mahpak	22	13	3	38
Sinnorit-Mahpak	6	1	0	7[33]
Azla	18	0	1	19
Other	2	0	0	2[34]

---

[28]Psa 39:2; 108:8; Job 9:22.

[29]*Sinnorit-Mereka* in Psa 2:7;   *Mahpak* in Psa 5:5 (replaces *Maqqeph*); *Little Shalsheleth* in Psa 65:2; 72:3; and Prov 1:9.

[30]*Sinnorit-Mereka* in Psa 18:1;   *Little Shalsheleth* in Psa 34:8;   68:15; and 137:9.

[31]Psa 66:15 (note that BHS has *Mereka* and *Metheg* transposed);

Sinnor

The name *Sinnor* means a "canal" or "water-channel." The accent mark, like the *Zarqa* used in the prose books, consists of a vertical stroke with its top bent sharply toward the left to form the appearance of a walking cane. In some printed editions it has the appearance of a backwards English "S" reclining on its back (`~`). The accent is postpositive, being placed above the last letter of a word regardless of which syllable is stressed. Thus the stress must be determined by the ordinary rules of Hebrew phonology. In some manuscripts, the mark is repeated above the stressed syllable when the location of the stress might be uncertain. The shape of the mark is the same as that for the conjunctive *Sinnorit* which is distinguished from this one by its position above the beginning or middle of the word.

A *Sinnor* segment is the near subordinate segment in the domain of *Ole-WeYored* and is subject to replacement by its lawful substitute *Little Rebia*. Its companion remote segment is *Great Rebia*. The syntax of the *Sinnor* segment is similar to that of a *Dechi* segment except that it does not transform *Legarmeh* into *Virtual Legarmeh*. In Hebrew order, the syntax of the segment is

----

67:2; 68:11; 83:9 (note that the last three have *Mahpak-Metheg* as well).

¹¹Psa 4:8; 76:4; 78:25; 119:84.

¹²Psa 28:8; 32:5; 48:9; 68:25; 74:10; 79:12; Job 14:3.

¹⁴*Little Shalsheleth* in Psa 3:3; *Tarcha* in Psa 125:3.

$$
\text{(Rule 7a)} \qquad SIN = \begin{cases} Sin \\ Sin + (LEG) \\ Sin + (LEG) + PAZ \end{cases}
$$

where "Sin" represents the word-unit bearing the accent *Sinnor*, "LEG" represents the domain of the near subordinate segment *Legarmeh*, and "PAZ" represents the domain of the remote subordinate segment *Pazer*. SIN is often empty, having only one word-unit (Sin); it may be fractional, having only Sin + LEG (#3); or it may be full, having Zaq + LEG + PAZ (#1). A LEG segment usually intervenes between Sin and PAZ (#1), but is lacking occasionally (#2).[35] LEG repeats at times (#3, #4). Table 67 provides a numerical summary of the structures of the *Sinnor* segment.

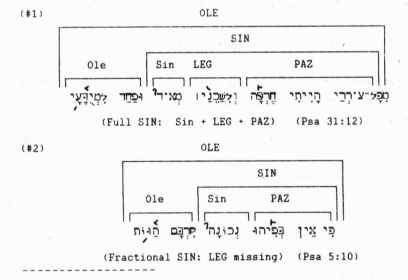

(#1)   OLE

(Full SIN: Sin + LEG + PAZ)   (Psa 31:12)

(#2)   OLE

(Fractional SIN: LEG missing)   (Psa 5:10)

----

[35] In five places *Legarmeh* is lacking between *Pazer* and *Sinnor* with no intervening conjunctive that may be regarded as v-leg (Psa 5:10; 31:11; 56:14; 126:2; 132:11).

(#3)

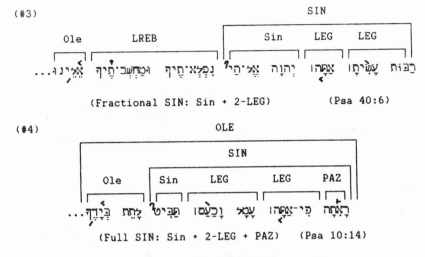

(Fractional SIN: Sin + 2-LEG)   (Psa 40:6)

(#4)

(Full SIN: Sin + 2-LEG + PAZ)   (Psa 10:14)

TABLE 67
Numerical Summary of the Structures
of the *Sinnor* Segment

	Psa	Job	Prov	Total
Sin only	118	10	8	136
Sin + LEG	88	7	6	101
Sin + 2-LEG	2	0	0	2[36]
Sin + LEG + PAZ	5	1	0	6[37]
Sin + PAZ	5	0	0	5[38]
Sin + 2-LEG + PAZ	1	0	0	1[39]
Total	219	18	14	251

----

[36] Psa 40:6; 55:20.

[37] Psa 31:12; 32:6; 39:13; 75:9; 84:4; Job 7:20.

[38] Psa 5:10; 31:11; 56:14; 126:2; 132:11.

[39] Psa 10:14.

Sinnor may have only one conjunctive serving it, and it must always be *Munach* or *Mereka*.[40] In a few places *Sinnor* has two conjunctives,[41] but the second one is understood to replace an expected *Maqqeph*. These are not regarded as instances of *Virtual Legarmeh*. In fact, *Virtual Legarmeh* does not occur in a *Sinnor* segment. In Hebrew order, the rule is

(Rule 7b)   Sin = sin + [mun/mer]

According to Wickes[42] the conjunctive is *Mereka* when the stress is on the first syllable of the word, or when the first letter of the stressed syllable has a *Daggesh*;   and it is *Munach* otherwise. This is true with the following exceptions: (1) it is *Mereka* when the stress is on the second syllable and the first syllable has vocal *Shewa*;[43]   (2) it is *Munach* rather that *Mereka* when a monosyllabic particle precedes the word even though not joined by *Maqqeph*;[44]   (3) in a few

----

[40] In Psa 79:6, BHS and BHK have an *Azla* serving *Sinnor*, whereas B and MG have *Azla-Legarmeh* as expected.   L is probably defective here.   In Psa 31:20, BHS and BHK have a *Mahpak* serving *Sinnor* contrary to expectation, whereas B has *Mereka* and MG has *Munach*.

[41] Psa 14:7 (= 53:7); 24:10; 60:2; 79:6; Job 31:7; 32:2.

[42] Wickes, I, 81-82.

[43] So in Psa 14:4 (= 53:5); 31:21; 32:9; 42:10; 48:3;   57:5; 77:3;   79:13; 99:4;   101:7; 128:3; 144:11.   In addition, *Mereka* replaces *Munach* in Psa 17:4; but this is an instance where *Sinnor* replaces *Great Rebia*, and the *Mereka* serves the displaced *Great Rebia* as though it were still there (see discussion under *Great Rebia*).

[44] Psa 24:10; 60:20.

instances *Munach* occurs under a letter with *Daggesh*.[43]

Also, Wickes stated that *Munach* becomes *Mahpak* when *Paseq* follows. But this is not confirmed in BHS, because the only instances of *Paseq* before *Sinnor* (Psa 68:21 and Prov 1:22) have *Munach* serving *Sinnor*. Table 68 provides a numerical summary of the conjunctives that serve *Sinnor*.

TABLE 68
Numerical Summary of the Conjunctives
Serving *Sinnor*

	Psa	Job	Prov	Total
Sin + mun	59	8	4	71
Sin + mer	46	1	4	51
Exceptions	2	0	0	2[44]
Total	107	9	8	124

Little Rebia

The name *Little Rebia* means "little quarter or resting." The accent mark consists of a prominent diamond-shaped dot placed above the first letter of the stressed syllable of the word (like the *Rebia* used in the prose books). The same mark is used with *Rebia Mugrash* and for *Great Rebia*. However, *Little Rebia* is distinguished from *Great Rebia* by its unique syntactic position and conjunctive that serves it: *Little Rebia*

----

[43]Psa 14:7 (= 53:7); 59:1; 116:16; Job 7:21; 31:7.

[44]In Psa 31:20 *Mahpak* serves *Sinnor*, but it likely replaces *Maqqeph*. In Psa 79:6 *Azla* serves *Sinnor*, but B and MG have *Azla-Legarmeh* as expected.

appears immediately before *Ole-WeYored*, governing its near subordinate segment, and having *Mereka* as the conjunctive that serves it; whereas *Great Rebia* governs remote subordinate segments in the domain of *Rebia Mugrash*, *Athnach*, and *Ole-WeYored*,[47] and it has its own set of conjunctives that serve it (which does not normally include *Mereka*).

A *Little Rebia* segment is the alternative for a *Sinnor* segment, the near subordinate segment in the domain of *Ole-WeYored*. A *Little Rebia* segment substitutes for a *Sinnor* segment when the *Ole-WeYored* that governs it has no conjunctive serving it.[48] The syntax of the *Little Rebia* segment is the same as that of the *Sinnor* segment except that *Little Rebia* never actually governs a remote subordinate *Pazer* segment, and the conjunctives serving *Little Rebia* are not exactly the same as those serving *Sinnor*. In Hebrew order the syntax of the segment is

(Rule 8a)   LREB = LReb + [LEG]

where "LReb" represents the word-unit bearing the accent *Little Rebia*, and LEG represents an optional near subordinate *Legarmeh* segment. LREB is usually empty, consisting only of the word-unit bearing the accent *Little Rebia*. Occasionally LREB is fractional,

----

[47]Wickes (I, 77, n. 1) regarded *Little Rebia* and *Great Rebia* to be the same except for their relative disjunctive force. Thus he discussed their dichotomy and conjunctives in the same chapter. But many of the exceptions to his rules of conjunctives are due to the uniqueness of *Little Rebia* in this area.

[48]In five instances (Psa 15:5; 35:10; 42:5; 79:4; Prov 30:9) *Mereka* intervenes between *Little Rebia* and *Ole-WeYored*, but these all are places where *Mereka* replaces an expected *Maqqeph*.

consisting of LReb + LEG (#1), but it is never full.
Table 69 provides a numerical summary of the structures
of the LREB segment.

(#1)   OLE

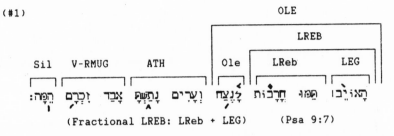

(Fractional LREB: LReb + LEG)   (Psa 9:7)

TABLE 69
Numerical Summary of the Structure
of the *Little Rebia* Segment

	Psa	Job	Prov	Total
LReb only	131	19	14	164
LReb + LEG	22	4	4	30
Total	153	23	18	194

Little Rebia may have only one conjunctive serving
it and that must be *Mereka* (unlike the conjunctives
that serve *Great Rebia*). In a few instances a second
conjunctive (*Mahpak*) is found, but in every case the
Mahpak marks a monosyllabic particle that could (and
probably should) be joined to the following word by
Maqqeph.[44] These are not regarded as instances of
Virtual Legarmeh. In fact, *Virtual Legarmeh* does not
occur in a LREB segment. Table 70 provides a numerical

----

[44]Psa 1:2;   20:7;   28:7; 35:20; 52:9; 55:13; 84:11; 90:17;
115:1; 116:8; 127:5; 135:6; 139:14; Job 14:7; 38:41; Prov 6:26;
23:5; 25:7.

summary of the conjunctives serving *Little Rebia*.   In
Hebrew order the rule is

(Rule 8b)   LReb = lreb + [mer]

TABLE 70
Numerical Summary of Conjunctives
Serving *Little Rebia*

	Psa	Job	Prov	Total
lreb + mer	93	17	14	124
Exceptions	1	1	0	2[30]
Total	94	18	14	126

Great Rebia

The name *Great Rebia* means "large quarter or
resting."   The accent mark consists of a prominent
diamond-shaped dot placed above the first consonant of
the stressed syllable of the word (like the *Rebia* used
in the prose books).   The same mark is used with *Rebia
Mugrash* and for *Little Rebia*.   *Great Rebia* is
distinguished from *Little Rebia* by its unique syntactic
position and the conjunctives that serve it: *Great*

----

[30] In Job 32:6, *Little Rebia* is served by *Tarcha* and *Mereka*,
providing a possible instance of *Virtual Legarmeh*. But this verse
is part of a prose section in Job, and this phrase embraces a long
proper name.   In BHS and BHK, Psa 1:2 has three conjunctives
serving *Little Rebia* (*Mahpak*, *Tarcha*, and *Mereka*).   The
monosyllabic particles אִם כִּי, which usually function as an
adversative conjunctive and are followed by *Maqqeph*, are marked
here by both *Mahpak* and *Tarcha*.   Here *Tarcha* stands in place of
the expected *Maqqeph*.   Note that B and MG have marked the word
כִּי with *Mahpak-Legarmeh*, suggesting that the two words function
separately, not as an adversative but as introducing an
explanatory conditional: "For if he delights . . ., he will be
like a tree . . ."

Rebia governs the remote subordinate segments in the domain of *Rebia Mugrash*, *Athnach*, and *Ole-WeYored*, and it has its own set of conjunctives that serve it; whereas *Little Rebia* governs the near subordinate segment of *Ole-WeYored* only, as a substitute for a *Sinnor* segment, and it is served only by *Mereka*, a conjunctive that rarely serves *Great Rebia*.

The companion near subordinate segment of *Great Rebia* is a *Dechi* segment in the domain of *Rebia Mugrash* and *Athnach*; and it is a *Sinnor* or *Little Rebia* segment in the domain of *Ole-WeYored*. *Great Rebia* never occurs without its companion near segment *Dechi* or *Sinnor* (or its substitute *Little Rebia*). It is repeated occasionally (see under *Athnach* and *Ole-WeYored*), and has no substitute. In Hebrew order the domain of *Great Rebia* is

$$(Rule\ 9a) \qquad GREB = \left\{ \begin{array}{l} GReb \\ GReb + (LEG) \\ GReb + [LEG] + (PAZ) \end{array} \right.$$

where "GREB" represents the domain of the *Great Rebia* segment, "GReb" represents the word-unit bearing the accent *Great Rebia*, "LEG" represents the near subordinate segment *Legarmeh* or *Virtual-Legarmeh*, and "PAZ" represents a *Pazer* segment. GREB is often empty, consisting only of GReb. It may be fractional, consisting of GReb + LEG (#1) or V-LEG (#3). It may be full, consisting of GReb + LEG + PAZ (#2). On rare occasions LEG may repeat (#1), and PAZ may repeat (#4). At times LEG is lacking. Table 71 provides a numerical summary of the structures of the GREB segment.

TABLE 71
Numerical Summary of the Structures
of the *Great Rebia* Segment

	Psa	Job	Prov	Total
GReb only	172	43	50	265
GReb + LEG	186	49	18	253
GReb + 2-LEG	4	0	0	4[51]
GReb + V-LEG + LEG	1	0	0	1[52]
GReb + LEG + PAZ	9	0	2	11[53]
GReb + V-LEG + PAZ	22	3	2	27[54]
GReb + LEG + 2-PAZ	0	0	1	1[55]
GReb + PAZ	12	1	3	16[56]
Total	406	96	76	578

(#1)   GREB

(Fractional GREB: GReb + 2-LEG)   (Psa 42:5)

----

[51] Psa 42:5, 9; 68:7; 144:1.

[52] Psa 55:24 (cf. B and MG).

[53] Psa 2:12;   4:2; 28:1; 68:31; 79:1; 90:10; 104:35;   106:48;
141:4; Prov 22:29; 23:29.

[54] Psa 11:2;   17:14; 22:25; 23:4; 27:6; 32:5; 35:13;   40:13;
44:4;   45:3; 59:6;   65:10; 69:14; 79:2; 99:5, 9;   106:23,   38;
123:2; 125:3; 138:2;   148:14; Job 10:15; 16:4; 24:14;   Prov 30:8,
33.

[55] Prov 30:4.

[56] Psa 7:6;   13:3; 50:1; 59:4; 68:28; 71:3 (cf.   B);   89:20;
90:4;   92:10; 127:2; 140:6; 141:5; Job 6:4; Prov 6:3; 7:23; 27:10.

(#2)

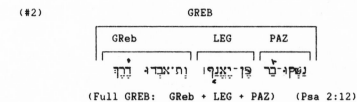

(Full GREB: GReb + LEG + PAZ)   (Psa 2:12)

(#3)

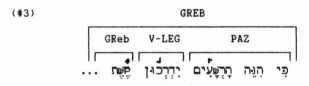

(Full GREB: GReb + V-LEG + PAZ)   (Psa 11:2)

(#4)

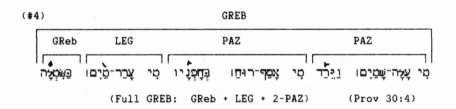

(Full GREB: GReb + LEG + 2-PAZ)   (Prov 30:4)

Great Rebia may be served by only one conjunctive,[57] either *Illuy, Mahpak,* or *Sinnorit-Mahpak.*[58] Table 72 provides a numerical summary of the

----

[57]Job 37:21 appears to have two conjunctives between *Legarmeh* and *Great Rebia,* but this is an instance of defective *Sinnorit-Mahpak* discussed in that section. In Psa 72:17 BHS and BHK have *Azla* serving *Great Rebia,* but this probably should be *Azla-Legarmeh* as in B and MG. In Job 32:11 and 34:33 *Great Rebia* has two conjunctives before it (*Mahpak* or *Illuy,* and *Azla*), but the *Azla* should be *Azla-Legarmeh* (cf. B and MG).

[58]*Mahpak, Sinnorit-Mahpak,* and *Illuy* function as musical variants depending on the phonology of the word bearing the accent. This same pattern operates with the conjunctives

conjunctives that serve *Great Rebia*.   In Hebrew   order
the rule is:

(Rule 9b)   GReb = $\left\{ \begin{array}{l} \text{greb} \\ \text{greb} + \left[\begin{array}{l} \text{ill} \\ \text{mah} \\ \text{sin-mah} \end{array} \right] \end{array} \right\}$

TABLE 72
Numerical Summary of Conjunctives
Serving *Great Rebia*

	Psa	Job	Prov	Total
None	255	67	60	382
greb + ill	52	8	5	65
greb + mah	34	5	2	41
greb + sin-mah	51	11	3	65
greb + mer	16	5	6	27
Total	408	96	76	580

According to Wickes,[59] the conjunctive usually is
Illuy when *Legarmeh* or *Pazer* precedes, but *Sinnorit-
Mahpak* if an open syllable immediately   precedes   the
stressed syllable.   This must be revised to state:

When *Legarmeh* or *Pazer* precedes:

(1) The conjunctive is *Illuy* if the stress is on
the   second syllable or later not following an
open syllable with a full vowel.[60]

----

serving *Legarmeh* and *Virtual Legarmeh*.   *Mereka* substitutes under
special conditions.

[59]Wickes, I, 79-80.

(2) The conjunctive is *Sinnorit-Mahpak* if an open
syllable (with a full vowel) immediately
precedes the stressed syllable.[60]

(3) The conjunctive is *Mahpak* if the word is
stressed on the first syllable.[62]

Also according to Wickes, the conjunctive usually
is *Mahpak* when *Legarmeh* or *Pazer* do not precede (that
is, at the beginning of the verse)[63] or when an accent
of equal or higher rank precedes[64] (that is, when GREB
is empty). This is true with few exceptions.[65]

----

[60] The only exceptions are found in Psa 60:10 (= 108:10), and
96:13, where *Mahpak* is expected. *Illuy* is used even when the
preceding syllable is joined by means of *Maqqeph* (Psa 40:13;
97:7; 148:13). In Psa 40:11, on the word לְבִּי BHS is lacking the
required *Great Rebia*; whereas BHK, B, and MG have it.

[61] Note the interesting cases where the open syllable occurs
as a short monosyllabic particle which might (and probably
should) be joined by *Maqqeph*: Psa 95:7; Job 32:5; 37:21. B and
MG have *Maqqeph* in Psa 95:7 and Job 37:21. Job 32:5 is a prose
section on which poetic accents are imposed.

[62] Psa 48:9; 54:5; 69:14; 93:4; 104:35; 108:9; 116:19; 125:3;
135:11; Job 16:4; 28:3. In Psa 41:7; 123:2 *Mahpak* appears on
the first syllable, but a word is joined with *Maqqeph* where
Illuy would be expected. In Psa 26:1, *Mahpak* appears where
Illuy would be expected, but the preceding *Legarmeh* is on the
short title; here the accentuation is as would be expected
at the beginning of the verse, that is, as though the title
were ignored. In Psa 148:14, *Mahpak* appears where *Illuy* is
expected.

[63] A few exceptions are found at Psa 9:14 (*Illuy* but
cf. B); 95:7 (*Sinnorit-Mahpak*); and 1:1, 32:2, 40:5, and Job 8:6
(all *Mereka*).

[64] Only once does *Athnach* precede *Great Rebia* (Psa 14:1), but
Great Rebia has no conjunctive serving it there. *Ole-WeYored*
appears only twice (Psa 60:2; 68:36).

[65] In Psa 9:14 BHS has *Illuy* serving *Great Rebia* after the
beginning of the verse; whereas B and MG have *Azla-Legarmeh*
instead of *Great Rebia*. In Psa 95:7 *Sinnorit-Mahpak* serves

Furthermore, Wickes stated that the conjunctive is
Mereka when another *Rebia* precedes. This is true
in four of the five instances where this happens.[66]
Several additional places exist where *Mereka* appears
to serve *Great Rebia,* but most are explained as
Mereka standing in place of *Metheg* where a *Maqqeph* is
expected but lacking.[67] A few others are explained
as *Mereka* standing in place of *Metheg* in a verb, where
the primary accent is lacking.[68] In five places
Mereka serves *Great Rebia* contrary to expectation or
explanation.[69]

In the few instances (cf. Psa 27:6) where more
than one conjunctive precedes greb, the remote
one is due to the presence of *Virtual Legarmeh.* When
only one conjunctive stands between *Pazer* and
Great Rebia, the conjunctive is a transformed
Virtual Legarmeh with no conjunctives of its own. When
such transformation occurs, *Legarmeh* is transformed
into the conjunctive that would normally serve *Great*

Great Rebia after the beginning of the verse, but note that this
is an instance of an unusual *Sinnorit-Mahpak.*

[66]Psa 17:1; 78:4; Prov 4:4; 27:10. In Job 32:5
Sinnorit-Mahpak serves *Great Rebia* after another *Great Rebia,*
but note that this occurs in a prose section with poetic accents
imposed. Wickes corrected the text in these cases.

[67]Psa 1:1; 18:16; 32:2; 40:5; 76:8; 82:5; 86:9; 88:6; 92:8;
110:4; Job 10:22; 34:19, 29; Prov 23:29; 28:10. In Psa 68:20,
Mereka appears to serve *Great Rebia,* but here the *Mereka* is part
of a defective *Ole-WeYored.*

[68]Psa 44:4; Job 14:9; 31:40.

[69]Psa 78:21 where *Sinnorit-Mahpak* is expected; Psa 108:8,
where *Illuy* is expected; and Job 8:6, Prov 22:17 (cf. B and MG),
and 28:22 where *Mahpak* is expected.

Rebia, that is, into *Mahpak,* *Sinnorit-Mahpak,* or *Illuy.* *Virtual Legarmeh* occurs only after *Pazer* or another *Legarmeh.* Table 73 provides a numerical summary of *Virtual Legarmeh* used with *Great Rebia.*

TABLE 73
Numerical Summary of *Virtual Legarmeh*
With *Great Rebia*

V-LEG transforms to:	Psa	Job	Prov	Total
Illuy	10	1	1	12[70]
Mahpak	4	1	0	5[71]
Sinnorit-Mahpak	8	1	1	10[72]
Mereka	1	0	0	1[73]
Total	23	3	2	28

----

[70]Psa 11:2;   17:14; 22:25; 27:6; 35:13; 40:13; 45:3;   55:24; 65:10;   79:2; Job 10:15; Prov 30:8.

[71]Psa 69:4; 123:2; 125:3; 148:14; Job 16:4.

[72]Psa 23:4;   32:5;   59:6;   99:5, 9; 106:23, 38;   138:2;   Job 24:14;   Prov 30:33.

[73]Psa 44:4;   note that in this strange accentuation *Mereka* replaces both *Maqqeph* and *Metheg,* and the normally stressed syllable is not marked. The rules of accentuation require an accent here to bear *Virtual Legarmeh.*

CHAPTER 15
Poetic Accents In Hierarchy IV

Hierarchy IV contains two disjunctives, *Legarmeh* and *Pazer*. *Legarmeh* governs the near subordinate segment in the domains of *Dechi*, *Sinnor*, and *Great Rebia*. Its companion remote subordinate segment in each of these domains is *Pazer*. Also included in this chapter is a discussion of *Paseq*.

Pazer

The name *Pazer* means "scattering." The accent mark, like the *Pazer* used in the prose books, consists of a vertical stroke with a horizontal arm midway on the right (⊢); in some printed editions the arm is bent upward at the elbow (Ϥ). It is placed above the first consonant of the stressed syllable of the word.

The domain of *Pazer* is limited to a near subordinate segment only. The depth of division of the verses in the poetic books is sufficiently limited so that a remote subordinate segment in the domain of *Pazer* is never required. In Hebrew order the domain is

(Rule 10a)   PAZ = Paz + [LEG]

where "Paz" represents the word-unit bearing the accent

Pazer and "LEG" represents an optional near subordinate *Legarmeh* segment.   *Pazer* is not used very frequently, only 91 times in the poetic books.   It is   used   most often in a *Great Rebia* segment, and it is used most often as the initial disjunctive of a verse.   Table 74 provides a numerical summary of the structures of the *Pazer* segment, and Table 75 a summary of the use of PAZ in the domains of the various disjunctives that   govern it.   Table 76   provides a numerical summary of the use of *Pazer* in the initial and non-initial position.

TABLE 74
Numerical Summary of the Structures
of the *Pazer* Segment

	Psa	Job	Prov	Total
Paz only	23	7	2	32
Paz + LEG-M	4	0	2	6
Paz + LEG-A	16	0	3	19
Paz + V-LEG	29	1	4	34
Total	72	8	11	91

TABLE 75
Numerical Summary of the Use of
Pazer in its Various Segments

	Psa	Job	Prov	Total
in DECH	11	2	1	14
in V-DECH	7	1	1	9
in SIN	11	1	0	12
in GREB	43	4	9	56
Total	72	8	11	91

TABLE 76
Numerical Summary of the Use of
Pazer in its Verse Position

	Psa	Job	Prov	Total
Initial	46	6	6	58
Non-initial	26	2	5	33
Total	72	8	11	91

Pazer may be served by only one conjunctive, Always *Galgal*.[1] However, *Pazer* rarely has a conjunctive serving it when it follows a disjunctive of higher rank[2] or *Mahpak-Legarmeh*. The same is usually true following *Azla-Legarmeh*.[3] In Hebrew order, the rule is

(Rule 10b)   Paz = paz + [gal]

Occasionally more than one conjunctive serves *Pazer*; However, those before *Galgal* are due to the presence of

----

[1] In Psa 4:3, 59:6, and 71:3, *Mereka* serves *Pazer* (but cf. B and MG); in Psa 89:20, *Mahpak* serves *Pazer* but I suspect that it should be *Mahpak-Legarmeh* (note also that *Mereka* replaces *Metheg* here); in Psa 32:5, *Azla* serves *Pazer*, but *Galgal* replaces *Metheg* in the same word with *Pazer*; I suspect that the accent should be *Azla-Legarmeh*, or *Virtual Legarmeh*, as the parallel clause suggests. In Psa 11:2 and 28:5 BHS and BHK have *Mahpak* serving *Pazer*, whereas B and MG have *Galgal* as expected.

[2] In Job 16:4, *Galgal* serves *Pazer* after *Ole-WeYored*; this is the only such occurrence.

[3] Three times *Pazer* is served by *Galgal* after *Azla-Legarmeh* (Psa 84:4; 127:2; Prov 27:10).

Virtual Legarmeh.   For musical reasons, *Legarmeh* cannot
stand on the first word before *Pazer.*   When *Legarmeh*
would be due there,   it is transformed into *Galgal,* the
conjunctive that normally serves *Pazer.*   Table 77
provides a numerical summary of the conjunctives that
normally serve *Pazer.*

TABLE 77
Numerical Summary of Conjunctives
Serving *Pazer*

	Psa	Job	Prov	Total
None	37	6	7	50
Galgal	31	2	4	37
Other	4	0	0	4[4]
Total	408	96	76	580

Legarmeh

The name *Legarmeh* means "break" or "to itself."
Legarmeh appears in two forms: *Azla-Legarmeh* and
Mahpak-Legarmeh.   The accent is represented by two
marks: (1) a mark like *Azla* or *Mahpak* on the stressed
syllable of the word, and (2) a vertical stroke like
Paseq immediately following the word.   It is as though
the *Paseq* transforms the conjunctive *Azla* or *Mahpak*
into a weak disjunctive.

Wickes[5] regarded the two forms to be musical

----

[4] *Mereka* in Psa 4:3, but here it replaces *Maqqeph* (cf.   B);
also in Psa 71:3 (MG has *Galgal*); *Mahpak* in Psa 11:2, 28:5, and
89:20, but B and MG have *Galgal* in all three;   *Azla* in Psa 32:5,
but *Galgal-Metheg* is present on the same word (B and MG have
Mahpak-Metheg).

[5] Wickes, I, 92-93.

variants of the same disjunctive. *Azla-Legarmeh* is used whenever the disjunctive is served by a conjunctive. When no conjunctive is present, then *Mahpak-Legarmeh* is used if the stress is on the first or second syllable, and *Azla-Legarmeh* is used if the stress is later in the word than the second syllable. Furthermore, *Mahpak-Legarmeh* is always used when called for before *Silluq*.

There are no disjunctives subordinate to *Legarmeh*. Therefore *Legarmeh* has no domain of its own; its segment is always empty. *Legarmeh* governs the near subordinate segment in the domains of *Dechi*, *Sinnor*, *Little Rebia*, and *Great Rebia*; and contrary to the usual expectation of the rules of hierarchic governance, *Legarmeh* also serves this role in the domain of *Pazer*. It also has an auxiliary function before *Silluq*, *Athnach*, and *Rebia Mugrash*.[*] The rule is

(Rule 11a) $$\text{LEG} = \left\{ \begin{array}{l} \text{Leg-M} \\ \text{Leg-A} \end{array} \right\}$$

where "Leg-M" represents *Mahpak-Legarmeh*, and "Leg-A" represents *Azla-Legarmeh*.

Mahpak-Legarmeh

Mahpak-Legarmeh is used before every disjunctive accent in the books of poetry except *Ole-WeYored* and

----

[*] *Mahpak-Legarmeh* appears to precede *Ole-WeYored* in Psa 68:20; however, this must be understood to be regular *Mahpak* followed by *Paseq*. The *Paseq* does not mark *Legarmeh*, but calls attention to the redundancy in the text. The same is true in Prov 30:15; the *Paseq* calls attention to a diminutive letter and redundancy.

Great Shalsheleth.   Table 78 provides a numerical summary of the contexts in which *Mahpak-Legarmeh* is used.

TABLE 78
Numerical Summary of the Use of
Mahpak-Legarmeh

BEFORE:	Psa	Job	Prov	Total
Dechi	26	1	2	29
V-DECH in ATH	21	7	3	31[7]
V-DECH in RMUG	1	0	0	1[8]
Sinnor	44	5	2	51
Little Rebia	14	2	4	20
Great Rebia	57	16	7	80
Pazer	4	0	2	6
Azla-Legarmeh	4	0	0	4
Silluq	21	5	3	29
Athnach	3	0	3	6[9]
Rebia Mugrash	2	0	0	2[10]
Total	197	36	26	259

----

[7] Psa 5:5; 10:13; 16:10; 18:50; 24:4; 31:15; 44:24; 51:18; 73:8, 10, 28; 85:10; 86:9; 88:14; 89:50; 94:12, 14; 96:5; 109:25; 119:128; 127:1; Job 5:6; 11:15; 13:14; 18:2; 20:20; 27:13; 31:2; Prov 1:9; 22:3; 24:20.

[8] Psa 137:9.

[9] Psa 14:5; 62:11; 137:7; Prov 8:30, 34; 16:10.

[10] Psa 71:21; 109:28.

Mahpak-Legarmeh never has a conjunctive serving it.[11] Thus the rule is

$$\text{(Rule 11b)} \qquad \text{Leg-M} = \left\{ \begin{array}{c} \text{leg-m} \\ \text{V-Leg} \end{array} \right\}$$

where "leg-m" represents the word-unit bearing the accent *Mahpak-Legarmeh* and V-Leg" represents *Virtual Legarmeh*.[12]

Azla-Legarmeh

   Azla-Legarmeh is used before most of the disjunctives of the books of poetry: *Dechi*, *Virtual Dechi*, *Sinnor*, *Little Rebia*, *Great Rebia*, *Pazer*, and *Legarmeh*. Table 79 provides a numerical summary of the use of *Azla-Legarmeh* in various contexts.

   Azla-Legarmeh may be served by only one conjunctive,[13] either *Mahpak*, *Sinnorit-Mahpak*, or *Illuy*,[14] depending on the musical (rhythmic) context.

----

   [11]In Prov 6:3, according to BHS and BHK, Leg-M has two conjunctives serving it, *Azla* followed by *Mereka*. However, B and MG have Leg-A followed by Leg-M. This verse has other peculiar cantillation.

   [12]See discussion in a later section.

   [13]On rare occasions Leg-A has an apparent second conjunctive. In Psa 117:2 and 143:3, *Mereka* precedes *Sinnorit-Mahpak* serving Leg-A; however, in these instances *Mereka* stands in place of a missing *Maqqeph*. In Prov 24:31, *Azla* precedes *Sinnorit-Mahpak* serving Leg-A; this probably should be *Azla-Legarmeh*.

   [14]BHS has nineteen instances where *Mereka* serves Leg-A. Most of these are cases where *Mereka* stands in place of a missing *Maqqeph*: Psa 111:1; 112:1; 113:1; 135:1; 147:1; 148:1; 149:1; 150:1; all of these involve הַלְלוּיָהּ where the word is divided into הַלְלוּ יָהּ in BHS and BHK, where *Mereka* replaces *Maqqeph* and *Metheg*. B and MG have only one word with *Azla-Legarmeh* and *Metheg*. In

TABLE 79
Numerical Summary of the Use of
Azla-Legarmeh

BEFORE:	Psa	Job	Prov	Total
Dechi	24	1	5	30
Sinnor	52	3	4	59
Little Rebia	8	2	0	10
Great Rebia	143	33	14	190
Pazer	16	0	4	20
Mahpak-Legarmeh	2	0	0	2
Azla-Legarmeh	2	0	0	2
V-DECH in ATH	5	4	1	10[15]
V-DECH in RMUG	0	2	0	2[16]
Total	251	45	28	324

According to Wickes,[17] the conjunctive is *Mahpak* when
the stress is on the first syllable, or on the second
syllable following a closed syllable or a vocal
Shewa.[18] It is *Sinnorit-Mahpak* when an open syllable

----

addition see Psa 19:15; 35:10; 65:10; 137:1; Job 14:5; Prov 19:7;
25:20; 27:22; 30:9. In two cases *Mereka* accents a word with
unusual vocalization: Psa 7:6; 17:14 (so noted by Wickes).

[15]Psa 37:1; 106:1; 122:5; 138:1; 150:1; Job 4:5; 12:3;
24:17; 37:12; Prov 24:15.

[16]Job 3:26; 38:2.

[17]Wickes, I, 92.

[18]This is true in every instance. However, Wickes
erroneously assigned the case following vocal *Shewa* to *Illuy*. In

(with a full vowel, not *Shewa*) precedes the stressed
syllable, even when the stress is on the third syllable
or later.[19]   It is *Illuy* when the stress is on the
third syllable or later not following an open syllable
with a full vowel.[20]   Table 80 provides a numerical
summary of the conjunctives that serve *Azla-Legarmeh*.
In Hebrew order the rule is

(Rule 11c) $\text{Leg-A} = \begin{Bmatrix} \text{leg-a} \\ \text{V-Leg} \end{Bmatrix} + \begin{Bmatrix} \text{mah} \\ \text{sin-mah} \\ \text{ill} \end{Bmatrix}$

TABLE 80
Numerical Summary of Conjunctives
Serving *Azla-Legarmeh*

	Psa	Job	Prov	Total
None	53	3	6	62
Mahpak	112	33	10	155
Sinnorit Mahpak	47	5	7	59
Illuy	26	3	0	29
Mereka	14	1	4	19
Total	252	45	27	324

----

a few instances, *Mahpak* is found where *Illuy* is expected: Psa
48:9;   55:24;   69:14;   79:13;   103:22;   149:9;   and once where
Sinnorit-Mahpak is expected: Psa 146:7.

[19]This is true in every instance.

[20]This is true in every instance.

Virtual Legarmeh

According to Wickes[21] *Legarmeh* cannot stand on the first word before *Dechi* for musical reasons.   In such cases *Legarmeh* is transformed into the conjunctive that would normally serve in that context.   I refer to such a "transformed" *Legarmeh* as *Virtual Legarmeh*.   *Legarmeh* also seems to transform in a similar fashion before *Silluq, Great Rebia,* and *Pazer.* Table 81 provides a numerical summary of the contexts in which *Virtual Legarmeh* is used.

TABLE 81
Numerical Summary of the Use of
Virtual Legarmeh

BEFORE:	Psa	Job	Prov	Total
Dechi	56	28	21	105
V-Dechi	72	29	24	125
Great Rebia	23	3	2	28
Pazer	29	1	4	34
Silluq	26	6	3	35
Total	206	67	54	327

Before *Silluq, Dechi,* or *Virtual Dechi, Virtual Legarmeh* is transformed into *Munach.*   Before *Great Rebia,* it is transformed into *Illuy, Mahpak,* or *Sinnorit-Mahpak,* depending on the musical (rhythmic) context.   Before *Pazer,* it is transformed into *Galgal.* Table 82 provides a numerical summary of the

----

[21] Wickes, I, 83.

conjunctives to which *Virtual Legarmeh* is transformed
in various contexts.

TABLE 82
Numerical Summary of the Conjunctives
to Which *Virtual Legarmeh*
Is Transformed

	Psa	Job	Prov	Total
Sil + mun	25	6	3	34
Dech + mun	56	28	21	105
Paz + gal	29	1	4	34
Greb + ill	10	1	1	12[22]
Greb + mah	4	1	0	5[23]
Greb + sin-mah	8	1	1	10[24]
Greb + mer	1	0	0	1[25]
Ath + V-Dech + mun	58	28	22	108
Rmug + V-Dech + tar	4	0	0	4[26]
V-Rmug + V-Dech +mun	3	0	0	3[27]
V-Dech + other	8	0	0	3[28]

----

[22]Psa 11:2;   17:14; 22:25; 27:6; 35:13; 40:13; 45:3;   55:24;
65:10;   79:2; Job 10:15; Prov 30:8.

[23]Psa 69:14; 123:2; 125:3; 148:14; Job 16:4.

[24]Psa 23:4;   32:5;   59:6;   99:5, 9; 106:23, 38;   138:2;   Job
24:14;   Prov 30:33.

[25]It   transforms into *Mereka* in the strange case of Psa 44:4,
where *Mereka* replaces both *Maqqeph* and *Metheg*, and bears *Virtual-
Legarmeh*.   The   word   on which it stands has no   accent   on   its
stressed syllable, as though *Maqqeph* were present.

[26]Psa 47:8; 73:4; 119:52; 129:7.

The conjunctives that may serve *Virtual Legarmeh* are the same as those that serve *Azla-Legarmeh*, and for the same reasons.[27] The exception is that when V-Leg is transformed into *Galgal* before *Pazer*, then the conjunctive serving it is *Azla*; and *Virtual Legarmeh* is served by *Tarcha* before *Silluq*. Table 83 provides a numerical summary of the conjunctives that serve *Virtual Legarmeh*.

TABLE 83
Numerical Summary of Conjunctives
Serving *Virtual Legarmeh*

	Psa	Job	Prov	Total
V-Leg + mah	103	46	42	191[30]
V-Leg + sin-mah	27	6	4	37
V-Leg + ill	20	4	3	27
V-Leg + azl	16	1	1	18[31]
V-Leg + mer	5	3	1	9[32]
V-Leg + tar	26	7	3	36
V-Leg + other	1	1	1	3[33]
Total	171	82	52	305

----

[27] Psa 42:2; 47:5; 54:5.

[28] In an ATH segment it is *Little Shalsheleth* in Psa 65:2 and Prov 1:9; and it is *Tarcha* in Psa 89:52. In a RMUG segment, it is *mereka* in Job 11:6, and *Sinnorit-Mereka* in Psa 18:1; and it is *Little Shalsheleth* in Psa 34:8 and 68:15. In a V-RMUG segment it is *Tarcha* in Psa 125:3 and *Little Shalsheleth* in Psa 3:3. Once before *Silluq* it is *Mereka* in Psa 146:3, but cf. B and MG.

[29] In Job 34:37, V-Leg has two conjunctives, *Mereka* and *Sinnorit-Mahpak*, but here the *Mereka* replaces *Maqqeph* as fixed by the Masorah (Wickes, I, 87).

Paseq

The   name   *Paseq*   means   "cutting   off"   or
"interrupter."   The accent mark consists of a vertical
stroke (|)   immediately following a word,   or,   perhaps
more   accurately,   immediately preceding the   word   to
which it refers.

Paseq is used to transform *Shalsheleth, Azla,*   and
Mahpak into   their   corresponding   disjunctive   accents
Great Shalsheleth,   Azla-Legarmeh,   and *Mahpak-Legarmeh*
respectively.   In   these   contexts   *Paseq*   loses   its
independent   function   and   becomes   a   part   of   the
disjunctive   mark   itself.   In   other   contexts   it
functions independently of the accents that precede   or
follow it.

As   an   independent mark,   *Paseq* is   an   auxiliary
accent   in   that   it   does   not   affect   the   laws   of
hierarchic   governance;   the   syntax of Hebrew   accents
completely   ignores the presence of   *Paseq*.[34]   However,
Paseq   does   affect cantillation in that it requires   a
short   pause   between   the words it separates,   without
affecting the melody.   *Paseq* has no domain;   it governs

----

[30]Sometimes the *Mahpak* may be replacing *Maqqeph.*

[31]Usually   before *Pazer,*   but twice before *Virtual Dechi* (Psa
32:5;   Job 12:3).

[32]Psa 14:7   (= 53:7);   47:5;   60:2; 90:10;   Job 11:6;   31:7;
40:10;   Prov   23:29.   Sometimes the *Mereka* may   be   replacing
Maqqeph.

[33]*Tarcha* (Psa 31:2);   and *Munach* (Job 32:2--a prose section;
Prov 3:12--five conjunctives before *Athnach*).

[34]*Paseq* does affect the choice of musical alternatives in   a
few cases.

no words with or without accents, and consequently is
not served by conjunctives.

Wickes[35] suggested that *Paseq* has three functions
in the books of poetry:

> (1) the *Paseq* of euphemism "which occurs before or
>   after the Divine Name, to prevent its being
>   joined, in reading, to a word, which --in the
>   opinion of the accentuators--it was not
>   seemly."
>
> (2) the *Paseq* of euphony which was used "to insure
>   distinct pronunciation, when one word ends,
>   and the next word begins, with the *same
>   letter*."
>
> (3) the *Paseq* of emphasis.

It is interesting to note that *Paseq* always stands
immediately before a disjunctive accent except where it
separates two *Illuys*. Table 84 provides a numerical
summary of the use of *Paseq*.

----

[35]Wickes, I, 96-98.

TABLE 84
Numerical Summary of the Use of
Paseq

BEFORE:	Psa	Job	Prov	Total
Silluq	10	0	0	10[36]
Rebia Mugrash	4	2	0	6[37]
Athnach	23	4	3	30[38]
Ole-WeYored	2	0	1	3[39]
Great Rebia	1	0	0	1[40]
Little Rebia	1	0	0	1[41]
Sinnor	1	0	1	2[42]
Pazer	2	0	0	2[43]
Illuy	7	0	0	7[44]
Total	51	6	5	62

----

[36] Psa 5:7;   10:3;   40:16;   41:14; 58:7;   61:9;   66:18;   70:4;
72:19; 89:53.

[37] Psa 5:2; 86:8; 119:52; 143:9; Job 38:1; 40:6.

[38] Psa 5:5;   10:13;   18:50; 35:21; 44:24; 57:10;   59:2;   66:8;
67:4,   6;   74:18; 77:8; 78:65; 89:9, 50, 52; 94:3;   108:4;   113:4;
116:1;   119:156; 139:19, 21; Job 27:9, 13; 35:13; 40:9;   Prov 6:9;
8:21; 15:25.

[39] Psa 68:20; 85:9; Prov 30:15.

[40] Psa 92:10.

[41] Psa 20:7.

[42] Psa 68:21; Prov 1:22.

[43] Psa 59:6; 141:4.

[44] Psa 36:1;   47:1; 49:1; 61:1; 81:1; 85:1 (all titles);   also
55:24.

CHAPTER 16

The Poetic Conjunctive Accents

There are ten conjunctive accents, some of which serve a number of different disjunctives, and some of which are dedicated to the service of only a few. Unlike the disjunctives used in the prose books, the disjunctives used in the poetic books may have only one conjunctive serving them. Several of the conjunctives function as musical alternatives for one another.

Munach

The name *Munach* means "sustained." Like the *Munach* used in the prose books, the accent mark consists of a vertical and a horizontal stroke joined to form a right angle with the corner at the lower right like a reversed English "L" (⎤); it is placed below the first letter of the stressed syllable of the word and immediately to the left of any vowel there.

Munach is used more often than any other accent in the books of poetry. It may serve *Silluq*, *Athnach*, *Sinnor*, *Dechi*, *Virtual Dechi*, or *Legarmeh*:

(1)   It serves *Silluq* when the stress is on the first syllable, or when it represents *Virtual*

Legarmeh (that is, following *Tarcha*);   when
the stress in not on the first syllable the
musical alternate conjunctive is *Mereka*, but
it is always *Illuy* after *Legarmeh*.

(2) It serves *Athnach* following *Dechi*;   the
alternative is *Mereka*.

(3) It serves *Dechi* exclusively with no
alternative.

(4) In an *Athnach* segment, it serves *Virtual Dechi*
almost exclusively, with *Tarcha* or *Mereka*
substituting in rare occasions.

(5) It serves *Sinnor* when the stress is not on the
first syllable of the word, and when the first
letter of the stressed syllable does not have
a *Daggesh*;   in the other conditions, the
musical alternate is *Mereka*.

(6) Twice it serves *Virtual Legarmeh*: Job 32:2 (a
prose section), and Prov 3:12 (an unusually
long string of five conjunctives).

(7) It replaces *Metheg* in a few instances where it
could have served as a conjunctive if one were
needed.[1]

Table 85   provides a numerical summary of the use of
Munach.

Mereka

The name *Mereka* means "prolonged." Like the
Mereka used in the prose books, the accent mark
consists of a diagonal stroke with its top inclined to
the right like an English slash (/);   in some printed

----

[1]Psa 10:11;   18:16;   22:27; 60:3; 71:23; 104:7; Job 22:4;
27:7; 28:22; 39:26; Prov 7:13; 10:10; 14:31; 25:7.

TABLE 85
Numerical Summary of the Use of
Munach

SERVING:	Psa	Job	Prov	Total
Silluq	899	467	426	1792
Athnach	1476	685	646	2807
Dechi	733	257	395	1385
Virtual Dechi	494	231	129	854
Sinnor	59	8	4	71
Virtual Legarmeh	0	1	1	2
Total	3661	1649	1601	6911

editions it has a slight downward curvature. It is placed below the first letter of the stressed syllable of the word and immediately to the left of any vowel there.

Mereka serves most of the disjunctives: *Silluq*, *Rebia Mugrash*, *Great Shalsheleth*, *Athnach*, *Sinnor*, *Little Rebia*, *Great Rebia*, and *Virtual Dechi*. It appears to serve the others, but these cases are best explained by other reasons.[2] For further details see the discussions under the individual accents.

> (1) It serves *Silluq* when the stress is not on the first syllable, or when *Paseq* follows; when the stress is otherwise, the musical alternate is *Munach* with rare exceptions.

----

[1] It appears to serve *Dechi* in Psa 78:21; 125:2; Job 8:6; and 29:25; but these are instances of defective *Ole-WeYored* where the *Ole* is lacking. In Prov 10:10 it also appears serve *Dechi*, but the word bearing it has two accents, the expected *Munach* and the unusual *Mereka*.

(2) It serves *Rebia Mugrash* with no alternative.

(3) It serves *Great Shalsheleth* on rare occasions with no alternative.

(4) It serves *Athnach* as an alternative to *Munach* when not following *Dechi*.

(5) It serves *Virtual Dechi* in an ATH segment when v-dech is *Mereka*; and in a RMUG segment, it serves *Virtual Dechi* after *Athnach* or *Pazer*.

(6) It serves *Sinnor* when the stress is on the first syllable, or when the letter under which it rests has a *Daggesh*, or when the stress is on the second syllable and the first syllable is open with vocal *Shewa*; when the stress is otherwise, the musical alternate is *Munach*.

(7) It serves *Little Rebia* with no alternative.

(8) It serves *Great Rebia* after another *Rebia* in those few places where this occurs.[3]

(9) In still other places it replaces *Maqqeph* before the conjunctive serving *Legarmeh* or *Virtual Legarmeh*: Psa 55:20; 96:4; 117:2; 143:3; Job 34:27. In these places the law of conjunctives may be apparently violated in that more than one conjunctive may be found standing before a disjunctive; but the law views this use of *Mereka* as the equivalent of

---

[3] (Psa 17:1; 78:4; Prov 4:4; 27:10); an exception occurs in Job 32:5, a prose verse. In Psa 78:21 it serves where *Sinnorit-Mahpak* is expected; in Psa 108:8 where *Illuy* is expected; and in Job 8:6, Prov 22:17 and 28:22 where *Mahpak* is expected. It appears to serve *Great Rebia* in Psa 1:1; 18:16; 32:2; 40:5; 76:8; 82:5; 86:9; 88:6; 92:8; 110:4; Job 10:22; 34:19, 29; Prov 23:29; 28:10; but these are explained as *Mereka* replacing *Maqqeph*. It also appears to serve *Great Rebia* in Psa 68:20, but here the *Mereka* is part of a defective *Ole-WeYored*.

the *Maqqeph* for which it stands.

(10)   At times in BHS *Mereka* may be confused   with   a
        defective   *Ole-WeYored,*   where   the   *Ole*   is
        missing   and only the *Yored* (which looks   like
        Mereka) is present.[4]

(11) It replaces   *Metheg*   in a few instances where   it
     could   otherwise   serve as a conjunctive   if   one
     were needed.[5]

Table   86   provides a numerical summary of the use   of
Mereka, and Table 87 summarizes the places where *Mereka*
replaces *Maqqeph.*

Illuy

The name *Illuy* means "above."   The accent mark is
like   a   *Munach* but it is placed   above   the   stressed
syllable rather than below.   It has no   correspondence
in the prose books.   It may serve *Silluq,   Great Rebia,*
Azla-Legarmeh, and *Virtual Legarmeh:*[6]

(1) It serves   *Silluq* after   *Mahpak-Legarmeh;*   it
    bears   *Virtual Rebia Mugrash* when Rmug   has   a
    conjunctive   after   *Dechi,*   or   after   *Virtual*
    Dechi with a preceding *Great Rebia,*   or after
    the beginning of the verse in short titles.

(2) It serves   *Great Rebia* after *Pazer* or *Legarmeh*
    if   a closed syllable or an open syllable with

----

[4]Psa 30:12;   42:3;   55:20;   68:20;   78:21;   86:2;   118:27;
125:2;   Job 8:6; 29:25; 34:20; Prov 24:24; 30:15;   see discussion
under *Ole-WeYored* for further details.

[5]Psa 39:13;   40:13; 44:13; 89:20; 137:6;   Job 21:2;   35:14;
36:21;   37:19; 38:11; Prov 26:7.

[6]For further   details see the discussion under the individual
accents.

TABLE 86
Numerical Summary of the Use of
Mereka

SERVING:	Psa	Job	Prov	Total
Silluq	900	310	303	1513
Rebia Mugrash	675	245	252	1172
Great Shalsheleth	1	2	0	3
Athnach	506	157	123	786
Virtual Dechi	28	7	6	41
Sinnor	46	1	4	51
Little Rebia	94	18	14	126
Replace Maqqeph	40	9	12	61
Other	7	0	3	10[7]
Total	2297	749	717	3863

TABLE 87
Numerical Summary of Places Where *Mereka*
Replaces *Maqqeph*

BEFORE:	Psa	Job	Prov	Total
Ole-WeYored	4	0	1	5[8]
Great Rebia	16	5	6	27
Pazer	2	0	0	2[9]
Azla Legarmeh	10	1	4	15[10]
Virtual Legarmeh	4	2	0	6[11]
(V)-Leg + Conj.	4	1	1	6[12]
Total	40	9	12	61

Shewa precedes the stressed syllable.   It has
Mahpak   or   *Sinnorit-Mahpak*   as   musical
alternatives.

(3) It serves *Azla-Legarmeh* when the stress is on
the second or later syllable and not preceded
by an open syllable.   It has *Mahpak* or
Sinnorit-Mahpak as musical alternatives.

(4) It serves *Virtual Legarmeh* under the same
conditions as it serves *Azla-Legarmeh*.

(5) It replaces *Metheg* in a few instances where it
could otherwise serve as a conjunctive if one
were needed.[13]

Table   88   provides a numerical summary of the use of
Illuy.

----

[7] In Prov 6:3   *Mereka* erroneously appears before *Mahpak-
Legarmeh* (cf. B and MG). It serves *Azla-Legarmeh* in Psa 7:6 and
17:14 (where the words have unusual vocalization); also in 19:15;
65:10.   In Psa 90:10 and Prov 23:29 it serves *Virtual Legarmeh*.
In Psa 86:7, 118:5, 139:7, and Prov 10:10, it erroneously serves
Dechi.

[8] Psa 15:5; 35:10; 42:5; 74:9; Prov 30:9.

[9] Psa 4:3; 59:6; 71:3.

[10] Psa 111:1; 112:1;   113:1;   135:1;   147:1;   148:1;   149:1;
150:1 (all with Hallelujah); also 35:10; 137:1; Job 14:5; Prov
19:7; 25:20; 27:22; 30:9.

[11] Psa 14:7 (= 53:7); 47:5; 60:2; Job 31:7;   40:10--these may
be understood to be merely the conjunctive serving another accent
rather than a *Virtual Legarmeh*.

[12] Psa 55:20 (on *selah*); 96:4; 117:2; 143:3; Job 34:37; Prov
3:12.

[13] Psa 42:6, 12; 43:5; 45:5; 126:6;   except for the last
verse, it occurs in the same word with *Azla-Legarmeh*, a
disjunctive it regularly serves.

TABLE 88
Numerical Summary of the Use of
Illuy

SERVING:	Psa	Job	Prov	Total
Silluq	34	5	4	43
Great Rebia	52	8	5	65
Azla Legarmeh	26	3	0	29
Virtual Legarmeh	20	4	3	27
Other	14	0	2	16[14]
Total	146	20	14	180

Tarcha

The name *Tarcha* means "laboring, heavy, slow."
Like the *Tiphcha* used in the prose books, the accent
mark consists of a diagonal stroke with its top
inclined to the left (\). In some printed editions it
has a slight downward curvature. It is placed under
the first consonant of the stressed syllable and to the
left of any vowel in that position. *Tarcha* may be
confused with *Dechi* when the stress is on the first
syllable of a word. Actually *Dechi* should appear
before the first letter of the word, and *Tarcha* should
appear under it, but the printed editions are not

----

[14]It serves *Rebia Mugrash* in Psa 137:9, *Virtual Rebia Mugrash*
in Psa 3:3, and *Athnach* in Prov 1:9 and 6:27--all after *Little
Shalsheleth* according to the rule of *Little Shalsheleth*. It
serves *Virtual Rebia Mugrash* in eight short titles (Psa 36:1;
44:1; 47:1; 49:1; 61:1; 69:1; 81:1; 85:1) where v-rmug = *Illuy*.
It serves *Virtual Dechi* in a *Virtual Rebia Mugrash* segment
immediately after *Athnach* when the stress is on the second
syllable after an open syllable with a full vowel (Psa 4:8; 76:4;
78:25; 119:84).

consistent in this regard. In doubtful places the context must decide.

Tarcha serves as a conjunctive for *Virtual Rebia Mugrash, Virtual Dechi,* and *Virtual Legarmeh*:

  (1) *Tarcha* serves *Virtual Rebia Mugrash* with few exceptions.

  (2) It serves *Virtual Dechi* when *Virtual Dechi* has been transformed into *Mereka* in an *Athnach* segment.[15]

  (3) It serves *Virtual Legarmeh* before *Silluq* exclusively.

  (4) In some instances *Tarcha* replaces *Metheg* where it could otherwise serve as a conjunctive if one were needed[16]

Table 89 provides a numerical summary of the use of *Tarcha*.

·Galgal

The name *Galgal* means "wheel." Like the *Galgal* used in the prose books, the accent mark consists of two diagonal strokes joined at the bottom to form a small angle like an English "v." It is placed below the first consonant of the stressed syllable and immediately to the left of any vowel in that place. *Galgal* may serve either *Ole-WeYored* or *Pazer.* Yeivin noted that early manuscripts distinguished between the

----

[15] In one instance it serves when v-dech = *Azla* (Psa 125:3).

[16] Psa 31:17;   32:7;   45:15;   51:11; 76:3;   77:13;   104:23; 105:9;   107:14;   116:5;   118:13; 138:7;   145:4;   Job 7:21;   8:16; 17:11;   28:17; 29:5; 31:12; 33:16; 37:8;   Prov 1:31;   3:17;   8:21; 22:20;   30:1. In all instances it appears in the same word with a *Munach* serving *Silluq* after *Rebia Mugrash.* This may suggest that *Virtual Legarmeh* is present in these places.

TABLE 89
Numerical Summary of the Use of
Tarcha

SERVING:	Psa	Job	Prov	Total
V. Rebia Mugrash	499	268	232	999
Virtual Dechi	56	10	5	71
Virtual Legarmeh	26	7	3	36
Other	1	3	2	6[17]
Total	579	288	242	1112

Galgal that serves *Ole-WeYored* and the one that serves *Pazer*; whereas later manuscripts tended to confuse them, and printed editions make no distinction.[18]

(1) *Galgal* serves *Ole-WeYored* when the stress is on the second or later syllable; it has *Mahpak* as an alternative.

(2) It serves *Pazer* with no alternative.

(3) At times *Galgal* replaces *Metheg* where it could otherwise serve as a conjunctive if one were needed.[19]

Table 90 provides a numerical summary of the use of *Galgal*.

- - - - - - - - - - - - - - - - - -

[17] In BHS it serves *Silluq* four times (Job 12:15; 19:14; 34:21; Prov 17:14); whereas B and MG have *Mereka* or *Maqqeph* as expected. In BHS it serves *Athnach* in Prov 3:4; whereas in B and MG it serves *Virtual Dechi* as expected. In Psa 31:2 *Tarcha* replaces *Maqqeph* (cf. B and MG).

[18] Yeivin, *Tiberian Masorah*, 266.

[19] Psa 5:11; 14:4; 28:3; 29:9; 32:5; 37:7; 44:4; 53:6; 65:10; 142:7.

TABLE 90
Numerical Summary of the Use of
Galgal

SERVING:	Psa	Job	Prov	Total
Ole-WeYored	164	13	5	182
Pazer	31	2	4	37
Total	195	15	9	219

Mahpak

The name *Mahpak* means "inverted." Like the *Mahpak* used in the prose books, the accent mark consists of two diagonal strokes joined at the left (<). It is placed below the first consonant of the stressed syllable and immediately to the left of any vowel that may be there. *Mahpak* may serve *Ole-WeYored*, *Great Rebia*, *Azla-Legarmeh*, and *Virtual Legarmeh*:

(1) *Mahpak* serves *Ole-WeYored* when the stress is on the first syllable; it has *Galgal* as an alternative.

(2) It serves *Great Rebia* when the stress is on the first syllable of the word whenever *Pazer* or *Legarmeh* precedes; and it usually serves when the stress is anywhere in the word if *Pazer* or *Legarmeh* does not precede.

(3) It serves *Virtual Dechi* in a *Virtual Rebia Mugrash* segment when the stress is on the first syllable.

(4) It serves *Azla-Legarmeh* or *Virtual Legarmeh* when the stress is on the first syllable, or on the second syllable following a closed syllable or a vocal *Shewa*.

(5) It occasionally accents a monosyllabic particle with which a *Maqqeph* is expected but lacking. In these places the law of conjunctives may be apparently violated in that more than one conjunctive may be found standing before a disjunctive; but the law views this use of *Mahpak* as the equivalent of the *Maqqeph* for which it stands.

(6) It occasionally stands in place of *Metheg* where it could otherwise serve as a conjunctive if one were needed.[20]

Table 91 provides a numerical summary of the use of *Mahpak*.

TABLE 91
Numerical Summary of the Use of
Mahpak

SERVING:	Psa	Job	Prov	Total
Ole-WeYored	14	1	1	16
Great Rebia	34	5	2	41
Virtual Dechi	22	13	3	38
Azla-Legarmeh	112	33	10	155
Virtual Legarmeh	90	44	38	172
Sub. for Maqqeph	21	2	6	28[21]
Total	293	98	60	451

----

[20]Psa 9:17; 13:6; 18:16; 27:11; 36:7; 43:1; 50:3, 16; 53:5; 55:20; 65:6, 9; 67:2; 68:11, 20, 21, 36; 79:11, 13; 83:9; 106:48 (twice); 146:5; Job 16:4; Prov 7:22; 9:7; 24:24; 29:13; also note the strange case at Psa 146:3.

Azla

The name *Azla* means "proceeding." Like the *Azla* used in the prose books, the accent mark consists of a diagonal stroke with its top inclined to the left like an English back-slash (\); in some printed editions it has a slight upward curvature. It is placed above the first consonant of the stressed syllable of a word.

Azla is a rather rare conjunctive that serves only the virtual disjunctives:[11] *Virtual Rebia Mugrash, Virtual Dechi,* and *Virtual Legarmeh:*

(1) *Azla* serves *Virtual Rebia Mugrash* following real *Dechi.*

(2) It serves *Virtual Dechi* in a *Virtual Rebia Mugrash* segment when the stress is on the second syllable or later following a closed syllable or an open syllable with vocal *Shewa.*

(3) It serves *Virtual Legarmeh* before *Pazer.*

(4) It occasionally accents a monosyllabic particle with which a *Maqqeph* is expected but lacking. In these places the law of conjunctives may be apparently violated in that more than one conjunctive may be found

----

[11] Before *Rebia Mugrash* (Prov 27:1, 19); before *Sinnor* (Psa 31:20); before *Little Rebia* (Psa 1:2; 20:7; 27:6; 28:7; 35:20; 52:9; 55:13; 84:11; 90:17; 115:1; 116:8; 127:5; 135:6; 139:4; Job 14:7; 38:41; Prov 6:26; 23:5; 25:7); before *Pazer* (Psa 89:20); before *Virtual Legarmeh* + a conjunctive (Psa 22:25; 23:4; 32:2; 65:2; 137:3; Prov 3:12). Note that other instances of *Mahpak* may also be substitutes for *Maqqeph.*

[12] In several instances it probably should be *Azla-Legarmeh:* Psa 13:3; 22:25; 23:4; 27:6; 31:12; 32:5; 56:3, 10; 62:13; 72:17; 75:4; 79:6; 90:10; 106:48; 125:3; 137:3; 138:2; 141:4; Job 12:3; 32:11; 34:33; Prov 6:3; 24:31; 27:10 (cf. B and MG); this is also possible in Psa 5:12; 14:3; 106:38; 122:4; 123:2.

standing before a disjunctive; but the law
views this use of *Azla* as the equivalent of
the *Maqqeph* for which it stands.
Table 92 provides a numerical summary of the use of
Azla.

TABLE 92
Numerical Summary of the Use of
Azla

SERVING:	Psa	Job	Prov	Total
V-Rebia Mugrash	3	0	1	4[13]
Virtual Dechi	18	0	1	19[14]
Virtual Legarmeh	14	1	0	15[15]
Other	5	0	4	9[16]
Total	40	1	6	47

- - - - - - - - - - - - - - - - - - -

[13]Psa 4:7; 109:16; 125:3; Prov 8:13.

[14]Psa 3:5;   24:6;   42:2; 47:5; 52:7; 54:5; 55:10; 56:1, 3;
59:6; 61:5; 62:13; 75:4; 81:8; 84:9; 89:5, 36, 49; Prov 3:27.

[15]Psa 5:12; 13:3; 22:25; 23:4; 27:6; 31:12; 68:31; 106:38,
48; 122:4; 123:2; 137:3; 138:2; 141:4; Job 12:3.

[16]Before *Mahpak-Legarmeh* + conj.:   Prov 6:3; here *Azla* with
Mereka stands in place of *Maqqeph* with *Azla-Legarmeh* (cf. B and
MG); this is the only place in BHS and BHK where *Mahpak-Legarmeh*
has a conjunctive; L is probably defective here.   Before *Azla-
Legarmeh* + conj.:   Prov 24:31; before *Virtual Legarmeh* + conj.:
Psa 56:10; 90:10; Prov 23:29; before *Pazer* + conj.: Prov 27:10
(all five of these probably should be *Azla-Legarmeh*).
     In BHS it serves *Sinnor* in Psa 79:6; but here it should be
Azla-Legarmeh (cf. B and MG). In Psa 32:5 it serves *Pazer,* but
this too should be *Azla-Legarmeh*.   Note that the word with *Pazer*
has a *Galgal* instead of *Metheg,* suggesting the same conclusion;
else why should not the *Azla* be the expected *Galgal*?   In Psa
72:17, BHS and BHK have it serving *Great Rebia,* but this too
probably should be *Azla-Legarmeh* (cf. B and MG).

Little Shalsheleth

The name *Little Shalsheleth* means "small triplet or chain." Like the disjunctive accent *Great Shalsheleth*, the accent mark consists of a vertical, three-stepped zigzag line placed above the first consonant of the stressed syllable, but without the following *Paseq*. *Little Shalsheleth* is very rare, occurring only eight times in the entire Hebrew Bible.[27] It always serves *Virtual Dechi*, and always functions as *Virtual Legarmeh*. It affects changes in the accents that follow it, and is served by the conjunctives that normally serve *Azla-Legarmeh*.[28] It probably is used to attach some special meaning to the passage in which it occurs, because in every instance it stands where another conjunctive is expected.

It affects the conjunctive after it bearing *Virtual Dechi* as follows:

(1) If the stressed syllable follows an open syllable with a full vowel, then the conjunctive becomes *Sinnorit-Mahpak* in a RMUG segment (Psa 34:8; 68:15), and it becomes *Sinnorit-Mereka* in an ATH segment (Psa 65:2; 72:3).

(2) Otherwise the conjunctive becomes *Illuy* (Psa 3:3; 137:9; Prov 1:9; 6:26).

----

[27] Psa 3:3; 34:8; 65:2; 68:15; 72:3; 137:9; Prov 1:9; 6:27.

[28] An exception is found in Psa 34:8 where *Sinnorit-Mahpak* is expected (cf. B and MG); in Prov 6:7 the interrogative prefix is ignored, otherwise *Illuy* is expected.

Sinnorit

The name *Sinnorit* means "canal or water channel." Like the disjunctive accent *Sinnor* and like *Zarqa* used in the prose books, the accent mark consists of a vertical stroke with its top bent sharply toward the left to form the appearance of a walking cane. In some printed editions it has the appearance of a backwards English "S" reclining on its back (~). But differing from the similar disjunctive accents, *Sinnorit* is prepositive, being placed above and before the first letter of the word; whereas the others are postpositive. *Sinnorit* also differs in that it is not a separate accent, but rather augments another conjunctive, either *Mereka* or *Mahpak*.

When the *Sinnorit* augment is required on a word with the stress on its first syllable and the preceding word is joined by *Maqqeph*, the *Sinnorit* rests on the word joined by *Maqqeph* and the *Maqqeph* is dropped. Wickes stated the rule:

> Two words joined by Maqqeph are regarded for the purposes of accentuation as *one* word. If, now, Sinnorîth falls on the first of two such words, the Maqqeph is dropped. . . . Sinnorîth joins the words so closely together, that Maqqeph is no longer needed.[19]

Sinnorit-Mereka

Sinnorit augments *Mereka* eighteen in the books of poetry. It augments *Mereka* eleven times when it is preceded by an open syllable with a full vowel.[30]   It

----

[19]Wickes, I, 23; emphasis his.

[30]Psa 41:14, 72:19, and 89:53 (after the double *amens* that close the first three books of the Psalms); 65:2 and 72:3 (both

does so twice even when *Mereka* is on the first syllable and *Sinnorit* is on a preceding monosyllabic particle where *Maqqeph* is expected but lacking.[31]   Five times BHS and BHK have *Mereka* on one word and *Sinnorit* on the preceding word, whereas B and MG have different accents.[32]   The augmentation is not consistent throughout the text, but occurs in only these few instances, suggesting that the *Sinnorit* in these cases may attach some special meaning to the passage.

Sinnorit-Mereka serves *Silluq, Athnach, Rebia Mugrash,* and *Virtual Dechi.* Table 93 provides a numerical summary of the use of *Sinnorit-Mereka.*

TABLE 93
Numerical Summary of the Use of
Sinnorit-Mereka

SERVING:	Psa	Job	Prov	Total
Silluq	9	1	0	10[33]
Athnach	4	0	0	4[34]
Rebia Mugrash	2	0	0	2[35]
Virtual Dechi	2	0	0	2[36]
Total	17	1	0	18

----

follow *Little Shalsheleth* with its special meaning);   also Psa 5:7; 10:3; 70:4; 118:25 (twice); Job 20:27.

[31]Psa 18:20   and 22:9 (both have a similar expression of deliverance).

[32]Psa 2:7; 5:5; 18:1; 31:22; 66:20.

[33]Psa 5:7;   10:3;   18:20;   22:9; 41:14; 70:4; 72:19;   89:53; 118:25;   Job 20:27.

Sinnorit-Mahpak

Sinnorit augments *Mahpak* whenever the stressed syllable is preceded by an open syllable with a full vowel; this is true even when the stress falls on the third or later syllable.[37] Thus *Sinnorit-Mahpak* serves essentially the same disjunctives as *Mahpak*:[38]

(1) *Sinnorit* augments *Mahpak* serving *Virtual Dechi* in a *Virtual Rebia Mugrash* segment.

(2) It augments *Mahpak* serving *Great Rebia*.

(3) It augments *Mahpak* serving *Azla-Legarmeh* or *Virtual Legarmeh*.

(4) It augments *Mahpak* following *Little Shalsheleth* according to musical context.

Table 94 provides a numerical summary of the use of *Sinnorit-Mahpak*.

----

[34] Psa 5:5; 65:2; 72:3; 118:25.

[35] Psa 31:22; 66:20.

[36] Psa 2:7; 18:1.

[37] I have checked every instance of *Sinnorit-Mahpak*. In six instances in BHS and BHK, *Mahpak* appears on the first syllable of a word and *Sinnorit* appears on a preceding monosyllabic particle with no other accent mark of its own where *Maqqeph* is expected but lacking: Psa 95:7; 147:20; Job 18:19; 32:5; 37:21; Prov 6:3; in most of these cases B and MG have the expected *Maqqeph*. In Psa 42:9 and 62:9 the same phenomenon occurs with a preceding multisyllabic word having no other accent of its own where *Maqqeph* is expected but missing. In Psa 68:20 *Sinnorit-Mahpak* seems to serve defective *Ole-WeYored*; however, this should be regarded as *Sinnor* followed by *Mahpak* with *Paseq*. The *Paseq* marks redundancy in the text.

[38] Twice *Sinnorit-Mahpak* occurs on the same word with *Great Rebia* (Psa 20:6; Job 6:10), and once it occurs together with a *Metheg* on the ultima (Job 31:35).

TABLE 94
Numerical Summary of the Use of
Sinnorit-Mahpak

SERVING:	Psa	Job	Prov	Total
Virtual Dechi	6	1	0	7[39]
Great Rebia	51	11	3	65
Azla Legarmeh	47	5	7	59
Virtual Legarmeh	27	6	4	37
Other	7	0	2	9[40]
Total	138	22	16	176

----

[39] Psa 28:8; 32:5; 48:7; 68:25; 74:10; 79:12; Job 14:3.

[40] It serves *Rebia Mugrash* in Psa 31:16:   34:8;   68:15; 79:3;
116:14; 135:21;   Prov 7:7. It serves *Virtual Rebia Mugrash* in Psa
68:20.   It serves *Athnach* in Prov 6:3.   In all these cases it is
bearing *Virtual Dechi*.   It is possible that these unusual
instances of *Sinnorit-Mahpak* may attach some special meaning to
the text as in the case of *Sinnorit-Mereka*.

CHAPTER 17
Interpreting the Poetic Accents

In the books of poetry the use of the accents is more greatly influenced by poetic structure than in the prose books. This is particularly true for the disjunctives in hierarchy II (*Athnach* and *Ole-WeYored*). These high ranking accents are found most often marking the end of poetic lines. In long verses containing numerous poetic lines the remote disjunctive (*Rebia*) is used to mark the end of some lines. When disjunctives in hierarchies II and III are both used to mark poetic structure, their segments may be of equal par syntactically, logically, or rhetorically; although the hierarchy II disjunctives sometimes may mark breaks of some greater significance.

Interpreting Poetic Structure

In poetry, grammatical syntax and poetic structure are usually in harmony. So the accents can usually be expected to reflect the syntactic relationships as well as poetic structure. However, whenever grammatical syntax and poetic structure fail to harmonize, the accents usually agree with the poetry rather than the syntax. The interpreter must keep this in mind when struggling with difficult passages. Interpretation should always agree with the syntax of the Hebrew language whenever the poetic structure is in disharmony. The poetic structure supplies literary nuances in such cases.

Interpreting The Disjunctives

As in the prose books, the remote poetic disjunctives (*Ole WeYored*, *Athnach*, *Great Rebia*, and *Pazer*) unambiguously mark the end of the segments they govern. Again this is not true for the near disjunctives (*Rebia Mugrash*, *Dechi*, *Sinnor*, *Little Rebia*, and *Legarmeh*). As in the case of the near disjunctives of the prose books, these accents may be found standing in place of (1) an expected conjunctive accent, (2) its own subordinate, (3) or its own remote companion accent. The interpreter should be careful not to attribute greater disjunctive value to the near disjunctives than their context allows.

Interpreting Virtual Disjunctives

Three near disjunctive accents (*Rebia Mugrash*, *Dechi*, and *Legarmeh*) are subject to transformation as described above. Whenever a disjunctive accent is served by more than one conjunctive accent, the condition can be explained by the law of transformation, or by the substitution of a conjunctive for *Maqqeph* with a monosyllabic particle. Whenever the laws of hierarchic governance expect the presence of a near disjunctive, it will be there virtually (as a transformed conjunctive). The interpreter should be mindful of these facts when struggling with apparent difficulties. Virtual disjunctives should be interpreted as though they were the corresponding real disjunctive.

Interpreting the Conjunctives

Except for those conjunctives that may be representing a virtual disjunctive, all conjunctives are of equal conjoining value. There is no hierarchy among the poetic conjunctives. Also there are no ordered ranks among the poetic conjunctives. The poetic disjunctives may be served by only one conjunctive at the most. If more than one conjunctive accent precedes a given disjunctive, it is due to the presence of a virtual disjunctive or a substitute for *Maqqeph* as explained above.

The author sincerely hopes that the present exposition of the syntax of the Masoretic accents will be of benefit to the reader in his efforts to determine the rabbinic interpretation of Hebrew Scripture. Such an interpretation has its roots in the recesses of antiquity and should not be lightly ignored. Only in those places where the evidence indicates that the ancient accentuation has been altered should an expositor entertain other explanations.

BIBLIOGRAPHY

BIBLIOGRAPHY

Books

Biblia Hebraica. Edited by R. Kittel. Stuttgart: Privileg. Wurtt. Bibelanstalt, 1937.

Biblia Hebraica Stuttgartensia. Edited by K. Elliger and W. Rudolph. Stuttgart: Deutsche Bibelgesellschaft, 1967/77.

Bohlius, Samuel. *Scriptinium Sensus Scripturae Sacrae ex accentibus* (1636).

Brewer, Mordecai. *The Biblical Accents as Punctuation.* Jerusalem: Hamador Hadati, 1958.

Butin, Romain. *Ten Nequdoth of the Torah,* rev. ed. Library of Biblical Studies. New York: KTAV, 1969.

Cohen, Miles B. *The System of Accentuation in the Hebrew Bible.* Minneapolis: Milco Press, 1969.

Driver, S. R. *A Treatise on the Use of the Tenses in Hebrew,* 3rd ed. London: Oxford University Press, 1892.

Florinius, C. *Doctrina de Accentuatione divina* (1667).

Haik-Vantoura, S. *La Musique de la Bible Révelée.* Paris: Dessain et Tolra, 1976.

Hughes, John J. *Bits, Bytes & Biblical Studies.* Grand Rapids: Zondervan, 1987.

Kautzsch, E., Ed. *Gesenius' Hebrew Grammar,* 2nd ed. Revised by A. E. Cowley. London: Oxford University Press, 1910.

Lee, S. *A Grammar of the Hebrew Language.* London: Duncan and Malcolm, 1844.

Books Continued

Mason, P. H., and H. H. Bernard. *An Essay, Practical Hebrew Grammar*. Cambridge: J. Hall and Son, 1853.

O'Connor, M. *Hebrew Verse Structure*. Winona Lake, IN: Eisenbrauns, 1980.

Waltke Bruce K., and M. O'Connor. *An Introduction to Biblical Hebrew Syntax*. Winona Lake, IN: Eisenbrauns, 1990.

Watson, Wilfred G. E. *Classical Hebrew Poetry*, *JSOT* Supplement 26. Sheffield: JSOT Press, 1984.

Weil, G. E. Ed. *Massorah Gedolah Iuxta Codicem Leningradensem B19a*, 4 vols. Rome: Pontifical Biblical Institute, 1971.

Weil, G. E., P. Riviere, and M. Serfaty. *Concordance de la Cantilation du Pentateuque et des Cinq Migillot*. Paris-Nancy: CNRS, 1978.

----------. *Les Cantilations des Premiers Prophetes*. Paris-Nancy: CNRS, 1981.

---------. *Les Cantilations des Livres Poetique*. Paris-Nancy: CNRS, 1982.

----------. *Les Cantilations des Derniers Prophetes*. Paris-Nancy: CNRS, 1982.

----------. *La Cantilation des Ouvrages Bibliques en Aramean*. Paris-Nancy: CNRS, 1983.

Wickes, William. *Two Treatises on the Accentuation of the Old Testament*, rev. ed. 1881-87; reprint, New York: KTAV, 1970.

Würthwein, Ernst. *The Text of the Old Testament*. Trans. by Erroll F. Rhodes. Grand Rapids: William B. Eerdmans, 1979.

Yeivin, Israel. *Introduction to the Tiberian Masorah*. Trans. and ed. by E. J. Revell. Society of Biblical Literature Masoretic Studies, Number 5. Missoula MT: Scholars Press, 1980.

מקראות גדולות, 5 Vols. New York: Pardes Publishing House, Inc., תשי״א.

Journal and Encyclopedia Articles

Allony, Nehemiah. "The Book of Vocalization (Kitab Al Musawwitat)
of Moses Ben Asher." *Leshonenu* (1983) 47(2):85-124.

Aronoff, M. "Orthography and Linguistic Theory: The Syntactic
Basis of Masoretic Hebrew Punctuation." *Language*   (1985)
61:28-72.

Breuer, Mordecai. "Toward the Clarification of Problems in the
Masoretic Accents." *Leshonenu* (1979) 43(4):243-53.

----------.   "Toward the Clarification of Problems in Biblical
Accents and Vocalization: The *Ga'ya* for Improvement of
Reading." *Leshonenu* (1979) 44(1):3-11.

----------.   "Clarifying Problems in the Accents and Vowel Signs
of the Biblical Text." *Leshonenu* (1985) 48/49(2/3):118-31.

Cohen, M. B. "Masoretic Accents as a Biblical Commentary."
Journal of the Ancient Near Eastern Society (1972) 4:2-11.

Christensen, Duane L.   "Prose and Poetry in the Bible: The
Narrative   Poetics of Deuteronomy 1, 9-18."   *ZAW* (1985)
97:179-189.

----------. "Narrative Poetics and the Interpretation of the Book
of Jonah."   *Directions in Biblical Hebrew Poetry.*   Ed.
Elaine R. Follis. *JSOT* Supplement (1987) 40:29-48.

Christensen Duane L.,   and M. Naruchi.   "The Mosaic Authorship of
the Pentateuch."   *Journal of the Evangelical Theological
Society* (December 1989) 32(4):465-71.

Dotan, Aharon. "The Minor *Ga'ya.*" *Textus* (1964) 4:55-75.

Herzog, Avigor.   "Masoretic Accents (Musical   Rendition)."
Encyclopedia Judaica (1971).

Margolis, Max L. "Accents in Hebrew." *The Jewish Encyclopedia.*

Revell, E. J. "The Oldest Evidence for the Hebrew Accent System."
Bulletin of the John Rylands Library (1971-72) 54:214-222.

----------.   "The Oldest Accent List in the *Diqduqe Hate'amim.*"
Textus (1973) 8:138-159.

---------.   "Aristotle and the Accents."   *Journal of Semitic
Studies* (1974) 19:19-35.

Journal Articles (continued)

----------. "The Hebrew Accents and the Greek Ekphonetic Neumes."
Studies in Eastern Chant (1974) 4:140-70.

----------. "The Diacritical Dots and the Development of the
Arabic Alphabet." *Journal of Semitic Studies* (1975) 20:178-
80.

----------. "Biblical Punctuation and Chant in the Second Temple
Period." *JSL* (1976).

----------. "Pausal Forms and the Structure of Biblical Poetry."
Vetus Testamentum (1981) 31:186-199.

Waltke Bruce K.   "The New International Version and Its Textual
Principles in the Book of Psalms."   *Journal of the
Evangelical Society* (March 1989) 32(1):25-26.

Weisberg, David.   "The Rare Accents of the Twenty-One Books."
Jewish Quarterly Review (April 1966) 56(4):315-36, (July
1966) 57(1):57-70, (January 1967) 57(3):227-38.

Werner, Eric. "Trop and Tropus: Etymology and History." *Hebrew
Union College Annual* (1975) 46:289-96.

Yalon, H. "Metiga." *Leshonenu* (1964-65) 29:24-26.

Yeivin, Israel.   "Some Manifestations of Milra' Tendency in
Hebrew." *Eretz-Israel* (1958) 5:145-49.

----------. "A Unique Combination of Accents." *Textus* (1960)
1:209-10.

INDICES

SUBJECT AND NAME INDEX

SCRIPTURE INDEX

STUDIES IN THE BIBLE AND EARLY CHRISTIANITY